TRANSLATION SERIES

TRANSLATION OF
CONTEMPORARY JAPANESE
SCHOLARSHIP
ON
SOUTHEAST ASIA

INDOCHINA
IN THE
1940s AND 1950s

EDITED BY TAKASHI SHIRAISHI AND MOTOO FURUTA

T0349769

VOLUME II

Southeast Asia Program
180 Uris Hall
Cornell University
Ithaca, New York 14853-7601

Project Leader
  George Kahin

Participating Researchers
  Takashi Shiraishi
  Motoo Furuta

Assistant Researchers
  Saya Shiraishi
  Sadako Taylor

Translation
  EDS (Tokyo)

Editing and Production
  Donna Amoroso
  Audrey Kahin
  Roberta Ludgate
  Dolina Millar

Published under the auspices of the Toyota Foundation

CONTENTS

INTRODUCTION

Born as "Southern Studies" (*Nampo Kenkyu*) in the interwar years, Southeast Asian studies in Japan is now passing from the second to the third generation, while the fourth generation of scholars in their twenties and early thirties is now emerging on the horizon. The preceding generations have produced excellent works, only some of which are available in English. Tatsuro Yamamoto's classic, *Recherches sur l'histoire de l'Annam,* and the "Overseas Chinese" studies by scholars affiliated with the East Asia Economic Research Bureau of the Manchurian Railway are among the best works of the first generation, while the writings of such scholars of the second generation as Akira Nagazumi, Yoneo Ishii, and Toru Yano represent Japanese scholarship on Southeast Asia at its best.[1] These and other studies, cross-bred with non-Japanese language works on Southeast Asia, have formed a beautifully mestizo scholarly tradition of Japanese research on Southeast Asia, now rebaptized as *Tonan Ajia Kenkyu* (Southeast Asian Studies), in which the succeeding generation of Japanese Southeast Asianists, among whom I belong, have worked over the last twenty years.

Yet each·generation of Japanese scholars working on Southeast Asia carries its own historical birth marks. Many members of the first generation entered "Southern Studies" in the 1930 when Japan was starting its fatal southward expansion. No wonder, then, that one of the major contributions of these scholars lay in their work on the "Overseas Chinese" and on the anti-Japanese Chinese national salvation movement in Southeast Asia.[2] Members of the second generation started to study Southeast Asia in the 1950s and early 1960s when Japan was notable by its absence from the region and when American scholarship was fast replacing the old colonial studies of Southeast Asia. Akira Nagazumi, the first Japanese to obtain a PhD in Southeast Asian history at an American university, thus clearly marked the coming-of-age of the second generation.

---

[1]Tatsuro Yamamoto, *Recherches sur l'histoire de l'Annam* (Tokyo: Yamakawa, 1950); Mantetsu Toa Keizai Chosakyoku, *Tai-koku ni okeru Kakyo* [Chinese in Thailand] (Tokyo, 1939); *Firipin ni okeru Kakyo* [Chinese in the Philippines] (Tokyo, 1939); *Ranryo Indo ni okeru Kakyo* [Chinese in the Dutch Indies] (Tokyo, 1940); *Eiryo Marai, Biruma oyobi Goshu ni okeru Kakyo* [Chinese in British Malaya, Burma and Australia] (Tokyo, 1941); *Futsuryo Indo-shina ni okeru Kakyo* [Chinese in French Indochina] (Tokyo, 1943); Akira Nagazumi, *The Dawn of Indonesian Nationalism: The Early Years of the Budi Utomo, 1908-1918* (Tokyo: Institute of Developing Economies, 1972); Yoneo Ishii *Jozaha Bukyo no Seiji-Sakai-gaku: Kokkyo no Kozo* (Tokyo: Sobunsha, 1975) Translated by Peter Hawkes, under the title *Sanha, State, and Society: Thai Buddhism in History* (Honolulu: University of Hawaii Press, c. 1986); Toru Yano, *Tai Biruma Gendai Seijishi Kenkyu* [A Study of Thai and Burmese Political History] (Tokyo: Sobunsha, 1968) and *"Nashin" no Keifu* [The Lineage of "Southward Expansion"] (Tokyo: Chuo Koronsha, 1975).

[2]Aside from the works on "Overseas Chinese" cited in n. 1, see also Toa Kenkyujo, Dai 3 Chosa Iinkai, *Nan'yo Kakyo Konichi Kyukoku Undo no Kenkyu* [A Study on the Nanyang Chinese Anti-Japanese National Salvation Movement] (Tokyo: Toakenyujo, 1944).

The third generation of Japanese Southeast Asianists, some of whose works appear in this and future volumes of this series, also display special characteristics. In terms of age they are now in their forties, and they entered Southeast Asian studies in the mid-1960s to early 1970s, when Japan was fast returning to Southeast Asia, and there were expanding opportunities for conducting research in the region and/or graduate studies abroad. Many of this generation spent one or more of their formative years outside Japan—in Southeast Asia, in the US, in Australia, and in Europe. They viewed a knowledge of all the languages needed for their studies as a self-evident requirement, "translation works [those based on non-Japanese works]" were no longer acceptable, and many were well aware of most recent research by non-Japanese Southeast Asianist. Yet when they first entered Southeast Asian studies Southeast Asia was still remote and it remained so for some time. Scholars of this generation felt themselves fortunate to visit the region once in five years; library collections on Southeast Asia were poor, a book or a journal article had to be pursued from one library to another. Besides, there were few places where one could learn Southeast Asian languages. At the same time, events were moving swiftly in Southeast Asia: the killings and the establishment of the New Order in Indonesia in 1965-1966, the American war in Vietnam, the 1969 riot in Malaysia, the anti-Japanese movement and the revolution in Thailand in the early 1970s, the anti-Japanese riot in Jakarta in 1974. Since then things have changed very much. But scholars of the third generation have not forgotten this past and the contrast it presents with the way things now are. And this memory still leaves its marks on many of their studies—in the questions they ask, on the approaches they take, and on the sources they use.

The essays included in the four volumes of the present series, *Contemporary Japanese Scholarship on Southeast Asia*, are chosen to illuminate the scholarship of this third generation, especially in fields where few Japanese works are available in English. The studies included in the first volume, *Reading Southeast Asia*, were attempts to read Southeast Asian "texts" in the broader sense. The essays in the present volume explore Japanese and Vietnamese language sources on Vietnam in the 1940s and 1950s and represent a collective effort by the Japanese authors to make their own contribution to our understanding of Vietnamese history: the four works on the 1940s by Motoo Furuta, Masaya Shiraishi, Yukichika Tabuchi, and Minami Yoshizawa are based on Japanese sources, while the two essays by Furuta and Hirohide Kurihara are based on their archival research in Hanoi.

Most of the works to be included in the third volume were originally written by the research group led by Hajime Shimizu at the Institute of Developing Economies. Building on Toru Yano's pioneering work on Japan's southward expansion they investigate the origins of the Japanese presence in Southeast Asia. And, finally, the fourth volume will include works on Suharto's New Order in Indonesia, the country where since the late 1960s the Japanese presence in the form of aid, investment, and trade has been the most pronounced in Southeast Asia.

This project to make Japanese works on Southeast Asia available to English readers has been carried out by a team at Cornell, headed by Professor George McT. Kahin and funded by the Toyota Foundation. All the draft translations were done by the EDS (Editorial and Design Services) in Tokyo. For all this, I would like to thank Ms. Kazue Iwamoto of the Toyota Foundation who first brought up the idea; Ms. Yoshiko Wakayama who patiently saw the project through to completion; Ms. Suzanne Trumbull and her colleagues at the EDS who put so much work into the translation effort; Dr. Audrey Kahin, without whose effort this project would have gone nowhere; Dr. Sadako Taylor who checked the draft translations with great care; and Roberta Ludgate, Donna Amoroso, and Dolina Millar who contributed to the project in many and valuable ways.

Finally, many Japanese scholars of the third generation owe an enormous intellectual debt to the late Prof. Akira Nagazumi in whose seminar some of us, including myself, were initiated into Southeast Asian studies and whose works set a standard to which all of us have had to live up. His untimely death in 1988 was an enormous loss for us all. But his works are still with us, and his soft voice, his gentle and quiet manner, and his rigorous scholarship are still in our memory. To his memory we would like to dedicate this book.

Takashi Shiraishi
Ithaca
March 1992

1

THE NISHIHARA MISSION IN HANOI, JULY 1940

Minami Yoshizawa

I. PERSPECTIVES OF ANALYSIS

INTERNAL DISSENSION AND THE EXPANSION OF THE WAR

In late September 1940, when the Japanese army began its occupation of northern Indochina in a two-pronged approach, overland from Lang Son and by sea from Do Son, Major General Issaku Nishihara, stationed in Hanoi as the leader of a mission directly assigned by Imperial Headquarters, telegraphed the following message to the vice-minister of war and the assistant chief of the Imperial Army General Staff in Tokyo: "Because it will be absolutely necessary to provide the chief commanding officer occupying French Indochina with a new organization to conduct diplomatic negotiations after action is taken around Lang Son, [two illegible characters] I request that selection of personnel and so on be initiated today. For the past three months, we have tried to conduct friendly negotiations. Granting the [illegible character] above not only will undermine trust in Imperial diplomacy but also is something that I personally, and as a member of the Imperial Army, cannot condone. Please take this into consideration."[1]

This text is most interesting. The troops that took action around Lang Son were the Kwantung [Guangdong] Army and the Nanning Army, stationed in Guangdong and Guangxi, respectively—army units on the southern edge of the expanded China front. Nishihara and his men in the Nishihara Mission in Hanoi, charged with undertaking diplomatic negotiations with the government of French Indochina, had "for the past three months . . . tried to conduct friendly negotiations," but now that China-based troops had taken action, that is, had occupied French Indochina, Nishihara was requesting that army headquarters relieve him and his group of their negotiating duties and transfer authority to "the chief commanding officer" of the occupying forces. Nishihara and his men did not consent to the execution of military action by the garrison army. Nishihara's comment that he "personally, and as a member of the Imperial Army," could not condone the military occupation was unusual for a telegram because it conveyed emotion. Nishihara, the leader of the group that had, in fact, laid the groundwork for the Japanese army's occupation—peaceful or otherwise—of Indochina, was asking that headquarters relieve him of his duties when the occupation actually occurred.

---

[1] Document 46.

A close study of the documents dealing with the occupation of northern French Indochina reveals not only Nishihara's frustration (the reasons for which are also important) but also the deep rifts within the group planning and prosecuting the war and thus involved in expanding the war. Why was expansion of the war possible under such conditions, and what was the nature of the disunity within the war-leadership group? These were my first questions.

In his postwar memoirs Major General Raishirō Sumita, Nishihara's successor in Hanoi, describes Major General Kyōji Tominaga, head of the First Department of the Army General Staff, and his associates as "the little gang of hawks in charge of army operations" and the actual ringleaders of military occupation, and praises Nishihara and himself, who opposed the hawks and engaged in negotiations, as the "moderate and impartial" doves who "adhered throughout to principles."[2] Although this evaluation reflects the self-serving character typical of memoirs, nevertheless it forces one to consider whether the military occupation of northern French Indochina and the disunity within the group that executed it can be explained adequately in terms of hawks versus doves and the identification of the hawks as the ringleaders (and, conversely, the identification of the doves as those opposing the ringleaders), and whether this schema of two opposed factions was indeed the crux of the problem.

Analysis of the Vietnam War is another focus of my historical research. Here, too, the pattern of hawks versus doves within the leading councils of the United States, the instigator of that war, must be considered. The nature and role of the doves can be viewed in a variety of ways, but at least some of the doves, while remaining within the group planning and prosecuting the war, also identified themselves with forces outside that group in thought if not in deed (this led ultimately to doves divorcing themselves from the war-leadership group by resigning in protest), and in extreme cases even established links of some sort with the antiwar movement, whose goals and activities were totally incompatible with those of the war leaders. Therefore the dovish faction, if indirectly, generated a force that was able to act to block expansion and continuation of the war. Naturally, elucidation of the way in which the conflict between the hawkish and dovish factions within the US war-leadership group developed, the way in which relations between the two groups evolved, and the impact that these factors had on the conduct of the war necessitates consideration of the relationships that pertained among the government, the military, big business, Congress, and mass movements within the context of the US political system.

It should be self-evident that, although we may apply the terms "hawks" and "doves" to the Japanese context, the situation in Japan at the time of the occupation of French Indochina differed considerably from that in the United States at the time of the Vietnam War. Specifically, consideration of the circumstances surrounding the Japanese army's occupation of northern French Indochina in 1940 and of southern French Indochina in 1941 makes it clear that the conflict between the faction advocating the use of force, which took the initiative in the occupation, and the faction advocating negotiations, or "peaceful occupation," and also the conflict between the faction advocating southern expansion and that advocating war against the Soviet Union, or northern expansion, was a tussle, both covert and overt, among birds of a

---

[2] Raishirō Sumita, "Futsuin shinchū to Sumita kikan no katsudō" [The occupation of French Indochina and the activities of the Sumita Mission], in Masaki Miyake, ed., *Shōwashi no gumbu to seiji* [The military and politics in the history of the Shōwa era], vol. 3 (Tokyo: Daiichi Hōki Shuppan, 1983), p. 238.

feather; this being the case, none of the parties to the conflict could possibly have acted to block expansion or continuation of the war.

THE SYNERGISTIC EFFECT OF SECTIONALISM

The sectionalism within the group planning and prosecuting the war, and the conflicts generated thereby, is well known. So far, historical research has concentrated on the nature of this dissension and its effect on the expansion and continuation of the war. One of the major perspectives of such analysis has been the so-called leadership theory: the attempt to determine what individual, or which of the conflicting factions, within the group planning and prosecuting the war played the leading role in the expansion and continuation of the war. This perspective naturally leads to identifying the "leader" (either an individual or a faction) as having had prime responsibility for expanding and continuing the war and the individuals or factions opposing this "leader" as having worked to block expansion of the war.

Typical of this approach are the work of Ikuhiko Hata[3] and the hundred-plus volumes of the *Senshi sōsho* [War history library] compiled by the Defense Agency's War History Office. Let us consider part of the latter, *Daihon'ei rikugunbu Dai Tōa sensō kaisen keii* [The Imperial Headquarters Army Department and the circumstances leading to the Greater East Asia War],[4] which devotes many pages to the occupation of French Indochina and is cited frequently in this paper. In its own fashion, this work directly addresses the issue of conflict within the group planning and prosecuting the war and taking the initiative in conducting the war. One may be tempted to think that a work emanating from the War History Office of the Defense Agency would not pursue the question of responsibility for the prosecution of the war, but this is not the case. The initiative taken by Tominaga in the Army General Staff's First Department, through his arbitrary actions, and by Colonel Kenryō Satō and other staff officers of the Kwantung Army in pushing for the military occupation of northern French Indochina is examined, and an attempt is made to pinpoint responsibility.

In my opinion, however, the leadership theory is seriously flawed for two reaons. First, it has a strong tendency to oversimplify the conflict between those advocating the exercise of force and those advocating negotiations into a conflict between two fixed policies, expansion and nonexpansion of the war. The truth is that, while there was always sectionalist conflict within the group planning and prosecuting the war, the points of policy at issue were not as clear-cut as, for example, expansion versus nonexpansion of the war, and for this reason the various sections' policies, despite the battles of rival proponents, were not always consistent. For example, the navy's advocacy of peaceful rather than military occupation actually reflected a policy not of nonexpansion of the war but of a different kind of expansion. The statements of Yōsuke Matsuoka, minister for foreign affairs at the time of the occupation of southern French Indochina, provide a classic illustration of this sort of inconsistency.

---

[3] Ikuhiko Hata, "Futsuin shinchū to gun no nanshin seisaku (1940–1941)" [The occupation of French Indochina and the army's policy of southern expansion (1940–1941)], in Nippon Kokusai Seiji Gakkai [Japan Association of International Relations], Taiheiyō Sensō Gen'in Kenkyūbu [Study Group on the Causes of the Pacific War], ed., *Taiheiyō sensō e no michi* [The road to the Pacific War], vol. 6 (Tokyo: Asahi Shimbunsha, 1963).

[4] Defense Agency, War History Office, *Daihon'ei rikugunbu Dai Tōa sensō kaisen keii* [The Imperial Headquarters Army Department and the circumstances leading to the Greater East Asia War], 4 vols. (Tokyo: Asagumo Shimbunsha, 1973, 1974).

Although he consistently opposed the mainstream within the group planning and prosecuting the war, he shifted his stance with dizzying rapidity, advocating first southern expansion, then southern expansion while reducing the scope of the China front, then postponement of southern expansion, and finally cessation of southern expansion and promotion of northern expansion. In short, that opposition to expansion of the war did not necessarily mean advocacy of nonexpansion and that the focal points of opposition over policy were neither clear nor consistent were hallmarks of the sectionalism within the war-leadership group, but these points are overlooked by exponents of the leadership theory.

The second major flaw in this theory is that, while it acknowledges conflict within the war-leadership group, too often it fails to recognize this as a dynamic process. Let us take the conflict between the faction advocating the exercise of force and the faction advocating negotiations. The usual interpretation of exponents of the leadership theory is that Tominaga and the army units on the scene strongly advocated the exercise of force and took the initiative in executing the occupation, either ignoring or dragging in their wake the advocates of negotiations—Nishihara and the navy units on the scene. According to this simplistic interpretation, expansion of the war was instigated by the hard-line proponents of military force, while those who opposed this policy, including the advocates of negotiations, either acted as a deterrent or passively acquiesced.

When we analyze the actual dynamics of this opposition, however, we find that it was not simply a matter of one faction—the hard-liners, for example—taking the lead in expanding the war; in fact, the various factions vied for leadership of the expansion effort, and the friction thus generated strengthened the impulse toward expansion. In other words, the existence of hard-liners within the war-leadership group was not the decisive factor in expansion of the war; the decisive factor was, rather, the synergistic interaction of internal conflicts.

Viewing these conflicts as expressing not a static relationship of opposing positions but a dynamic process of competitive relationships among factions culminating in expansion of the war allows us to explain the occupation of French Indochina in a more realistic fashion. If we adopt this perspective, we see the negotiation faction not as a deterrent to the war expansion instigated by the military-force faction but as an active, competitive participant in that process. This is why I take a jaundiced view of the frequent protestations of people formerly affiliated with the Imperial Navy that the navy's role in the conflict between army and navy was one of opposing the "tyranny of the army" through constant efforts to "avert war."[5]

As I have already said, the leadership theory seeks to identify those who played the most active role in expanding the war, the ringleaders. In this sense, it also endeavors to fix responsibility. By focusing solely on the responsibility of the ringleaders, however, it disregards the complicity of those who opposed the ringleaders. For example, in proposing Tominaga as the ringleader *Daihon'ei rikugunbu*, compiled by former officers of the Imperial Army, weakens its analysis of the role of the army leadership as a whole. Similarly, the War History Office's *Daihon'ei kaigunbu Dai Tōa senso kaisen keii* [The Imperial Headquarters Navy Section and the circumstances

---

[5] See, for example, Takeo Shimmyō, ed., *Kaigun senso kentō kaigi kiroku* [Records of navy conferences to consider war] (Tokyo: Mainichi Shimbunsha, 1976).

leading to the Greater East Asia War],[6] prepared by former officers of the Imperial Navy, while mentioning Tominaga, identifies the army as a whole as the ringleader; thus, despite the many navy documents cited, this work fails to provide an incisive analysis of the navy's role.[7]

But the greatest flaw in the leadership theory is that despite its search for culprits it lets the archcriminal slip through its fingers. It pays no attention whatsoever to the structural factors that generated discord in the group planning and prosecuting the war or to the way in which these factors functioned. Any such analysis, I believe, must lead ultimately to examination of the emperor system.

THE ROLE OF THE EMPEROR SYSTEM AND MAINTAINING ORDER BY PARALLEL ARGUMENT

In a 1981 paper, Keiichi Eguchi, discussing past studies of the Manchurian Incident which marked the beginning of the Fifteen-Year War, notes that according to the theory of "emperor-system fascism" Japan's leadership was basically united. Although there were conflicts among the military, elder statesmen *(genrō)*, political parties, big business, and so on, these were temporary, localized, relative, and tactical; ultimately, the ruling stratum united in promoting fascism and an external war of aggression. His objection to this theory is that it "explains that the birds of a feather all came from one nest, but not why they pecked one another so viciously, inflicting such bloody wounds."[8]

Amplifying this criticism in a 1982 paper, Eguchi notes again that "one of the greatest problems" in study of the Manchurian Incident lies in the way in which one perceives "the conflicts and rifts in Japan's external policies" occasioned by army field units' embarking on the exercise of force by means of a stratagem while the government professed a policy of nonexpansion.

> It is a fact that in the end the conflicting and divided parties were united in the policy of aggression and that a consensus of state organs and the ruling stratum was established, but emphasizing the fact of unity and consensus alone leads to overlooking the questions of why the conflict preceding unification and the rifts preceding consensus arose and persisted.

He applies a scalpel of sharp analysis to the conflicts and rifts in the group planning and prosecuting the war, concluding that they were "rooted in the highly contradictory dual character of Japanese imperialism, self-reliance as a military power on the one hand and economic dependence on the United States and Britain on the other,

---

[6] Defense Agency, War History Office, *Daihon'ei kaigunbu Dai Tōa sensō kaisen keii* [The Imperial Headquarters Navy Section and the circumstances leading to the Greater East Asia War], 2 vols. (Tokyo: Asagumo Shimbunsha, 1979).

[7] One reason for this lopsidedness is probably that army histories are written or compiled by people formerly affiliated with the Imperial Army and navy histories are written or compiled by people formerly affiliated with the Imperial Navy. Such histories thus reflect even today the conflict and rivalry generated by army and navy sectionalism. A comparative study of such works as the War History Office's *Daihon'ei rikugunbu* and *Daihon'ei kaigunbu* or of Makoto Ikuta, *Nippon rikugunshi* [A history of the Japanese army] (Tokyo: Kyōikusha, 1980) and Saburō Toyama, *Nippon kaigunshi* [A history of the Japanese navy] (Tokyo: Kyōikusha, 1980) reveals that to a greater or lesser extent the authors are writing as apologists for the services with which they were once affiliated.

[8] Keiichi Eguchi, "Manshūjihen ki kenkyū no saikentō" [Reexamining studies of the time of the Manchurian Incident], *Rekishi hyōron* [Historical review], no. 377 (September 1981), p. 4.

and are to be seen as the expression of the conflict between the two external policies based on this dual character"[9] (cooperation with the United States and Britain to accommodate the system established by the Washington Conference on the one hand and an Asian Monroe Doctrine necessitating conflict with the United States and Britain on the other).

Eguchi's "dual imperialism" theory appears to have received favorable notice from some scholars of Japanese history.[10] I, for one, searching for a way to explain the dissension within the war-leadership group at the time of the occupation of French Indochina, found his thesis suggestive, since it supports thinking of the occupation, which was an expansion of the war, in terms of the conflicts dividing the group planning and prosecuting the war. I should, however, note one way in which the focus of Eguchi's interest differs from mine. He is concerned with *why* such dissension occurred, whereas at this time my interest is focused on *how* it evolved. Nevertheless, I do not believe that these are mutually exclusive concerns.

When the development of dissension within the war-leadership group is viewed from this perspective, two points demand attention. The first is the group's composite organization *(yoriai-jotai)*. Imperial Headquarters, part of the war-leadership group, was itself a composite of the Army General Staff and Naval General Staff. And the membership of the Nishihara Mission, which was directly attached to Imperial Headquarters, was drawn from the Army General Staff, Naval General Staff, and Ministry of Foreign Affairs. These organizations were set up to coordinate different sections' views and unify policy and action, but cursed as they were by their composite nature, they functioned instead to amplify disunity—temporarily concealed at best—as members with disparate views vied with one another.

The second point has to do with the war-leadership group's decision-making process, which was dominated by the parallel presentation of pros and cons *(ryōron heiritsu)*; the policies finally adopted also gave opposing views equal weight and set them forth in parallel fashion *(ryōron heiki)*. Whatever the controversy—forcible occupation versus peaceful occupation, southern expansion versus northern expansion, war against Britain and the United States versus negotiations with Britain and the United States—there was no logical debate by means of which a consensus could be achieved (no mechanism for such debate was provided), and no firm leadership decision to endorse one or the other viewpoint. This was true from the tactical level all the way up to the strategic and state-policy level. In the circumstances, the expedient of "respecting" opposing views was the dominant mode of "resolving" disagreement. A classic example of this approach is seen in the joint instructions issued by the assistant chiefs of the army and navy general staffs: these documents did not stipulate a single course of action agreed upon by the army and navy but merely set forth the two sets of views.

A decision-making process that shrank from dealing with opposing views either by adopting one or the other on the grounds of greater efficacy or by achieving agreement through logical debate to settle points of contention, and that relied in-

---

[9] Keiichi Eguchi, "Jūgo nen sensōshi kenkyū no kadai" [Problems in the study of the history of the Fifteen-Year War], *Rekishigaku kenkyū* [Journal of historical studies], no. 511 (December 1982), p. 9.

[10] See, for example, Nobuyoshi Tazaki, "Shōwa senzen ki kenkyū o meguru jakkan no mondai" [Some problems in regard to the study of the prewar period in the Shōwa era], in Junnosuke Sasaki and Susumu Ishii, eds., *Shimpen: Nihonshi kenkyū nyūmon* [An introduction to the study of Japanese history: New edition] (Tokyo: Tokyo Daigaku Shuppankai, 1982).

stead on "consensus" policies that were nothing but a patchwork of contradictory views, necessarily produced policies that remained merely theoretical and abstract. Moreover, because policies arrived at in this manner set forth two viewpoints, giving equal weight to both, any given policy could obviously generate two courses of action. Because no choice between opposing views had been made, it was possible to initiate and justify conflicting courses of action on the basis of the same policy.

In this way, the conflict among different sections of the group planning and prosecuting the war resulted in an increasingly violent oscillation between confrontation and "consensus" or compromise that exacerbated friction and strengthened the impulse toward war. Indeed, because of its amplificatory effect this motion should be likened to that of a screw spiraling forward rather than that of a pendulum swinging back and forth.

What underlay the war-leadership group's composite makeup and its penchant for a method of decision making that gave equal weight to opposing views, characteristics that determined its pattern of internal dissension? I will address this question by examining the way in which the emperor system functioned and the role of the emperor. Because of the magnitude of this theme, I will limit my discussion to the context of the issues raised so far. Specifically, I will address two issues: the functioning of the emperor system in relation to sectionalism and the role of the emperor in relation to let-both-arguments-stand decision making.

My thinking in regard to the first issue, the functioning of the emperor system in relation to sectionalism, owes a great deal to Masao Maruyama's well-known views, expressed in the following three passages:

> What determined the everyday morality of Japan's rulers was neither an abstract consciousness of legality nor an internal sense of right and wrong, nor again any concept of serving the public; it was a feeling of being close to the concrete entity known as the Emperor, an entity that could be directly perceived by the senses. It was therefore only natural that these people should come to identify their own interests with those of the Emperor, and that they should automatically regard their enemies as violators of the Emperor's powers.[11]

> Sectionalism . . . derived from a system according to which every element in society was judged according to its respective connexion, in a direct vertical line, with the ultimate entity. This involved a constant impulse to unite oneself with that entity, and the resultant sectionalism was of a far more active and 'aggressive' type than that associated with feudalism.[12]

> Each unit finds refuge in the limits of its authority; since every such attempt involves an effort by the respective unit to link itself vertically with the prestige of the Emperor, the various units (with their limited authority) are trans-

---

[11] Masao Maruyama, *Zōhoban: Gendai seiji no shisō to kōdō* (Tokyo: Miraisha, 1964), p. 21. The translation of this passage is by Ivan Morris in the English version of Maruyama's book, *Thought and Behaviour in Modern Japanese Politics: Expanded Edition*, ed. Ivan Morris (London: Oxford University Press, 1969), p. 13.

[12] Ibid., p. 23. The translation of this passage is by Ivan Morris in *Thought and Behaviour*, p. 15.

formed into something absolute and their relations with each other become infinitely complex.[13]

The reason that each section was able confidently to act independently, thus exhibiting the pluralized nature of the political system, was its belief that it was linked directly to the emperor, the sole ultimate authority. In this paper, incidentally, I use the term "sectionalism" narrowly, to refer to the pluralized political forces that defined themselves in terms of their direct links with the emperor and to their mutually exclusive nature.

The uniqueness of the emperor's ultimate authority and the pluralism of the political forces emanating therefrom constituted a contradiction peculiar to the emperor system. Two methods had to be employed to "resolve" this contradiction: one was to emphasize the uniqueness of the emperor's ultimate authority; the other was to recognize and "respect" the pluralism of the political forces.

Let us first examine the second method, which sought to integrate pluralized political forces under the single ultimate authority of the emperor while "respecting" their pluralism. This necessitated a composite organizational makeup, a policy-making process that gave equal weight to opposing arguments, and therefore the formulation of policies that set forth both sides of disputed issues. Because building a "consensus" of pluralized political forces while giving equal weight to opposing arguments upheld the contradictory relation between the uniqueness of the emperor and the pluralism of political forces, the result was an entire order (*chitsujo*) premised upon the equal-weight method. For the group planning and prosecuting the war, upholding this order was an imperative. It is not surprising that "consensus" building premised on "respect" for pluralized political forces was unable to unify these forces.

What about the other method, which emphasized the uniqueness of the emperor's ultimate authority? As the sole holder of power, the emperor was "theoretically . . . in a position to bring about the ultimate integration of the pluralized political power."[14] Let us consider this in connection with the central governing apparatus. It is well known that the Constitution of the Empire of Japan (the so-called Meiji Constitution) invested the emperor with powerful and sweeping prerogatives.[15] It also stipulated that the exercise of these prerogatives required the advice of ministers of state. This placed constitutional limits upon the scope of the emperor's authority, but at the same time, because ministers of state were required to take total responsibility for the execution of the imperial prerogatives, the emperor was placed outside the sphere of legal and political responsibility, thus enabling him to remain "sacred and inviolable" (Article 3).

One imperial prerogative, however, was unconditional: the prerogative of supreme command did not necessitate the advice of ministers of state. Instead, the General Staff (eventually divided into the Army General Staff and Naval General Staff) was invested with the right to report directly to the throne concerning matters

---

[13] Ibid., p. 124. The translation of this passage is by Ivan Morris in *Thought and Behaviour*, p. 123.

[14] Ibid., p. 125. The translation of this passage is by Ivan Morris in *Thought and Behaviour*, p. 124.

[15] See Saburō Ienaga, *Rekishi no naka no kempō* [The constitution in a historical context], vol. 1 (Tokyo: Tokyo Daigaku Shuppankai, 1977), pp. 62–74.

of supreme command. This direct vertical link with the emperor enabled the General Staff to execute all matters having to do with supreme command. "Independence of the prerogative of supreme command" *(tōsuiken no dokuritsu)* is the phrase used to describe the fact that this prerogative did not depend on the advice of ministers of state. In regard to this prerogative, at least, "it is fair to regard the emperor as an absolute monarch with dictatorial powers who had no leeway to behave as a constitutional monarch."[16]

The independence of the prerogative of supreme command, together with the expansion of its scope over time, led to a division between state affairs and supreme command, that is, between the government and the military, and further between the War Ministry, which was in charge of administering military affairs, and the General Staff (the Imperial Headquarters Army Department), which was in charge of exercising supreme command (this division between administrative and general-staff functions applied to both the army and the navy). Although the emperor's prerogative of supreme command applied, of course, to the army and the navy alike, in 1903 the Naval General Staff split off from the General Staff. From then on, the army and navy general staffs were on an equal footing, each linked directly to the emperor, which made the two services independent of each other. In this way the government, the army, and the navy, by virtue of their separate direct links with the emperor, came to possess independent spheres of competence and became separate entities competing with and checking one another.

Given this structure, when dissension among the three arose (disagreements because of sectionalism were frequent), only the emperor could mediate or arbitrate. When expansion of the war became inevitable, dissension among the government, the army, and the navy grew still more pronounced and became chronic. The need to unify political power required the emperor to assume an expanded role as absolute monarch. Without unified state policies the war could not be prosecuted, much less won. However, it is important to note that "even in regard to the exercise of the prerogative of supreme command, which is construed as having been intended to enable the emperor legally to act as an absolute monarch, the emperor did not in fact impose his individual will in order to wield his potential as an absolute monarch."[17]

The establishment of a mechanism whereby the government, the army, and the navy could achieve "consensus" is a good example. The institution of Imperial Headquarters–government liaison conferences in 1937, the substitution of Imperial Headquarters–government liaison discussions in 1940 to promote unity, and the reversion to liaison conferences the following year testify to the difficulty of achieving consensus. But as a rule the emperor neither attended such meetings nor issued direct imperial decisions. Instead, the emperor's judgments and will were made known and implemented through a process that, though tortuous, was invested with the coercive power of absolute authority: conferences of the war-leadership group to coordinate opinions, followed by communication between members of that group and the emperor in the form of private reports to the throne *(naisō)*, formal reports to the throne *(jōsō)*, imperial questions *(gokamon)*, and imperial conferences *(gozenkaigi)*. Simple consultations among some ministers and representatives of the army and navy general staffs took precedence over cabinet meetings and became the actual mechanism for determining important state policies even in regard to matters that

---

[16] Ibid., p. 70.

[17] Ibid., pp. 71–72.

did not involve the prerogative of supreme command because for the emperor, in time of war, that was the most expedient and efficient way of gaining "consensus" among the government and the two military services.

The role of the emperor in the governing apparatus can also be explained in terms of his divine authority. To preserve his "sacred and inviolable" status, it was necessary that he not become caught up in the rivalries and conflicts of the pluralized political power but remain above the fray, a transcendental entity. Because, as I have noted, unification of political forces required the emperor to expand his role as an absolute monarch, remaining in a transcendental position was contradictory. Resolution of this contradiction was attempted by using the emperor's very transcendence of the political sphere as a kind of disguise behind which he could exercise effective and real authority for unification, in other words, by deifying him still more. As the impulse toward war expansion grew, it became essential "to bring about the ultimate integration of the pluralized political power." In accordance with this necessity, the emperor had to express his intentions and act explicitly as an absolute monarch. Ceremonial and formalistic embellishments became more important than ever to maintain the fiction that the emperor was aloof from the pluralized political power. I may add that in discussing the emperor's responsibility for the war, obviously what should be examined is not the fiction of his transcendence but the reality of his power.

The emperor could not openly display the attributes of an absolute monarch but had to rely on a number of embellishments and disguises. This testified to an inherent contradiction in efforts to resolve the dilemma between the pluralization of different policy groups maintaining their own lines of authorization to the emperor and an emperor whose authority was emphasized as ultimate, unique, and absolute.

Viewed thus, dissension within the group planning and prosecuting the war can be seen as inevitable and insoluble. But there were of course "safety valves" to vent some of the pressure of this insoluble conflict. One was the thorough repression of the antiwar and antiestablishment movements within Japan, the only true opposition; the other was the prosecution of a war of aggression overseas.

II. THE SURVEILLANCE ACTIVITIES OF THE NISHIHARA MISSION

Contemporary documents refer to the Nishihara Mission variously as a "surveillance group," a "study group," or a "group dispatched to French Indochina." Nishihara himself, after taking up his duties in Hanoi, referred to the group in telegrams to army headquarters in Tokyo mainly as the Nishihara Mission. The mission was called a surveillance group because the main official reason for dispatching this band of military specialists was to observe the blockade of supplies to Chiang Kai-shek by conducting surveillance in Vietnam, on the Chinese border, and in other key locations.

On June 22, 1940, a message titled "Proposal to France Concerning the Dispatch of a *Surveillance Group*" (emphasis added) was handed by Masayuki Tani, the vice-minister for foreign affairs, to Charles Arsène Henry, the French ambassador in Tokyo. The first paragraph read: "The Imperial Government [wishes to] send . . . thirty military specialists and ten diplomatic personnel *to observe* the blockade of supplies moving through French Indochina to China"[18] (emphasis added). The

---

[18] Document 5.

function of the military specialists that Japan wished to send to French Indochina was to be limited to surveillance.

To cite another example, on June 24 Captain Kuranosuke Yanagisawa, an Imperial Headquarters naval staff officer, was named head of the group's navy contingent by the Imperial Headquarters Navy Section. His orders, issued by the chief of the Naval General Staff, stated: "As head of the Imperial Headquarters Navy Section contingent, you are ordered to carry out *surveillance* of the French Indochina blockade of supplies to Chiang Kai-shek"[19] (emphasis added).

Since the ostensible reason for sending military specialists to Hanoi was "to carry out surveillance of the blockade of supplies to Chiang Kai-shek," the group was called a "surveillance group" or "study group." Let us now consider the surveillance activities of this group of military specialists.

Japan first disclosed the composition of the surveillance group it was sending to Hanoi—thirty military specialists and ten diplomatic personnel—in the "Proposal to France Concerning the Dispatch of a Surveillance Group"[20] of June 22. The army contingent, headed by a major general, included eleven field and company officers and eleven warrant officers and noncommissioned officers, a total of twenty-three personnel.[21] The navy contingent was headed by a captain and included two commanders or lieutenant commanders, one special-duty officer, and three petty officers, a total of seven personnel.[22] Nishihara, the leader of the army contingent, also commanded the entire group. Thus Yanagisawa, the leader of the navy contingent, was under Nishihara's command. The Nishihara Mission "received orders from the chiefs of the Army General Staff and Naval General Staff to act as an organization dispatched by Imperial Headquarters."[23] However, because it included both army and navy personnel, it perpetuated the army-navy conflict that existed at central headquarters.

Three of the ten diplomatic personnel in the group were from the Japanese consulate general in Hanoi.[24] The remaining seven were sent directly from the Foreign Ministry in Tokyo. The course of later negotiations between Japan and French Indochina indicates that the Japanese consul general in Hanoi at that time, Rokurō Suzuki, acted as the representative of the ten diplomatic personnel, which means that the Hanoi consulate general also came under the command of Imperial Headquarters once the Nishihara Mission arrived. Thus, because of the structure of the Nishihara Mission, the discord that characterized the relationship between the military and the Foreign Ministry at central headquarters was replicated in Hanoi. However, this discord cannot be viewed as a conflict between equals. Throughout the Japanese army's occupation of Indochina, the consulate general in Hanoi disliked and distrusted the local Japanese military authorities and put up weak, sporadic resistance. But it was never able to act autonomously or implement its own proposals, because it was merely an appendage of the military organization. The inclusion of consulate general

---

[19] Document 7.

[20] Document 5.

[21] Document 9.

[22] Document 8.

[23] Suketaka Tanemura, *Daihon'ei kimitsu nisshi* [Imperial Headquarters secret war diaries] (Tokyo: Daiyamondosha, 1952), p. 16.

[24] Document 5.

personnel in the Nishihara Mission was the first step in the consulate general's fall to ancillary status.

Also noteworthy is the relationship between the Nishihara Mission and the Japanese forces stationed in southern China, mainly Guangdong. The document "Imperial Headquarters Army Department Members of the Group Dispatched to French Indochina" stipulated that three members, in addition to the eleven field and company officers sent from headquarters, were to be staff officers of the Kwantung Army or the Nanning Army.[25] The Kwantung Army had its headquarters in Guangzhou, Guangdong Province, while the Nanning Army (the Twenty-second Army) was based in Nanning, Guangxi Province. These two armies, situated at the southern edge of a war front that had expanded throughout China, were the units most eager to use military force against French Indochina. Three staff officers of those units were named to serve concurrently as staff officers of the Nishihara Mission.

In a secret message to the Naval General Staff, Yanagisawa wrote that Colonel Kenryō Satō, assistant chief of staff of the Kwantung Army, and Colonel Masutarō Nakai of the Nanning Army were ordered to serve concurrently as Nishihara Mission staff officers.[26] Nakai went to Hanoi immediately to join the group, but Satō, known as "a hard-liner on French-Indochina strategy,"[27] remained in Guangzhou for a while. Nishihara met with Satō in Guangzhou on his way to Hanoi, and Yanagisawa noted: "Major General Nishihara seemed relieved that Colonel Satō had a more moderate attitude than he had expected."[28] This short passage gives a glimpse of the three-way tug-of-war involving army headquarters, local army units, and the navy, which tried to check the conflict between the other two, that was emerging within the Nishihara Mission even as Nishihara was on his way to Hanoi. (Satō eventually went to Hanoi, and I will describe later the disturbance he created within the Nishihara Mission.) Thus, the Nishihara Mission incorporated the conflict between the those favoring negotiations and the hard-liners or, stated more simply, the conflict between army headquarters and field units.

Because of its mixed membership, the Nishihara Mission incorporated multiple strands of conflict between the army and the navy, between the military and the Foreign Ministry, between the hard-liners and the negotiators within the army, and also between central headquarters and units in the field. These structural rifts in the Nishihara Mission made Japan's policy toward French Indochina extremely contra-dictory and tortuous. What is more, they did not have the effect of blunting the activities of the military or checking its aggressive behavior. On the contrary, they exacerbated the military's thirst for invasion and had the effect of expanding the war.

The first contingent of the surveillance group headed by Nishihara arrived in Hanoi on June 29. The remaining members arrived on July 3, bringing the group to full strength.[29] On the morning of July 1, two days after arriving in Hanoi, Nishihara, together with Yanagisawa, Ryūji Koike, and Shigeru Yosano (a secretary in the Hanoi consulate general who was a member of the Nishihara Mission), met with Governor General Georges Catroux.[30] Nishihara handed Catroux a "Proposal to the French

---

[25] Document 9.

[26] Document 16.

[27] Ibid.

[28] Ibid.

[29] Document 35.

[30] Document 16.

Indochina Authorities" concerning establishment of the surveillance group. The main points were as follows:

"1. We wish to establish surveillance posts in Haiphong, Tien Yen, Lang Son, Cao Bang, Ha Giang, and Lao Cai.

"2. Each surveillance post will be staffed by one officer and six clerks, interpreters, and others.

"3. We wish to have surveillance personnel assume their duties at each post on July 2.

"4. In carrying out their duties, surveillance personnel may move in border areas other than those in the vicinity of their posts. We request your approval of this.

"5. We request your approval to carry out communications between surveillance posts and headquarters in Hanoi by coded telegrams and by sending personnel back and forth."[31]

That afternoon Yanagisawa, Koike, and Yosano began detailed negotiations with French Indochinese officials over these conditions, all of which were approved the same day. Personnel left for the six surveillance posts at 8:00 A.M. (10 A.M. Japan time) on July 2.[32] However, only three or four men left for each post that day; the others left on July 8.[33] Although they were few in number, they were the first Japanese military personnel to set foot in the strategic area of northern Indochina.

Let us examine the significance to Japan of the locations of the observation posts.

On June 17 Catroux, acceding to Japanese demands, had begun to blockade all supplies—not only weapons and ammunition but also trucks and gasoline—passing through French Indochina en route to Chiang Kai-shek. Ambassador Henry in Tokyo relayed this news to Foreign Vice-Minister Tani on June 19.[34] On June 25 Imperial Headquarters, in a secret message, "The Situation with Regard to Enemy Imports of Materiel: The Effects of French Indochina's Blockade of Goods on Supplies to Enemy Forces," had declared that "the French Indochina blockade has cut imports [of supplies] to Chungking by more than half." The Japanese judged that the blockade was continuing and was having a major impact on the Chiang regime's ability to resist. But at the same time, the analysis stated that it was not believed that "the enemy [the Chiang regime] will succumb immediately" and emphasized the need to formulate additional measures so that Chiang would "not be given a chance to work out countermeasures."[35]

Sending the Nishihara Mission to French Indochina was one such measure. The six Japanese surveillance posts were located at points believed to be major unloading, marshaling, and border-crossing points for supplies to Chiang. This can be seen from previous studies conducted by the Japanese.

On October 28, 1938, the Japanese government had protested to France about Chiang's supply routes through Indochina and had requested that the border be closed and a Japanese team be sent to investigate the situation. France, however, refused these requests. In December that year the Third Department of the Naval General Staff drew up a document, "French Opinion on the China Incident," that analyzed Chiang's supply routes through Indochina thoroughly for the first time.

---

[31] Document 14.

[32] Document 16.

[33] Document 20.

[34] Document 4.

[35] Document 10.

According to this document, there were four supply routes: the route to Kunming via the Vietnam-Yunnan railroad, the route to Longzhou via the Lang Son railroad, the route to Longzhou via Tien Yen and Lang Son, and the route to Longzhou via Mong Cai and Dongxing.[36] In June 1940 the Third Department drew up another report, "Current Status of Imports of Supplies for Chiang via French Indochina and Burma," which is believed to have supplied some of the data used by the Nishihara Mission in its activities. The main marshaling points named in that report were Dong Dang, Na Cham, That Khe, Cao Bang, Shuikouguan, Pingerguan, Trung Khanh, Haiphong, Hanoi, Viet Tri, Yen Bai, and Lao Cai.[37]

Let us examine these supply routes and marshaling points in relation to the six surveillance posts established by the Japanese. It is clear that the surveillance posts and the group's headquarters in Hanoi covered all these routes and marshaling points almost completely. However, the surveillance posts were set up half a month after the blockade went into effect. Imperial Headquarters also knew that French Indochina was maintaining the blockade and that the blockade was having an adverse effect on the Chiang regime. In addition, personnel at the surveillance posts reported to headquarters in Hanoi that the blockade was definitely being carried out: "Each observation post reported that the supply-route blockade was in effect."[38]

Therefore, as far as observation of the blockade went, the surveillance posts had little significance from the start. Japan knew this very well but set them up nevertheless, not only because the posts were in important locations along Chiang's supply routes but also because these locations were strategically important positions in northern Vietnam.

One of the six posts, Tien Yen, was closed only two weeks after being set up because it was found to lack importance as either a supply or a strategic point. How did Japan see Tien Yen's role as a point on Chiang's supply routes before sending observers there? "French Opinion on the China Incident" is precise on this point. Supplies transferred to junks off Haiphong were conveyed along the coast to Tien Yen, where they were loaded onto trucks and taken to Lang Son. Sea transport to Tien Yen was handled by a French-owned and -operated company. After Japanese forces advanced to Guangdong, a number of ships bound for Hong Kong called at Paihai, transshipping goods offshore, the goods then being taken to Tien Yen. Thus, the Third Department of the Naval General Staff identified Tien Yen as an important unloading point in December 1938.

Incidentally, the document noted that travel by Japanese in the area was "difficult even for consulate personnel." This means that it would have been difficult for anyone actually to go to Tien Yen and gather information there, so Tien Yen's role in a supply route to Chiang may have been overestimated, a point I will examine later. Be that as it may, Japan asked to be allowed to set up a surveillance post at Tien Yen on the basis of this research.

The Tien Yen surveillance post was manned by a team headed by Lieutenant Commander Takeshi Fukuoka. After seeing off Fukuoka and his party on the night of July 2, Yanagisawa, the head of the navy contingent and Fukuoka's immediate superior, wrote to Captain Takeji Ono, directly assigned to the head of the First Department of the Naval General Staff: "Tien Yen is an overwhelmingly Chinese town, and

---

[36] Document 2.

[37] Document 13.

[38] Document 24.

I am concerned about the safety of our men's housing. . . . Depending on the situation, I may transfer them elsewhere or order them to return to headquarters."[39] Yanagisawa was thinking of recalling the party the very night it went out because Tien Yen was "overwhelmingly Chinese" and thus dangerous.

The diplomat Yosano, however, disagreed with Yanagisawa's assessment. In a July 9 telegram to Minister for Foreign Affairs Hachirō Arita, he maintained that it was the French Indochina authorities who were reluctant to send the surveillance group to Tien Yen: "I am sure of the sincerity of the governor general and the military commander in maintaining the supply-route blockade, and they have been very cooperative over assignment of the surveillance teams." However, "all the Chinese know Tien Yen, and the French Indochina authorities are very concerned that we will have difficulty operating our surveillance post."[40] It will be noted that Yosano does say that the French Indochina authorities were worried about the Chinese, and for the same reason as that given by Yanagisawa.

The French Indochina authorities probably raised difficulties about sending personnel to every surveillance post, not just Tien Yen. However, the decision to close down Tien Yen was not made because of concern on the part of French Indochina; it was made entirely on Japanese initiative. On July 16, exactly two weeks after the surveillance team had been dispatched, the Nishihara Mission in Hanoi sent the following telegram to Imperial Headquarters: "The Tien Yen surveillance post (commanded by Lieutenant Commander Fukuoka) reports that in two weeks of observation, it has been ascertained not only that there is no sign of this area's being used as a supply route to Chiang but also that the local roads and waterways are in no condition to be used for this purpose. Therefore, the Tien Yen post has been closed down, and its personnel have been assigned to patrol the areas around Mong Cai and Tien Yen."[41]

Thus, the Nishihara Mission decided to close down the Tien Yen post only two weeks after it had been set up because there was no evidence at all of Tien Yen's being part of a supply route to Chiang. While I believe that further research should be conducted to determine whether Tien Yen had at some earlier time been part of a supply route, the Nishihara Mission's message makes it clear that Tien Yen's role had been considerably overestimated in the December 1938 Naval General Staff report.

In his July 2 message, Yanagisawa wrote that Tien Yen was closed down because Chinese were living in the area and he was worried about the safety of the group. Let us weigh the validity of this assertion. Certainly Tien Yen, a coastal town, was, along with Mong Cai, a border town heavily populated by Chinese, but it was not the only such town. The other border towns with surveillance posts—Lang Son, Cao Bang, and Lao Cai—also had large Chinese populations.

A man named Toshiyo Yamada, who was living in Hanoi at the time, wrote the following about Lang Son and other border towns in a secret report sent to the head of the Third Department of the Naval General Staff: "Because there are so many Chinese there, the observers based in Cao Bang, Lang Son, and Lao Cai are in consider-

---

[39] Document 16.

[40] Document 24.

[41] Document 37.

able danger."[42] Thus, the Japanese military authorities were fully aware that the observers in Lang Son, Cao Bang, and Lao Cai were exposed to "considerable danger," since there were just as many Chinese there as in Tien Yen. But even though the supply routes to Chiang had been blockaded and there was no longer such a pressing need to monitor movements, the observers were not removed from these three posts because they were in strategic military locations. Lang Son and Cao Bang were contact points between the Nishihara Mission and the Kwantung and Nanning armies in Guangdong and Guangxi. Lao Cai was seen as a base from which to bomb Chiang's forces. These considerations point to the real reason the Tien Yen surveillance post was shut down. The observers were pulled out not because of the danger posed by the large Chinese population or because the observation post there was no longer needed but because Tien Yen was relatively unimportant in strategic terms.

Thus, by mid-July one surveillance post had been shut down. The five others remained, all located in strategic military spots in northern Vietnam: Haiphong, Lang Son, Cao Bai, Ha Giang, and Lao Cai. Four of the posts were commanded by army officers: Lang Son by Lieutenant Colonel Oka (Infantry), Cao Bang by Major Yokoyama (Infantry), Ha Giang by Major Yasumura (Air Service), and Lao Cai by Major Sakai (Infantry).[43] The fifth post, Haiphong, was commanded by a navy officer, Commander Jun'ichi Negi.[44]

The second paragraph of the "Proposal to the French Indochina Authorities" set the complement of each post at seven, one officer and about six clerks, interpreters,

---

[42] Document 12. Since Yamada gave his address in this report as "Imperial Consulate General, Hanoi," it is clear that he stayed at the consulate general while he was in Hanoi. His report dated June 22, 1940 (Document 6), is also extant. Both reports were addressed to the head of the Third Department, Naval General Staff, so Yamada was probably connected with the navy. He was probably one of the people in Hanoi making preparations for the arrival of the Nishihara Mission. A report prepared by the Third Department of the Naval General Staff in June 1940, "Current Status of Imports of Supplies for Chiang via French Indochina and Burma" (Document 13), contained information based on Yamada's reports.

[43] Document 52.

[44] Document 16. Commander Negi was killed in an airplane crash on July 7, less than a week after assuming command of the Haiphong surveillance post (Documents 25, 35). Following is a brief description of the incident. On July 6 the Army General Staff sent the Nishihara Mission an urgent message that part of the Japanese fleet would visit Guangzhou Bay on July 7 and Haiphong on July 10. When Catroux was told, he "became very agitated" and balked, saying, "Threatening me with the imminent arrival of ships of the fleet is like holding a gun to my head during negotiations" (Document 22). Some of the members of the Nishihara Organization, including the navy contingent, concluded that the fleet should call off its uninvited visit, since such a visit would not advance negotiations with French Indochina. One of these men was Negi. He "immediately wrote a draft telegram asking that the Imperial fleet not enter French territory until the Nishihara Organization requested it to do so" and submitted it to Yanagisawa, his superior. But Yanagisawa "held the message back because the date in question was the next day and it would be hard for Tokyo to rescind an order already issued." Instead, he "decided to send a liaison officer to Guangzhou Bay, and Commander Negi volunteered to go himself" (Document 25). Negi left Hanoi at 8:30 A.M. on July 7 for Guangzhou Bay aboard a twenty-passenger plane provided by French Indochina. But radio contact was lost at 10:00 A.M. Negi's body was washed up on the western shore of the Leizhou Peninsula on July 8. His plane had been shot down by a Japanese navy plane. As far as extant records show, Negi was the first Japanese military man to die in Indochina. Moreover, his plane was shot down by the Japanese military. His death is an episode that should be included on the first page of any history of the Japanese military in Indochina, since it seems to presage the ultimate fate of the Japanese military.

and others. According to another source, each post was staffed by eight people: the commanding officer, one code clerk, three sentries, one interpreter, one clerk, and one supernumerary.[45] At any rate, each post had a staff of seven or eight, not a very large number. Naturally, the clerks and supernumeraries had been brought from Japan.[46] Each post was equipped with one automobile and one motorcycle with sidecar, provided by the French Indochina authorities.[47]

The French Indochina authorities placed liaison officers in the posts to handle communications with the Japanese. The liaison officers at Haiphong, for example, were a coal mining company president (given the rank of army captain),[48] a Hanoi University professor (lieutenant), and a minister who had served at a church in Mikawashima, Tokyo (corporal).[49] Some of them had lived in Japan, and most of them understood Japanese. The professor, who was the liaison officer for the team in Hanoi, had "worked as an adviser to the Foreign Ministry in the past and [was] a knowledgeable Japanophile."[50] Another typical character was Major Thiébaut, who was assigned to Nishihara. Thiébaut, a French military attaché in Tokyo, had accompanied Nishihara to Hanoi.[51] Nishihara appeared to trust Thiébaut and would negotiate important points with him, which he would then take to the governor general. Thus, French nationals who were pro-Japanese or knowledgeable about Japan played an important role in the early stages of negotiations between Japan and French Indochina.[52]

---

[45] Document 52.

[46] Document 9.

[47] Document 52.

[48] This "coal mining company president (captain)" is almost certainly the person referred to in one document as "Captain Bourgouin [phonetic], the pro-Japanese manager of the Hong Gai coal mine, who is responsible for liaison with Commander Negi" (Document 25). He was aboard the same plane as Negi on July 7 and died with him when the plane was shot down by the Japanese (see note 44 for details).

[49] Document 16.

[50] Document 12.

[51] Document 35.

[52] There was some conflict within the Nishihara Mission over such French nationals. Yanagisawa, head of the navy contingent, clearly expressed his displeasure at the close relations between Thiébaut and Nishihara in messages to the Imperial Headquarters Navy Section: "Who knows what will happen, since as usual Major Thiébaut is involved," and "Negotiations were carried out by the Nishihara-Thiébaut pair. I mentioned today to Colonel Koike that we must be very careful about this, and he agreed" (Document 17). Such comments reflected the conflict between the army and the navy, of course, but they went beyond that, since even Koike, who was an army officer and Nishihara's right-hand man, agreed with Yanagisawa. "Colonel Koike just handles the paperwork. Nishihara often writes telegrams without consulting Koike and takes them to the telegraphers' office himself. Given Major General Nishihara's character, perhaps this cannot be helped, but I consulted [with Colonel Koike and we agreed] that we should take precautions to ensure that nothing goes wrong in major matters" (Document 17). This passage shows that both army and navy members of the Nishihara Mission resented Nishihara's authoritarian personality and methods. Yanagisawa's dislike of Thiébaut may have stemmed from the suspicion and contempt of the French in general that were characteristic of ultranationalistic Japanese military men. Moreover, the sight of Nishihara speaking in a friendly manner in passable French (he had spent some time in France as a military attaché) to a Frenchman who should have been treated with hostility or disdain aroused disrespect for Nishihara among his subordinates. At any rate, the conflict over even such a matter as French nationals who were pro-Japanese or knowledgeable about Japan

The French Indochina authorities also agreed to two conditions concerning liaison: they authorized the installation of wireless equipment linking the Hanoi headquarters with each observation post, and they agreed to the installation of an undersea cable between Haiphong and Haikou.[53] Until then, the only way of contacting the Japanese troops in Guangdong had been via Tokyo;[54] the undersea cable would make it possible to communicate with them directly. The French Indochina authorities even permitted personal contact. A telegram from Foreign Minister Arita to ambassadors and consuls general dated July 22 read in part: "The French Indochina authorities have permitted liaison officers communicating between our forces that have reached Zhennanguan and the surveillance group to move back and forth across the border and also to deliver comfort supplies to our troops at Zhennanguan."[55] The surveillance post at Lang Son had also become a liaison and supply point between Japanese troops in China and the Nishihara Mission.

Because French Indochina permitted the Nishihara Mission to engage in activities that far exceeded surveillance functions, it was natural for the authorities in Tokyo to regard Governor General Catroux and his colonial administration as cooperative and conciliatory. One Foreign Ministry document noted that the French Indochina authorities "are intent on showing as much goodwill as possible and are very cooperative."[56]

The French Indochina authorities did not meekly accede to every Japanese demand relating to surveillance activities, however. It is known that Catroux sometimes resisted Japanese demands or made his displeasure evident. When he met with Nishihara on July 9, he said: "The observers at the surveillance posts often engage in reconnaissance and other activities distasteful to the French Indochina authorities out of boredom."[57] Nevertheless, the authorities accepted as many of the Japanese demands relating to the Nishihara Mission's activities as possible, apparently in the hope of being able to avoid giving in to other demands, particularly strong military demands to station Japanese troops from China in northern Vietnam (Tonkin). That this was a vain hope was seen when Japan later forcibly occupied French Indochina, but in July 1940 French Indochina, still hoping for the best, accepted most of Japan's demands concerning its surveillance teams.

The Nishihara Mission surveillance network, with headquarters in Hanoi and five surveillance posts in coastal areas or on the Chinese border, was laid out in a fan-shaped pattern that covered most of northern Vietnam. The limited, direct aim of this network was to oversee and maintain the blockade on supplies bound for Chiang, in other words, to form a southern front against Chinese resistance. Had installing a surveillance network remained the goal of the Nishihara Mission, its activities could have been regarded as falling within the scope of "settling the China Incident." However, its activities took on a broader significance: to covertly observe movements within French Indochina and maintain contact with the Japanese army units in southern China positioned on Indochina's northern border, and to pressure the

---

within the Nishihara Mission illustrates how much deeper and more numerous than we can imagine were the divisions in that group.

[53] Document 48.

[54] Document 25.

[55] Document 39.

[56] Document 48.

[57] Document 35.

French Indochina authorities, through military intimidation, to facilitate the Japanese army's preparations for occupying French Indochina.

Here, too, there was conflict between those who wanted to restrict the Japanese army's occupation to the aim of "settling the China Incident" and those who wanted to use the occupation chiefly as a pretext for expanding the front southward, which would contribute incidentally to settlement of the China Incident.

In Tokyo, meanwhile, Prime Minister Fumimaro Konoe formed his second cabinet, and an Imperial Headquarters-government liaison conference adopted the "Outline of Measures to Deal with Changes in the World Situation," described as "the most significant policy decision in the process leading to the decision to wage war against the United States and Britain."[58] Many people have attributed these moves to the initiative of the army, especially the staff officers at central headquarters. It is certainly true that army leaders influenced the government's decisions, but this does not mean that there was no opposition in Tokyo or in the field. The complex infighting was never resolved. The friction and contradictions that resulted only internalized and obscured the conflict, further intensifying it in the end. It is fair to say that this conflict pushed the entire political and military policy structure to take a more aggressive stance toward the outside world.

As far as the Nishihara Mission itself was concerned, from the start it internalized the multiple conflicts that I have described. Its surveillance network soon acquired strong new overtones as a means of paving the way for the military occupation of French Indochina. This process shows that the hard-line faction within the army became dominant within the Nishihara Mission as well, but the opposing faction neither sat quietly as a spectator nor died out. In fact, when the Nishihara Mission's activity reached its peak, at the time that Japanese troops advanced from Lang Son and Do Son to occupy northern French Indochina, the struggle between the hard-liners and their opponents was intense. Indeed, it is wrong to say that the occupation was forced through *despite* severe conflict. Rather, the occupation took place precisely *because* this conflict existed.

The surveillance network more than fulfilled its purpose of preparing for occupation by Japanese forces. It also acquired yet another role: to detect undercurrents of national awareness and nationalist movements among the Vietnamese and to prepare ways of dealing with them. Initially, the Japanese were more interested in what was occurring among ethnic Chinese residents of Indochina and important representatives of the Chiang regime in Hanoi, but they had to penetrate Vietnamese society more deeply in forcing through the occupation.

In the next section I will discuss the second of the Nishihara Mission's three roles, especially as it relates to the first round of negotiations between the Japanese and the French Indochina authorities, which took place in July 1940.

III. The Japanese Demand for Troop Transit

The conclusion of a defense alliance was the main theme of the July 1940 negotiations. The following telegram from the Nishihara Mission to Imperial Headquarters is on file in the Foreign Ministry Archives: "The governor general of French Indochina has made the following proposals:

---

[58] Akira Fujiwara, *Tennōsei to guntai* [The emperor system and the military] (Tokyo: Aoki Shoten, 1978), p. 47.

"The government of French Indochina is willing to enter into a defense (?) alliance with Japan and establish a joint front against Chiang Kai-shek if Japan agrees to respect French Indochina's territorial integrity.

"If this alliance is concluded, several minor issues that are now becoming problems must be resolved quickly.

"Nevertheless, we ask that the Government make overtures."[59]

This message indicates that the proposal to "enter into a defense alliance" to "establish a joint front against Chiang Kai-shek," on the condition that "Japan agrees to respect French Indochina's territorial integrity," was made by the governor general. The sole purpose of this proposal was to get Japan to agree "to respect French Indochina's territorial integrity." The offer to "establish a joint front against Chiang Kai-shek" was merely bait with which to tempt Japan into agreeing.

I should mention in passing that it is not clear when this message was sent. The text preserved in the Foreign Ministry Archives was typed on Imperial Army letterhead and dated July 6, 1940, but we do not know whether this is the date on which the message was sent or the date on which it was received. However, the chronological table of negotiations between the Nishihara organization and the French Indochina authorities compiled by Captain Ōno of the Naval General Staff included the entire text of this message in the entry for July 6, with the remark that it was sent on July 5.[60] In addition, a message dated July 7 from Yanagisawa in Hanoi to Ōno in Tokyo stated: "If the Japan-French Indochina defense alliance proposed on the fifth comes about, it will be easy to settle everything in Japan's favor."[61] A report from Yosano also stated: "Major General Nishihara reported to me on the fifth that the governor general of French Indochina wants to enter into a defense alliance with Japan against Chiang Kai-shek."[62] This information, taken together, suggests that Catroux proposed the defense alliance to the Japanese on July 5, that the telegram quoted above was sent the same day, that it was received in Tokyo on July 6, and that it was also circulated to the Foreign Ministry.

The question mark after the word "defense" in the telegram was added either by Imperial Headquarters, which received the message, or by the army. This question mark hints at the puzzlement felt in Tokyo on seeing the words "defense alliance" for the first time in the frequent communications between the Nishihara Mission and Tokyo. However, Imperial Headquarters reacted swiftly. On July 7 Nishihara was sent the following instructions, signed by both assistant chiefs of staff: "The army and navy wish to enter into a defense alliance against China. To make this possible, we want terms that will allow us, for the purpose of joint defense, to station troops in French Indochina and use various military facilities there."[63]

Imperial Headquarters was enthusiastic about the proposal of a defense alliance against China because it saw this as an opening for Japan "to station troops in French Indochina and use various military facilities there." These were the very points on which Japan and French Indochina had differed so sharply, and there had also been discord among the Japanese on how to accomplish them.

---

[59] Document 21.

[60] Document 43.

[61] Document 22.

[62] Document 35.

[63] Document 43.

This was not the first time that Nishihara had been so instructed. He had received similar instructions from Shigeru Sawada, assistant chief of the Army General Staff, before leaving Tokyo. These instructions have been quoted in other books, but they are cited here as well because of their importance: "Once supplies for the Nanning Army passing through French Indochina have been arranged, work toward obtaining permission as soon as possible for our troops to transit French Indochina and use airfields there."[64]

The Japanese wanted French Indochina to agree to three points: supplying the Nanning Army, allowing the transit of Japanese troops, and permitting the use of airfields. Since the French Indochina authorities had already agreed to the first point,[65] the Nishihara Mission's main task now was to win approval of the second and third points, as the July 7 message from the two assistant chiefs of staff stated.

Sawada has been portrayed variously as a supporter of peaceful occupation who was in sharp conflict with hard-line elements within the military[66] and as a weakling incapable of leading the hard-liners, such as Kyōji Tominaga, head of the First Department of Imperial Headquarters, and the staff officers of the Kwantung Army, and who looked the other way as the war expanded.[67] Others believe that Tominaga and the Kwantung and Nanning army staff officers were much more hot-headed than the Second Department of the Army General Staff, the Army Ministry, and the navy, and tried to have the second and third points in Sawada's instructions approved immediately.[68] These arguments attempt to pinpoint responsibility for the expansion of the war that led to the occupation of northern Indochina. But emphasizing the responsibility of the unilateral actions of Tominaga and the other hardliners and the incompetence of Sawada leads to deemphasizing the role played by the Second Department of the Army General Staff, the Army Ministry, the navy, and those in favor of peaceful occupation, thus bypassing completely the issue of their responsibility.

This problem illustrates the limitations of a methodology that concentrates on establishing which individual or faction of the group planning and prosecuting the war played the leading role and holds a particular individual or faction responsible. A more effective methodology involves examining the way in which the war expanded through the conflicts and contradictions among the various factions within the war-leadership group. Naturally, the instructions Sawada sent from Tokyo did not express his ideas alone. They should be seen as a distillation of the conflict between the hard-liners and those favoring peaceful occupation that intensified the

---

[64] Ibid.

[65] Yanagisawa's July 4 message to Captain Ōno contained the following passage: "The army unit that advanced [from Nanning] to Zhennanguan [the Twenty-first Brigade of the Fifth Division occupied Zhennanguan on June 29] is having great difficulty obtaining food supplies. Through Major Thiébaut, Nishihara negotiated with General Martin, the [French Indochina] army commander, . . . and the governor general. Staff officer Amano, stationed at the front, was brought to Hanoi by military plane, and after various matters were discussed, it was agreed that food would be supplied from here. The governor general also sent two truckloads of rice, meat, vegetables, fruit, cigarettes and other goods as comfort supplies" (Document 17).

[66] Tanemura, *Daihon'ei kimitsu nisshi*, p. 28.

[67] Jun Tsunoda, ed., *Nitchū sensō 3* [The Sino-Japanese War 3], vol. 10 of *Gendaishi shiryō* [Sources of contemporary history, 1925–1945] (Tokyo: Misuzu Shobō, 1964), "Kaisetsu" [Commentary].

[68] Defense Agency, *Daihon'ei rikugunbu*, vol. 2, pp. 76–77.

impulse to expand the war. Sawada himself appears to have had neither the will nor the opinions required to exercise effective leadership over the competing factions under him. So while he behaved like a supporter of peaceful occupation, his stance in fact contributed to intensifying the impulse toward war expansion. In this sense, his role at central headquarters was similar to that of Nishihara in the Nishihara Mission.

On July 7 and 8 Nishihara and his men were busy dealing with the crash of the plane carrying Commander Negi,[69] but on July 9 Nishihara, acting on instructions received from the assistant chiefs of staff, "explained [to Catroux] that the transit of Japanese troops through French Indochina and the use of airfields would facilitate their occupation of Yunnan."[70] Nishihara was asking the French Indochina authorities to let Japanese troops transit French Indochina and use airfields there to enable Japan to occupy Yunnan, a step deemed necessary to "settle the China Incident."

Catroux replied: "You say 'transit,' but the rear guard would remain in French Indochina. This would amount to semipermanent occupation of our territory. The same goes for the airfields. This would probably affect our relations with the United States and Britain. I cannot assume responsibility for causing problems in international relations."[71] This was a clear refusal, on the grounds that letting Japanese troops transit French Indochina and use airfields there would lead to semipermanent occupation, which would upset the United States and Britain.

French Indochina's intention in proposing a defense alliance against Chiang had always been to get Japan to agree to "respect French Indochina's territorial integrity." In other words, French Indochina wanted to stop the Kwantung Army from occupying Indochina. Japan, however, was trying to gain more than French Indochina was willing to give, taking advantage of French Indochina's proposal of an anti-Chiang defense alliance to press for permission to transit French Indochina and use airfields there, which it had wanted to do for a long time. This was also the decisive time for another actor—Colonel Kenryō Satō, assistant chief of staff of the Kwantung Army and concurrently a staff officer of the Nishihara Mission—to make his move.

After being assigned to the mission, Satō took his time leaving Guangdong, thus exerting silent pressure on French Indochina and simultaneously hampering Nishihara and the Navy.[72] He finally flew to Hanoi on July 11[73] and met with Catroux the

---

[69] See note 44.

[70] Document 35.

[71] Ibid.

[72] In his memoirs, Satō recalls the circumstances leading up to his arrival in Hanoi as follows: "On June 30, Major General Issaku Nishihara, head of the French Indochina surveillance group, landed in Guangdong on his way to Hanoi by plane. I had intended to go with him on the same plane, but he told me: 'Wait a while.' He explained: 'It was only decided afterward that you should take on duties with the surveillance group in addition to your present post, and the French haven't been advised yet. I'll handle this when I get to Hanoi, so please come later.' That was the excuse Nishihara gave, but in fact he probably wanted to avoid me. He thought I would be a thorn in his side.

"I cooled my heels in Guangdong, and at the beginning of July I received a telegram from Nishihara advising me: 'It looks as though Governor General Catroux of French Indochina is going to propose a Franco-Japanese defense alliance.' The telegram he sent to Tokyo had also come [to me] in southern China.

"Of course he did not ask me to go [to Hanoi], but I was overjoyed to see the telegram. I thought this defense-alliance proposal would give us the opportunity to occupy French Indochina at last, so I left immediately for Hanoi." Kenryō Satō, *Satō Kenryō no shōgen* [Kenryō Satō's testimony] (Tokyo: Fuyō Shobō, 1976), pp. 162–63.

next day, accompanied by Nishihara and Yosano, to present a proposal. According to Yosano, the meeting took place "at Satō's request."[74]

Before discussing this proposal, I would like to explain Satō's position in the negotiations. At the beginning of the written proposal, a French translation of which was handed to the French Indochina authorities, Satō described himself as follows:

> I have come to French Indochina on assignment to the surveillance team sent by the Imperial Government. Availing myself of the honor of meeting with the French Indochina authorities, as a staff officer of the Kwantung Army I wish to explain various matters from the standpoint of those forces and ask your understanding. Please consider what I say completely unofficial.[75]

Satō was able to meet Catroux because he was a member of the Nishihara Mission. But he addressed Catroux at that meeting not as a member of that group but as "a staff officer of the Kwantung Army . . . from the standpoint of those forces." Officially, then, the July 12 meeting took place between the Nishihara Mission and Catroux, but actually it marked the first round of negotiations between a staff officer of the Kwantung Army and the governor general of French Indochina. Without even asking whether it was agreeable to the governor general, Satō began the meeting by declaring that he represented the position of the Kwantung Army. Moreover, he was aware that his words were unusually direct, as indicated by his assuring Catroux that what he said was "completely unofficial."

Satō's written proposal noted that "our forces welcome your proposal of a defense alliance" and continued: "To achieve this, we would like to have your

---

According to these memoirs, Satō's arrival in Hanoi was delayed not of his own volition but by Nishihara. That may in fact have been the case, because Nishihara and Satō disliked and disagreed with each other from the start of the surveillance group's tour of duty. One indication that Nishihara did stop Satō from going to Hanoi to take up his duties with the Nishihara Mission is Nishihara's remark that the decision to assign Satō to the Nishihara Mission had been made "afterward" and that the French had not yet been advised of this. "Imperial Headquarters Army Department Members of the Group Dispatched to French Indochina," dated June 24 (Document 9), which was appended to a secret message from the Imperial Headquarters Navy Section (Document 7), clearly shows that a Kwantung Army staff officer was to be part of the group, so the decision to include Satō must have been made before June 24. However, there is no record of whether the Japanese had given the French advance notice of the Nishihara Mission's members. Be that as it may, Nishihara's excuse for not taking Satō with him to Hanoi—that the French had not been notified—was arbitrary, because a Nanning Army staff officer, Masatarō Nakai, did accompany Nishihara to Hanoi. Nishihara probably had his own reasons for not wanting Satō to go with him. It is also a reasonable supposition that Satō was content to stay in Guangdong for a while to see how negotiations would go, to see what cards Nishihara would play. Also, as I have mentioned, Satō in Guangdong, as a hard-liner who was biding his time, exerted considerable pressure on French Indochina and probably also constrained the actions of Nishihara and the navy contingent in the Nishihara Mission. Satō was waiting for the most effective moment to make his appearance. When word came from Hanoi about the proposal to form a defense alliance, Satō "thought this defense-alliance proposal would give us the opportunity to occupy French Indochina at last" and "left immediately for Hanoi," although "of course he [Nishihara] did not ask me to go." Satō had decided that the time was ripe to make an appearance.

[73] Yosano's July 15 report (Document 35) stated that Satō arrived in Hanoi on July 10, but this was a mistake. The date was actually July 11.

[74] Document 35.

[75] Document 30.

cooperation on the items listed separately, which we require for strategic purposes."
He thereupon proffered the "Outline of the Agreement Between Japan and French
Indochina," the main points of which were as follows:

1. "Japan and French Indochina will mount joint operations against Chiang Kai-
shek."

2. Joint operations will involve "Japanese forces attacking Chinese territory from
the direction of French Indochina," Japanese forces "defending French Indochina's
territory jointly with French Indochina forces," and "French Indochina forces defending French Indochina's territory."

3. "French Indochina will grant permission for troops and military supplies to
transit French Indochina and will provide other assistance necessary for joint operations."

4. "Japan will guarantee French Indochina's independence."[76]

Clearly, the most important point was the third, concerning the transit of
Japanese troops and supplies. When Satō explained the outline, the first thing he
stressed was the "vital importance" of Japanese troops being able to transit French
Indochina:

> Because of the need to apply direct pressure on Chungking, we have reached
> the conclusion that, together with troops pressing in from other areas, we ab-
> solutely must advance on Chungking from the direction of French Indochina
> as well. Also, because increasing numbers of Chinese troops are massing
> along the French Indochina border, we must use the railroad [one line miss-
> ing] to attack them. This has become a matter of vital importance to our
> forces. I would particularly like you to understand that this has become a
> matter of life and death to our forces in dealing with China militarily.

The line missing from the text probably referred to the use of airfields in French
Indochina.

Acting in an intimidating manner as a staff officer of the Kwantung Army, Satō
began by putting pressure on Catroux, stressing that the transit of troops and the use
of airfields and railroads was "a matter of vital importance" and "a matter of life and
death." Next Satō discussed Chinese troop movements, saying that "increasing numbers of Chinese troops are massing along the French Indochina border" and that
there was "a grave risk that the fighting will spill over into French Indochina, making
it a battlefield for Chinese and Japanese troops." He also envisioned the possibility
that "Chinese troops [would] attempt a military incursion of French Indochina" and

---

[76] Document 31. There is no documentary evidence indicating who was the author of the
"Outline of the Agreement Between Japan and French Indochina." In content, however, this
document is almost identical to the instructions given to Nishihara in Tokyo by the assistant
chief of the Army General Staff, the July 7 message to Nishihara from the army and navy assistant chiefs of staff, and the July 9 proposal from Nishihara to Governor General Catroux based
on that message. Therefore, the outline cannot have been drawn up by Satō and other Kwantung Army staff officers alone. It was drafted under the direction of central headquarters and
presented to French Indochina by Satō with headquarters' agreement. However, as I have
noted, the Nishihara Mission was probably not directly involved in drafting the document.
That Satō, not Nishihara, presented this outline of an agreement permitting the transit of
Japanese troops through French Indochina to the local authorities indicates the pressure being
applied to French Indochina as well as the growing contradictions within the war-leadership
group.

emphasized the risk that French Indochina would become "a battlefield." He concluded his analysis of the situation with a request for Japanese occupation of French Indochina: "If French Indochina permits Japanese forces to advance from the French Indochina border into Chinese territory, our surprise-attack strategy will make it impossible for large numbers of Chinese troops to violate the French-Indochina border, . . . which will eliminate the danger of French Indochina's becoming a battleground." He was saying, in effect, that permitting Japanese occupation would save French Indochina from becoming a battleground.

The French Indochina authorities were asking the Japanese to agree to "respect French Indochina's territorial integrity." Satō, on the other hand, making Japanese occupation of French Indochina a condition, declared: "I can assure you that the military has no designs on the territorial integrity of French Indochina." But though he assured the French Indochina authorities that Japan had no territorial ambitions, it is clear that his position was completely unacceptable to them. This was because French Indochina was pressing Japan to agree to "respect French Indochina's territorial integrity" to ward off occupation, while Japan would agree to "respect French Indochina's territorial integrity" only on the condition of occupation.

Satō was probably aware of the gap in the positions of the two sides. He maintained a bland expression but uttered the following forceful words: "However, if French Indochina refuses to let our troops transit and, as a result, we are unable to press Chungking directly from that direction, so that it takes time to deal with China, feeling in Japan will naturally run high. That would be unfortunate for both France and Japan."[77]

Japan was being self-serving and unreasonable in placing the blame for "tak[ing] time to deal with China," in other words, the worsening war situation between Japan and China, on French Indochina's "refus[al] to let our troops transit." However, this issue can be set aside for the moment. What is noteworthy is Satō's statement that "feeling in Japan will naturally run high," a veiled threat that Japanese attitudes toward French Indochina would harden. The "feeling" he was referring to was clearly not just the hard-line attitude within the lower echelons of the military but also the rising anti-French sentiment among the general public—although it should be remembered that this was organized and manipulated by those in power. How public opinion regarding the occupation of French Indochina was formed, or, more precisely, how it was manipulated by the government, is a subject for a separate discussion, but as Satō's words indicate, the hard-liners were not indifferent to public opinion. In fact, aroused public opinion gave added momentum to their actions, and they used this in turn to justify their actions.

The first reason Catroux turned down the Japanese proposals at the July 9 meeting was his fear of semipermanent occupation. To counter this objection, in the outline that Satō presented on July 12 a sentence was added stating that "the Japanese forces will immediately cease military use of French Indochina once the war with China is concluded." The second reason for Catroux's refusal was his fear that the United States and Britain would be strongly aroused if Japanese troops were allowed to pass through French Indochina. Satō's response to this point was extremely vague. At the end of his July 12 proposal Satō, requesting secrecy, stated:

---

[77] Document 30.

The proposals I have made are very important to planning our forces' strategy. Therefore, this must be kept absolutely secret from China or third countries. In particular, if this agreement [the Agreement Between Japan and French Indochina] is concluded, we must move some of our troops before it is announced, so please be careful not to reveal any information about the progress of this agreement to outsiders.

Satō said nothing of the effect he thought the transit of Japanese troops through French Indochina would have on Japan's relations with the United States and Britain in Indochina, Southeast Asia, and the Pacific. He was bent on making the transit of Japanese troops a *fait accompli* by keeping the agreement secret from the United States and Britain and thus urged French Indochina not to reveal the information. It was lack of insight into international conditions on the part of Japanese staff officers in China that led them to press for a *fait accompli* policy.

One passage in Satō's written proposal is of great interest for the light it sheds on relations between Japan and the indigenous people of Indochina:

I am fully aware of the French Indochina authorities' position toward governing the natives. When the natives see great numbers of our troops or military supplies passing through, they may misunderstand this to mean that by virtue of the agreement French Indochina has been occupied for the sake of the Japanese army or that its independence has been violated. This kind of misunderstanding would have a negative effect on governing the natives. However, if the natives fully understand that French Indochina and Japan are truly friends and that they have entered into an alliance as equals to carry out joint operations, this type of misunderstanding can be avoided.

Thus, we will cooperate in every way necessary, issuing any kind of declaration or proclamation in the name of the commander of the Japanese forces that the French Indochina authorities may desire.

This was the first Japanese reference to French Indochina's governing the indigenous people, another reason that the July 12 proposal is an important document. Satō's major concern, in regard to the transit of Japanese troops, was how the people of Indochina, especially those living in northern Vietnam, would react to seeing Japanese troops passing through at close quarters. The passage quoted above faithfully reflected Satō's concern. If people labored under the "misunderstanding" that the Japanese army had "occupied" French Indochina or that its "independence [had] been violated," this would have "a negative effect on governing" them. To avoid such a "misunderstanding," Satō promised to "cooperate in every way" with the French Indochina authorities. The tone of this passage clearly indicates that Japan agreed that France would continue to administer Indochina and that the French Indochina authorities and the Japanese army would cooperate in "governing the natives," that is, would rule Indochina jointly, which did in fact come about.

Recent research into the history of Japanese military rule during World War II has tended to credit the Japanese army with having "liberated" Southeast Asian peoples from the imperialist powers. The above passage, however, offers historical evidence to the contrary. In Indochina, from the time it prepared for occupation the Japanese army supported the French Indochina authorities, approved of their governing the indigenous people, in other words, their domination of the colony, and willingly cooperated with them.

Altogether, the Japanese army in Southeast Asia conspired with the colonial administrations, either establishing joint rule with them or removing them and establishing its own administration (including, of course, the bestowal of nominal, *pro forma* independence). From the viewpoint of the indigenous peoples, however, there was no significant difference between the two courses. Japan utilized both in setting up colonies through its war of aggression, choosing one or the other according to the circumstances. In this respect, Indochina was a typical case. Joint administration by France and Japan lasted more than four years. Finally, on March 9, 1945, the Japanese army staged a coup d'état, the so-called military disposition of French Indochina. Japan then established a government of its own choosing, installing the pro-Japanese cabinet of Tran Trong Kim and bestowing "independence" in April.[78]

Satō favored Japanese occupation of Indochina on the basis of acceptance of continued administration of the indigenous people by the French Indochina authorities, which set him apart from those who advocated the expulsion of France.[79] However, as I will discuss later, some Kwantung Army officers considered the very proposal of a defense alliance a delaying tactic by French Indochina and urged immediate military occupation. This view was just a hairbreadth from the argument for expulsion. In his first meeting with Catroux, on July 12, Satō did not go so far as to say this outright, but in subsequent negotiations he may well have threatened to remove France as the administrative power. Because the idea of removing France sur-

---

[78] See Minami Yoshizawa, "Nihon-Furansu shihai jiki no Betonamu chishikijin: 'Taingi' shi dōjin no dōkō o chūshin ni" [Vietnamese intellectuals during the period of joint rule by Japan and France: Trends among intellectuals connected with the journal *Thanh Nghi*], *Rekishi hyōron* [Historical review], no. 272 (January 1973).

[79] One of the strongest arguments for expelling France at the time was stated as follows: "We believe it is no longer possible for Japan to ensure the prosperity of the Indochinese people and the coexistence and coprosperity of the peoples of Southeast Asia by peaceful means. True coexistence and coprosperity between Japan and the peoples of this region [Indochina] can be achieved only by expelling France from this region, by force if necessary, to create new conditions. Therefore, we must be prepared to await the right opportunity to make our move. This should be our fundamental policy toward French Indochina" (Document 11).

Because this argument for expelling France did not sufficiently consider the ramifications such actions would have on Japan's relations with Britain and the United States, particularly the latter, it could not become the dominant view among Japan's political and military leaders. The July 1940 "Outline of Measures to Deal with Changes in the World Situation" adopted the position of a "shift toward placing priority on southern policy measures." This policy paper acknowledged "the possibility of exercising force depending on circumstances," but, with an eye toward relations with the United States, stopped short of mandating the expulsion of France from Indochina. Mamoru Shigemitsu, then ambassador to Britain, was carefully watching the international situation. He proposed the following argument for expelling France to Foreign Minister Arita: "Our diplomatic strategy must be to deal with the Empire's actions *one at a time*, while bearing in mind relations with the United States (and the Soviet Union). In the present delicate circumstances, we must avoid as far as possible having the United States, Britain, and other countries turn against us simultaneously. We must hold off putting pressure on Hong Kong and concentrate first on ridding China and Indochina of French influence, meanwhile trying to keep relations with the United States and Britain on an even keel" (Document 19; emphasis in the original). Shigemitsu was advocating that Japan follow a "diplomatic strategy" of dealing with "the Empire's actions *one at a time*," avoid rash actions that would turn both Britain and the United States against Japan at the same time, and concentrate on ridding China and Indochina of French influence. These views on expelling France lay behind the sentiment in favor of military occupation of French Indochina.

faced as an extension of the idea of occupying Indochina on the basis of continued French administration, the two concepts were not irrevocably opposed; in fact, depending on the circumstances, one could replace the other.

Above I have described how Satō promised to cooperate so that France could retain effective administrative control over the indigenous population, agreed to respect French Indochina's territorial integrity, and pledged that "the Japanese forces will immediately cease military use of French Indochina once the war with China is concluded." At the same time, he pressed the government of French Indochina to permit Japanese troops to pass through its territory.

Catroux continued to refuse, declaring, "I am prepared to [accept] all your other proposals, but as far as military *occupation* is concerned, since that lies outside the scope of my authority as governor general, I cannot make a decision on my own" (emphasis in the original). He continued:

The Japanese foreign minister should advise Ambassador Henry and the governor general of French Indochina secretly in writing whether he will declare [that Japan will undertake to do] the following:

1. Maintain the status quo in French Indochina.
2. Prevent the European war from spilling over into the Far East.
3. Restore peace quickly to East Asia.

The French and Japanese governments will cooperate fully to achieve these three goals. This notification, in the form of a declaration, will reassure the French, and at the same time the Japanese and French governments will negotiate the occupation rights of the Japanese forces.[80]

Catroux's response to Satō's proposal can be summed up by saying that he evaded the occupation issue, on the grounds that "that lies outside the scope of my authority as governor general" and that the matter should be negotiated by the French and Japanese governments, but accepted the other demands, receiving in exchange a pledge from Japan to issue a declaration or secret communiqué guaranteeing that Japan would "maintain the status quo in French Indochina."

IV. Sectionalism

How did the Nishihara Mission as a whole, its navy contingent, its diplomatic contingent (members of the Japanese consulate general in Hanoi), and the Kwantung Army, waiting on the other side of French Indochina's border with China, view the initial discussions in the first round of negotiations between Japan and French Indochina, in which a Kwantung Army staff officer also participated? Could all these factions possibly have had a uniform outlook on French Indochina?

First let us consider relations between Nishihara himself and central headquarters. On July 6 the Nishihara Mission received a telegram from the Army General Staff announcing that a Japanese navy ship would arrive at Haiphong on July 10. On July 8, when it was learned that Commander Negi's plane had been shot

---

[80] Document 34.

down,[81] the Nishihara Mission sent an urgent message to central headquarters requesting that the port call be postponed: "We request that you have the port call of the Japanese fleet on the tenth postponed for a while."[82] On July 9 headquarters replied: "In regard to the port call around the tenth, an Imperial order was issued on the eighth, and [the plan] *absolutely* cannot be changed now. Furthermore, this port call is absolutely necessary to secure communications with navy units. . . . We wish you to negotiate this point with the government general"[83] (emphasis in the original).

Determined to push through the port call as scheduled, headquarters flatly refused the Nishihara Mission's request. In the margin by the first mention of the word "absolutely" is the notation "Inserted by the army," an indication that there had been considerable debate over the issue at headquarters and that the army was adamant about having the port call go ahead. Japan also used this occasion to press the French Indochina authorities to facilitate direct communications between the Nishihara Organization and Japanese army units in China.

According to the July 6 telegram from the Army General Staff, a Japanese ship was to visit Guangzhou Bay (a territory leased by France) on July 7, but it was actually at 9:30 A.M. on July 10 that minesweeper no. 18 entered the bay. At 5:00 P.M. the same day, the *Nenohi*, a destroyer, steamed into Haiphong Harbor. One document stated that "liaison with the French Indochina authorities in connection with the port call was good,"[84] but a telegram sent by Nishihara, in Hanoi, to the Army General Staff on July 11 reported a completely different local reaction:

Having been notified that one ship of the Japanese fleet would call at Haiphong, I conveyed this information to the French Indochina authorities on July 10, but today, July 11, the governor general protested that two ships had arrived [in French territory]. I replied that since I am not trusted much at home I had not received any information and there was nothing I could do.[85]

This episode indicates the anger and suspicion with which the French Indochina authorities viewed the arrival of Japanese navy ships.

Still more remarkable is the excuse Nishihara gave the governor general, that he was "not trusted much at home"—inappropriate and baffling words from a man representing Japan in explaining a unilateral port call by his country's ships, a matter of state policy, to his negotiating counterpart. However, the French Indochina authorities offered no effective counterargument. The words exchanged by Nishihara and the governor general in the heat of the moment reveal the true political balance of power that prevailed between the imperialist power and the colonial power; while negotiations may have remained bogged down, the display of physical might symbolized by the arrival of the navy ships proceeded inexorably.

Considered from another perspective, Nishihara's excuse was an expression of his dissatisfaction with headquarters. But his dissatisfaction did not deter the ships from making a port call, nor had he any intention of trying to deter them. It is true that there was discord between headquarters and units stationed overseas, but—as

---

[81] See note 44 for details of this episode.

[82] Document 23.

[83] Document 26.

[84] Document 36.

[85] Document 28.

Nishihara's lament that "there was nothing I could do" shows—this was used to rationalize and acknowledge the various authoritarian measures taken by Japan as *fait accompli* and to force negotiating counterparts, who were also directly involved, to accept them. If Nishihara's excuse expressed his dissatisfaction with headquarters, it also brought home forcefully to the French Indochina authorities the reality of the Japanese ships' port call. I believe that his excuse admirably illustrates the theme that runs through this paper, that conflict within the Japanese war-leadership group not only did not deter expansion of the war but actually stimulated it.

Next let us examine relations within the Nishihara Mission. A message from the group received by the Army General Staff on July 14 described the July 12 negotiations between Catroux and Satō as follows: "Colonel Satō, accompanying Major General Nishihara, proposed a detailed agreement to the French Indochina authorities, from the standpoint of the army, on the right of Japanese forces to transit French Indochina and use military facilities there. He went over all the details and made strong demands."[86]

The "detailed agreement" clearly refers to the "Outline of the Agreement Between Japan and French Indochina." The comment that Satō proposed the outline to French Indochina "from the standpoint of the army" indicates that Nishihara was not consulted closely beforehand about the outline and that Satō proposed and explained it largely on the basis of his own judgment, differentiating himself from the Nishihara Mission. The phrase "strong demands" was not necessarily a criticism of Satō's aggressive attitude, but it does suggest a desire to distance the Nishihara Mission from Satō's approach to the negotiations. Nishihara undoubtedly found it most irksome to have Satō suddenly step in and play the leading role in negotiations with French Indochina. At that point there were no overt differences between the two men over Japanese policy toward French Indochina, but it must be assumed that their rivalry widened the gap between them. In fact, official telegrams and other documents from August onward reveal that the conflict between Nishihara and the Kwantung Army had by then become impossible to conceal.

Yanagisawa and the other navy members of the Nishihara Mission kept their distance from Nishihara[87] and showed still greater dislike of the Kwantung Army, and of Satō in particular.[88] The diplomatic members (consulate general officials) were quite hostile to the military as a whole, including both Nishihara and Satō, but at the same time their attitude was inconsistent and contradictory. In a July 9 telegram from Consul General Suzuki in Hanoi to Foreign Minister Arita, Suzuki went out of his way to note, regarding the content of this communication, that "some points have not yet been reported to the military, so please keep this confidential." Reflecting the conflict between the military and the Foreign Ministry, the consulate general and the Nishihara Mission were hiding information from each other and playing a game of one-upmanship.

---

[86] Document 34.

[87] See note 52.

[88] When Nishihara returned to Tokyo in late July for consultations with headquarters, Satō was the acting head of the Nishihara Organization. At that time Yanagisawa, head of the navy contingent, sent the following message to headquarters: "Since I do not consider that the acting head has the authority to make decisions, I intend to carry out my duties in the form of cooperation with him" (Document 40). These words show the navy contingent's dislike of Satō.

The telegram also contained the following passage: "French Indochina's true intention [is] to gain some kind of assurance from Japan that its territorial rights will not be violated. In that case, I believe they are prepared to enter into a defense alliance against Chiang Kai-shek *(we will also gain transit for our troops)*"[89] (emphasis added). According to this telegram, if Japan promised to respect French Indochina's territorial integrity, the French Indochina authorities were prepared to enter into a defense alliance that would enable "transit for our troops." However, as already mentioned, Catroux had refused Japan's request for troop transit, so this information was clearly mistaken. Though admittedly less than fully informed by the Nishihara Organization, the consulate general clung to a most rosy view of how French Indochina would react to Japanese initiatives.

Yosano, who caught the mistake, telegraphed Arita on the afternoon of July 10 to correct the error:

> I went with Major General Nishihara to meet with Governor General
> Catroux on the ninth. We verified his intentions on the defense alliance; he
> will probably never agree to it, because he believes that letting our troops
> transit French Indochina and so on will result in semipermanent occupation.
> Therefore, this message amends the passage [of Suzuki's July 9 telegram] in
> parentheses.

The latter part of Yosano's telegram is worth noting, as well: "I do not know which side brought up the matter of the alliance, but it might have been 'that tactic.' I have so much to tell you when I return to Japan. I know you are looking for my successor, and I hope you will decide on someone as soon as possible."[90]

As already noted, various documents indicate that the defense alliance was proposed by French Indochina, but even this basic information was unavailable to officials at the Hanoi consulate general. It is thus understandable that the consulate general was suspicious of the Nishihara Mission. It is not clear what the words "that tactic" *(rei no te)* refer to, but the diplomats' suspicion of the military is obvious. As Yosano's words "I have so much to tell you when I return to Japan" indicate, he had so much to say about, and was so dissatisfied with, relations between the consulate general and the Nishihara Mission and the situation within the Nishihara Mission itself that it was impossible to put it all in a telegram; therefore he asked the ministry to recall him so that he could talk face to face.

The ministry must have wondered what was going on to prompt this kind of message from a locally based official. A telegram dated July 13 from Arita to Suzuki stated:

> Lately Major General Nishihara has sent several messages to the Army
> General Staff about the [two illegible characters] of his meetings with the
> governor general about respecting French Indochina's territorial integrity
> and about the defense alliance, but I do not really know what is going on.
> Please have the deputy director or Yosano telegraph me immediately and
> frankly with all the details of this matter from the beginning, especially

---

[89] Document 24.

[90] Document 27.

French Indochina's intentions and your observations. (This has already been discussed with the military.)[91]

This seems to indicate that the Foreign Ministry had not been given all the information that the Nishihara Mission had been sending in its numerous messages to the Army General Staff. It also reveals that the Foreign Ministry's own source of information, the consulate general in Hanoi, was unreliable, as the episode about Yosano's having to send a telegram of correction suggests. Hence Arita's request that Suzuki have someone at the consulate general "telegraph me immediately and frankly with all the details of this matter." The word "frankly" (*enryo naku*) can be interpreted as meaning to speak without reservations toward the ministry, but given the notation that "this has already been discussed with the military," it should be taken to mean speaking without reservations toward the military.

It appears that Yosano's request to return to Tokyo for face-to-face talks was not granted immediately. Upon receiving the above telegram, he sent back quite a long message on July 14 describing what had occurred in connection with the question of a defense alliance.[92] He followed this on July 15 with a detailed fourteen-page report on negotiations between the Nishihara Mission and French Indochina from the group's arrival in Hanoi on July 1 to July 13, appending the July 6 "Memorandum from the Governor General of French Indochina" and the July 12 "Proposal by Colonel Satō" as references. He concluded this report by noting that "there is considerable dissatisfaction with the organization of the observer group. I think it would be best to report to you on the situation when I return to Japan,"[93] thus asking again to be recalled. Clearly he remained dissatisfied with the Nishihara Mission and the military.

I have described at some length the tug-of-war over information between the Foreign Ministry and the consulate general on the one hand and the Army General Staff and the Nishihara Mission on the other, as well as the problem of sectionalism. How far apart were the two groups' policies toward French Indochina? The numerous messages between the Foreign Ministry and the consulate general that I have quoted constituted a kind of log (including erroneous information) of negotiations between Japan and French Indochina. They contained no critical evaluation, analysis, or forecasts, but simply summarized Nishihara's and Satō's proposals to the French Indochina authorities. In fact, this record even seemed to approve of the hard-line approach.

Take, for example, a July 9 message from Suzuki to Arita: "Concerning the ... proposal by French Indochina [that "if (French Indochina) can gain some kind of assurance (from Japan) that its territorial rights will not be violated ... it is prepared to enter into a defense alliance against Chiang Kai-shek"], Major General Nishihara seems to be expecting a favorable answer from central headquarters. However, considering what has happened so far with our proposals to Germany and Italy,[94] the

---

[91] Document 32.

[92] Document 33.

[93] Document 35.

[94] In mid-June 1940, immediately after France surrendered to Germany, Foreign Minister Arita instructed Ambassador to Germany Saburō Kurusu and Ambassador to Italy Eiji Amou Temba to raise the issue of French Indochina with the German and Italian governments, respectively. His main instructions were as follows: "French Indochina serves as a major artery for supplying weapons and other materiel to the Chungking regime, which Japan is continuing to

recent international situation, the foreign minister's statement on June 29, and our policy toward the south so far, not only is it undesirable to promise to respect the French Indochina's territory at this time, but it would in fact be very difficult to do so because of hard-line views at home."[95]

As I have already mentioned, and as the above passage stated, Nishihara believed it would be acceptable to guarantee to respect French Indochina's territorial integrity if this meant that a defense alliance against Chiang could be concluded, and he was "expecting a favorable answer from central headquarters." However, Yosano, who wrote the telegram, opposed guaranteeing French Indochina's territorial integrity, calling it "undesirable" and adding that "hard-line views at home" would probably make it impossible in any case. This message expressed views even more hard-line than Nishihara's. Though it is true that the Foreign Ministry and the consulate general clashed with Imperial Headquarters, the Army General Staff, and the Nishihara Mission on every issue, this does not mean that the Foreign Ministry and the consulate general were moderate in regard to policy toward French Indochina.

Meanwhile, what moves were being made by the Japanese army units that had deployed troops directly north of the French Indochina border? On July 11, the day Satō arrived in Hanoi, the chief of staff of the Nanning Army sent the following telegram to the assistant chief of the Army General Staff:

1. We are planning to shift the main force of the Nakamura Group by around July 20, gradually assembling the troops at the French Indochina border.

2. French Indochina's proposal of a defense alliance may not spring from sincere motives. French Indochina is also being pressed by China, and there is reason to believe that the proposal is a tactic intended to delay occupation by our forces. Therefore, since it will probably take at least a month to conclude the alliance, continuing to negotiate while keeping an eye on the situation could hamper the activities of our forces.

3. For this reason, we should not take this course at this time. Instead, we should present the French with an ultimatum once the Nakamura Group is assembled and ask for their independent decision.

4. Even if a defense alliance is concluded, we should avoid being deceived by devious delaying tactics of the French, such as believing that they will allow our troops to transit as soon as this is approved in principle. We should exert pressure on France through the strength of our troops assembled at the border and take advantage of this opportunity to strike.[96]

---

suppress. The Japanese forces are trying very hard to sever supply links. That is why Japanese forces are conducting military activities even in areas bordering French Indochina. At the same time, for the sake of stability in Asia, . . . it is natural for Japan to have a strong interest in French Indochina, given its political, military, and economic importance, and I trust that the countries to which you are posted understand this, as well" (Document 3). This passage shows that the Japanese government was trying to obtain the prior approval of Germany and Italy to the dispatch of the Nishihara Mission to French Indochina and, ultimately, the Japanese army's occupation of French Indochina.

[95] Document 24.

[96] Document 29.

A noteworthy feature of this message is that, unlike the Nishihara Mission and the Army General Staff which believed that French Indochina's proposal was sincere and welcomed it as a good opportunity to bring about the occupation (though Yosano, as mentioned above, offered a different view), the Nanning Army felt that "French Indochina's proposal of a defense alliance may not spring from sincere motives" and saw it as "a tactic intended to delay." The Nanning Army was concerned that negotiations on the alliance might "hamper" its activities. It favored direct action to "avoid being deceived by devious delaying tactics of the French." Specifically, this meant assembling the main body of the Nakamura Group at Zhennanguan to put pressure on French Indochina and at the same time presenting an ultimatum to the French Indochina authorities to force them to agree to the Japanese army's occupation of French Indochina. The Nanning Army did indeed deploy its main force at Zhennanguan.

Because the Nanning Army considered French Indochina's proposal of a defense alliance a delaying tactic and did not feel that this should be the main subject of negotiations, it was at odds with the Nishihara Mission and was also suspicious of Colonel Satō of the Kwantung Army. The Nanning Army considered the conclusion of a defense alliance a delaying tactic because it saw through French Indochina's motives. But another reason for its unwillingness to accept the negotiations was its pride at being on the front line of Japan's French Indochina operation. We cannot ignore that, underlying the Nanning Army's belligerence was the weakness and shortsightedness of the decision-making process.

On July 19 the Kwantung Army telegraphed the assistant chief of the Army General Staff:

> 2. From our standpoint, whatever the main point of preparing and carrying out the Yunnan operation may be, we believe it is necessary to use it as a pretext to obtain occupation rights. If diplomatic negotiations on the matter drag on, we would like to have permission to negotiate directly with the French Indochina authorities, at least over the occupation rights of our forces.

> 3. Negotiations should take place between July 22 and July 31, around the time the Konoe Division arrives and the bulk of the Fifth Division is grouped near the border. The appropriate period for taking action would be early August or later, when military preparations are completed.[97]

The Nanning Army, which had advanced from Nanning to Zhennanguan, was the unit on the front line of the French Indochina operation, while the Kwantung Army, positioned behind the Nanning Army, was the headquarters for the operation. The Kwantung Army sent Satō, its assistant chief of staff, to Hanoi to negotiate with the French Indochina authorities on its behalf, but when negotiations foundered over French Indochina's refusal to let Japanese troops transit its territory, the Kwantung Army's hawkishness became overt. We can infer that the message quoted above reflected the Kwantung Army's true intentions.

Both central headquarters and Satō maintained that Japanese troops needed to transit French Indochina to mount operations against Chiang Kai-shek and empha-

---

[97] Document 38.

sized that they would transit only for that purpose. The Kwantung Army was franker, calling anti-Chiang operations "a pretext." It believed that it was "necessary" to "obtain occupation rights" from French Indochina and requested permission from the Army General Staff "to negotiate directly with the French Indochina authorities." A timetable was even proposed: direct negotiations with French Indochina from July 22 to July 31 and, if negotiations stalled, armed action in or after early August.

Central headquarters did not give the Kwantung Army an official go-ahead. But the content of the July 19 message indicated that the Kwantung Army was chafing to take independent action and did not expect the Nishihara Organization to get anywhere. This also led to disagreements with Satō, who was negotiating in Hanoi. The rift between Satō and the Kwantung Army was described by the navy's Yanagisawa in a report sent to Tokyo in early August:

> The chief of staff of the Kwantung Army [Major General Hiroshi Nemoto] has sent numerous messages urging decisive action, but [Colonel Satō] is assuming more and more authority in the negotiations. Since coming in contact with Colonel Koike, me, and diplomatic officials, Colonel Satō has gradually become more cautious, and the young Kwantung Army staff officers who come relaying information are apparently saying that Colonel Satō has softened.[98]

Taking Satō's behavior in Hanoi at face value and evaluating him as having "softened" "since coming in contact with" the Nishihara Mission was a lopsided view. He had his own interests as the representative of the Kwantung Army, and although he negotiated together with the Nishihara Mission, we should assume that he did not identify with it. Still, it is true that conflict began to arise between Satō, negotiating as the Kwantung Army representative, and his own unit. And the differences that arose within the Kwantung Army itself had the effect of exacerbating its belligerence.

Finally, I will touch briefly on the conflict between the army field units that took the initiative in the occupation of French Indochina and the navy, which championed the policy of southern expansion, in order to elucidate the roles of the two sides.

Since the Nishihara Mission was in disarray, Nishihara was recalled to Tokyo temporarily and Satō was named acting chief in his absence. On July 27, the day the order regarding Satō reached Hanoi, Yanagisawa, head of the navy contingent, sent the following message to navy headquarters: "What is headquarters' intention? Has it been decided that military force is to be used in the end? If so, Tonkin and so on are of little value to southern expansion. I believe that [military action] will have little meaning unless it extends to the vicinity of Saigon, in southern French Indochina."[99]

Competition for leadership of southern expansion was the real reason the navy clashed so strongly with army field units, which, along with one faction at army headquarters, were infatuated with military occupation of French Indochina. That the navy was keener than the army to expand the war southward was demonstrated by Yanagisawa's urging at this stage that army units be ordered to occupy southern as well as northern French Indochina. The navy being in competition with the army, the

---

[98] Document 42.

[99] Document 40.

more the navy opposed and sought to deter the army's exercise of military force, the more the army was spurred to such action.

V. Conclusion: The Impulse to War and "Liberation of the Peoples of East Asia"

Colonel Satō's arrival in Hanoi and his direct negotiations, as the representative of Kwantung Army, with Governor General Catroux complicated negotiations between Japan and French Indochina, which had been conducted until then by the Nishihara Mission. The chain of command was unclear, orders lacked consistency, and Nishihara became almost incapable of functioning. In mid-July he was recalled to Tokyo for talks with headquarters; Satō remained in Hanoi as acting head of the organization. The events up to this point constituted the first round of talks between Japan and French Indochina.

Around the same time, the second Konoe Cabinet replaced the Mitsumasa Yonai Cabinet and adopted the "Outline of Measures to Deal with Changes in the World Situation," thereby endorsing the policy of southern expansion. In French Indochina, Catroux was replaced by Admiral Jean Decoux, setting the stage for the second round of negotiations. Talks took place simultaneously in Tokyo and Hanoi. In Tokyo they concerned the conclusion of a military alliance between France and Japan, while in Hanoi Nishihara, who had returned, discussed local details of the alliance.

By then Japan had decided to occupy French Indochina. France was resigned to accepting this in order to preserve its influence there. The problem now was how and when to proceed with the occupation. In early September a military agreement with France was signed in Tokyo, while a similar agreement with French Indochina was signed in Hanoi. An obstacle arose, however. Immediately after the agreements were signed, the Nanning Army began conducting skirmishes across the French Indochina border. These actions were a shock not only to the French Indochina authorities but also to the Japanese, especially the Nishihara Mission.

The negotiations between Japan and French Indochina after these skirmishes may be called the third round. Its main purpose was to cajole and bully French Indochina into signing the local military agreement once again. Meanwhile, the Japanese were having great difficulty putting their own house in order. On September 30 they finally succeeded in getting the French Indochina authorities to sign, but they failed utterly to achieve coordination among themselves. This was because, at about the same time as the second signing of the agreement, the Kwantung and Nanning armies embarked on military action. Although this had been expected, it illustrated the deep divisions within the war-leadership group. Nishihara asked to be relieved of his duties. At the same time, a navy destroyer that was supposed to support the landing of Kwantung Army troops turned its back on them and sailed away.

In this paper I have concentrated on the first round of negotiations between the Japanese and French Indochina authorities.[100] I would like to conclude by discussing the attitudes of the various factions within the war-leadership group toward the peoples of Indochina and toward indigenous nationalist movements.

---

[100] The way in which sectional rivalry further intensified during the second and third rounds of negotiations, exerting a synergistic effect on the impulse to war and culminating in the occupation of French Indochina, is detailed in Minami Yoshizawa, *Sensō kakudai no kōzu: Nihongun no "Futsuin shinchū"* [The pattern of war expansion: The Japanese army's occupation of French Indochina] (Tokyo: Aoki Shoten, 1986), chaps. 2, 3.

On August 26, 1938, two years before the occupation of northern French Indochina, the Army General Staff issued a pamphlet more than a hundred pages long titled *The Peoples of Yunnan and Annam and Their Religion and Customs*. The pamphlet included the explanatory note: "This volume contains the March 1937 report by Suyama of the East Asia Economic Research Bureau [of the South Manchuria Railway]. The content covers the major points and is, we believe, of considerable value." To the best of my knowledge, this was the first comprehensive report on the peoples of the Indochinese Peninsula put together by the Japanese military. Such data were of keen interest to the military authorities, who were planning to cut off Chiang Kaishek's supply route from French Indochina to Yunnan.

The pamphlet classified the peoples of the Indochinese Peninsula into five categories: "the so-called barbarian tribes," Khmer and Cham (inhabitants of Champa), Thais and Annamese (Vietnamese), Chinese, and "other encroaching tribes" (supposedly less "barbarian" peoples than those in the first category, such as the Meo, Lolo, and Man [Yao]). The relatively detailed description of the first category of peoples emphasized the "barbarian" and "uncivilized" nature of the Moi and Kha (as they were known at the time) inhabiting the mountains of central Vietnam and the interior of the peninsula. The report also noted that "some tribes are extremely independent, occasionally greeting intruders with a hail of arrows."

Many pages were devoted to the ancient historical links between the "Annamese" and the Chinese, noting that "the Chinese tried to assimilate the Annamese but without success; they only conquered them, and have controlled them for a long period. However, the Annamese have adopted the literature, customs, technology, religion, and civilization of their Chinese conquerors."[101]

This report was not written with Japan's French Indochina policy directly in mind but was a compilation of data interpreted in the light of various anthropological and historical theories. What lessons the Army General Staff drew from the report is not known, but we can infer that army headquarters began collecting information on the peoples of Indochina by studying the most fundamental aspects of their cultures.

As the group planning and prosecuting the war debated military versus peaceful occupation of French Indochina and as public enthusiasm for southern expansion mounted, proposals for Japanese policy measures in the region became ever more grandiose, as demonstrated by the following excerpts from a 1940 proposal by Yasukichi Nagata of the Foreign Ministry, who had served as consul general in Hanoi from 1930 to 1933 and thus was probably counted among the ministry's French Indochina experts:

> The Annamese, who safeguarded their independence for a thousand years and were the sovereigns of the Indochinese Peninsula, the Cambodians, who once possessed a great culture, and the Laotians and other peoples of Indochina fell victim to French aggression some eighty years ago. . . . These peoples are now in a sorry state, having lost their erstwhile vigor, forgotten their culture, forfeited their wealth, and reverted to a primitive and uncivilized state. The majority of the land is given over to wild animals and poisonous snakes. France claims to be guiding and enlightening backward peoples and introducing them to European culture, but this is nothing but

---

[101] Document 1.

empty propaganda directed at the outside world. . . . This should be clear to anyone who compares the condition of these regions with that of Thailand, Korea, or Taiwan. . . . From the positive viewpoint of the growth of [Japan's] national strength, development and exploitation of their resources hold great promise. . . . Our ultimate objective should be to take advantage of this opportunity to grant the Annamese independence (whether Cambodia and Laos are to be subordinated to Annam can be considered later) and include them in our planned East Asian community. . . . People to plan Annamese independence should be assembled quickly and, in conjunction with the military, should organize a kind of provisional government for an independent Annam.[102]

After referring to Vietnam's history of independence and its culture, Nagata criticized French colonial rule, which he said had destroyed that legacy. He contrasted Vietnam, "primitive and uncivilized" and "given over to wild animals and poisonous snakes," with the "cultured" conditions of Japan's colonies of Korea and Taiwan. He advocated gathering together pro-independence patriots, inciting an independence movement, and incorporating an independent Vietnam in the Greater East Asia Co-Prosperity Sphere. His scenario combined the view of Annam as "primitive and uncivilized" with the idea of an independent Annam belonging to the Greater East Asia Co-Prosperity Sphere.

Advocating "Annamese independence" as he did, Nagata showed a keen interest in fomenting an independence movement under French rule. In a topical article headlined "Great Resources Lie Dormant in a Closed Country; Annamese Hatred Runs Deep," published in the July 3, 1940, issue of the newspaper *Tokyo Asahi Shimbun*, he wrote: "On the surface, [the Annamese] are acquiescing meekly to French rule; but deep down they nurse spirited feelings that sometimes burst forth like volcanic eruptions in independence movements and rebellions." He discussed the anti-French struggle in some detail, even referring to the Nghe Tinh Soviet movement of 1930. Needless to say, the aim of fanning the flames of "Annamese hatred" of the French was to foster a pro-Japanese independence movement, and thus to twist Vietnam's indigenous nationalist movement to Japanese ends.

Some within the military, too, argued strongly for using a Vietnamese nationalist movement as a pretext for occupation. A July 1940 Naval General Staff document advised occupying French Indochina by "taking advantage of France's loss of influence and using an Annamese nationalist movement or an anti-Japanese movement instigated by the Chungking regime among Chinese residents of French Indochina, on the pretext of protecting residents."[103] This provocative argument proposed exploiting unrest among the Annamese for the purpose of occupation.

In contrast to those who regarded a Vietnamese independence movement as potentially useful to Japanese interests were others who insisted that there was no possibility of an independence movement's arising in Vietnam, given the country's backward condition, and maintained that for this reason the Vietnamese were eager to come under Japanese protection. A typical expression of this argument, that the Annamese themselves wanted Japanese military occupation, is seen in a June 1940 secret message from Toshiyo Yamada in Hanoi to the Naval General Staff. Yamada

---

[102] Document 11.

[103] Document 15.

wrote that while it was possible that discontent would surface among Annamese civil servants, because of "their historical subservience" and also because "education is not widespread . . . it is extremely difficult to expect them to [be able to] unite the Annamese under their direction." Therefore, "it is unthinkable that they can generate an organized independence movement. . . . At least, I do not think they can generate a strong movement without outside direction." For these reasons, "some members of the intellectual class are now sincerely hoping for Japanese protection of the territory. . . . They are saying they want to be ruled by the Japanese, who are the same color as they." Moreover, "quite a few people in the lower classes believe the Japanese army will advance into the territory. Many ask, when they see someone Japanese, 'When is the Japanese army coming?'"[104]

Another typical expression of the argument that the Annamese actually wanted Japanese military occupation is seen in a July telegram from the Nanning Army, the field unit most actively involved in carrying out the occupation of northern French Indochina: "1. On the twenty-eighth of this month, at border marker three (eight kilometers south of Pingerguan), 104 Annamese soldiers bearing small arms voluntarily surrendered to us, so we took them into custody.

"2. The Annamese near the border are strongly hoping for Japanese military occupation."[105]

As the above examples indicate, Yamada and the Nanning Army, on the basis of their firsthand experience in the region, most bluntly advocated occupation on the grounds that this was what the Annamese themselves wanted.

Both those who believed in the possibility of a Vietnamese nationalist movement and those who dismissed it were united in rationalizing the occupation of French Indochina and pushing for its execution. Underlying their agreement was their concept of Annam as "primitive and uncivilized." Inevitably, this view of Annam as backward manifested itself as contempt toward the people of Vietnam.

Immediately after occupying northern French Indochina in September 1940, the force led by Major General Takuma Nishimura set up headquarters in a hotel in Do Son. On September 29 Shirō Haga, an attaché in the Hanoi consulate general, visited Nishimura there. Haga later described the scene as follows:

Drinking wine in a second-floor room cooled by breezes, the commander, Major General Nishimura (formerly chief of staff of the Eastern Army Defense Command), the chief of staff, Colonel [Isamu] Chō (commander of the Nomonhan force), and the others were in quite high spirits. The headquarters staff was put together in Tokyo. Because the troops are raw recruits of the Konoe Division stationed in Qin District, southern China, and have never been in combat, military discipline is strict right now, but the authorities are worrying about setting up recreation facilities, [ianjo], since there is no telling what [the troops] might do to women, brutish Annamese though they are.[106]

The phrase "brutish Annamese" expressed the true opinion of the invading colonial rulers. This contemptuous view of the Annamese as animals reflected the attitude toward Asia underlying the occupation of northern French Indochina, which

---

[104] Document 6.

[105] Document 41.

[106] Document 47.

was supposed to be a step toward the "liberation of the peoples of East Asia." But while the occupying Japanese army regarded the Annamese as mere animals, even the Japan of that time realized that it would not do to express such sentiments openly. A *Tokyo Asahi Shimbun* story on the occupation reported that "the townspeople of Dong Dang were not at all intimidated even at first sight of the troops who had executed the bold occupation, but dashed outdoors as if greeting long-awaited guests. Some people accorded the soldiers such a warm welcome that they offered them soft drinks and cigarettes."[107] News reports dwelt on the "warm welcome" of the Vietnamese masses and "the Annamese reliance on the strength of Japan, leader of East Asia."[108]

As we have seen, the Japanese view of Annam and its people was compounded of the idea of fostering an independence movement, the concept of Annam as backward, and contempt for the Annamese. Let us consider this complex view of Annam and the Annamese in the light of Japan's plans, at the time of the occupation, for dealing with the French Indochina government (destroying it or retaining and utilizing it) and relations with Britain and the United States.

Japan attempted to apply selectively two means of dealing with nationalist movements in the region. One was suppression of nationalist movements in general. The terms of Colonel Satō's July 12 proposal to Governor General Catroux permitted France to retain its influence in French Indochina in order to establish joint rule of the colony. The basic policy of joint rule was also followed at the time of the occupation of southern French Indochina in 1941. This policy had been adopted for two reasons. First, it was felt that retaining the pro-Vichy French Indochina governing apparatus would enable Japan to turn relations with Britain and the United States in Asia to its advantage. Second, it was calculated that preserving and making use of the French colonial government apparatus would be the cheapest, most skillful way to administer the territory. In connection with the second reason, it should be noted that Japan, in financial straits because of the war in China, planned to have "the French Indochina authorities supply" the massive funds needed to defray the cost of garrisoning Japanese occupation forces.[109] As long as Japan pursued the policy of joint rule through the use of the French colonial governing apparatus, it was obliged to pose as the oppressor of not only anti-Japanese but even anti-French nationalist movements.

The other means of dealing with nationalist movements was to weaken France's power to govern and, while preserving the form of joint rule, seize actual leadership. Eventually France would be expelled and Japan would rule alone. To accomplish this, Japan presented itself in the guise of a "liberator," encouraging nationalist movements that showed anti-French tendencies and attempting to sever the peoples of the region from French colonial rule. The "independence" Japan offered "the peoples of East Asia" would merely subsume them in the Greater East Asia Co-Prosperity Sphere and thus incorporate them in Japan's colonial dominion. Nevertheless, as long as Japan was advocating even nominal independence, it had to cultivate rather than suppress the latent nationalistic energy and cohesiveness of "the peoples of East Asia" while perverting these qualities to establish Japanese colonial rule. Viewed from the perspective of Asian peoples, this was one of the pitfalls of

---

[107] Dispatch from Dong Dang, *Tokyo Asahi Shimbun*, September 25, 1940.

[108] Ibid.

[109] Document 49.

movements that sought to make use of Japan's power to oust a European overlord, whether France or the Netherlands or Britain.

To the military hard-liners, whose first priority was to gain and expand colonies even at the risk of destroying the international balance of power, selective application of the two approaches discussed above was essential. The latter in particular was indispensable. The hard-liners were fanatical nationalists in the guise of supporters of nationalist movements.

What was the attitude of the Foreign Ministry, which was in conflict with the military? On July 5 Consul General Suzuki in Hanoi telegraphed Foreign Minister Arita: "The Annamese have always been spineless, so they are incapable of achieving independence, but they are pro-Japanese, as I have often reported."[110] This brief passage clearly expressed the Foreign Ministry's and consulate general's attitude toward the people of Indochina. Not only did Suzuki dismiss the Annamese as having "always been spineless," but he also evaluated them solely in terms of whether they were "pro-Japanese." This extremely contemptuous and static view of Asian peoples made identification with indigenous nationalist movements all but impossible. The Foreign Ministry advocates of negotiations and peaceful occupation, wishing to retain and utilize the French colonial apparatus and to avoid any major change in the international balance of power, were necessarily reluctant to encourage anti-French nationalist movements. Indeed, this faction held the most conservative view of indigenous peoples.

As we have seen, the military, like the Foreign Ministry, judged indigenous peoples solely in terms of whether they were sympathetic to Japan. Thus it would be simplistic to say that the Foreign Ministry's view of indigenous peoples conflicted with that of the military. Rather, tension arose because, of the two means of dealing with nationalist movements endorsed by the military, the Foreign Ministry espoused only the former, that is, suppression.

At the time of the occupation of northern French Indochina the Foreign Ministry faction favoring negotiations and peaceful occupation took the cautious stance of trying to retain the French colonial apparatus and avoid upsetting the balance between Japan on the one hand and Britain and the United States on the other. But when it came to the occupation of southern French Indochina a somewhat more complex division of interests within the war-leadership group occurred. In July 1941 Fujio Minoda, consul general in Saigon, sent the following telegram to the foreign minister: "The French Indochina authorities' retention of sovereignty, that is, control of government administration and the police, is the cancer of our policy measures vis-à-vis French Indochina. The same can be said with regard to economic negotiations, development of resources, and maneuvers concerning the Annamese and overseas Chinese. This time, therefore, we should take advantage of the slightest provocation by French Indochina to declare null and void the clauses guaranteeing respect for French Indochina's sovereignty and protection of its territorial integrity in the three agreements of August 30, September 4, and September 22 last year and in the peace treaty between Thailand and French Indochina, taking a totally different tack unbound by past [commitments]."[111]

Complaining that the French Indochina authorities' "control of government administration and the police" was the "cancer" of Japanese policy measures toward

---

[110] Document 18.

[111] Document 50.

French Indochina, and recommending that on "the slightest provocation" Japan should render "null and void" French Indochina's sovereignty, Minoda saw the occupation of southern French Indochina as the occasion for overthrowing the French regime there. Following this advice would mean welcoming Vietnamese nationalist movements; encouraging them would be necessary as well as advantageous.

Thus, the choice between suppression or support of Vietnamese nationalist movements was not a clear-cut one. The war-leadership group was not cleanly divided into two diametrically opposed factions, one determined to uphold suppression and the other advocating support. In the eyes of the group planning and prosecuting the war, both approaches were to be applied as appropriate; they were two aspects of a single state policy: expansion of the war in Asia.

This is demonstrated by two policy papers drawn up jointly by the Imperial Headquarters Army Department and Navy Section and issued on September 15, 1940. They presented policies premised on two scenarios. The first paper outlined policies to be followed in the case of an "independent occupation," a situation short of "general military conflict":

> For the time being, we will refrain from provocative propaganda likely to stir up French Indochina's past hostility and incite the natives to pro-independence uprisings, and we will direct [the Japanese authorities] to monitor French Indochina's attitude toward our occupation. We will also take care not to prematurely inflame the Japanese public, in order to avoid a change of heart in French Indochina that would make it less cooperative.[112]

As long as "peaceful occupation" remained possible, that is, as long as France remained willing to compromise, Japan would do nothing to "incite the natives to pro-independence uprisings": in other words, nationalist movements would be suppressed.

In the case of the second scenario, however, that is, if "general military conflict" became unavoidable, Japan would "commence propaganda efforts to [incite] successful pro-independence uprisings among the natives of Annam." More detailed policy guidelines followed:

> We will take special care to ensure that the natives support us. To accomplish this . . . we will direct [the Japanese authorities] to engineer plots and spread propaganda to induce public opinion to rise naturally in support of the Annamese people's right of national independence, liberation from their oppressed state, construction of a new East Asia, and spontaneous cooperation with East Asian liberation.[113]

Clearly, Japanese endorsement of "the Annamese people's right of national independence" was nothing but an expedient to seize Indochina from France in the event of "general military conflict."

The selective use of repressive and supportive means brought into play at the time of the occupation of northern French Indochina was repeated faithfully in connection with the 1941 occupation of southern French Indochina. When the French

---

[112] Document 44.

[113] Document 45.

refused to make concessions in the course of negotiations, strong anti-French sentiment flared; when France finally acceded to Japan's demands and so-called peaceful occupation was carried out, as if to reward this cooperation Japan issued the following policy guideline: "Refrain from comment likely to incite the natives to anti-French, pro-independence uprisings."[114]

As we have seen, Japan alternated between suppression and support of Vietnamese nationalist movements as circumstances dictated, both approaches being aspects of a single state policy aimed at expanding the war in Asia. While there was a general tendency for the faction favoring peaceful occupation and conciliation of Britain and the United States to opt for suppression and the faction urging military action and resistance to Britain and the United States to lean toward support, both factions were only contributing in different ways to the overall goal of expansion of the war in Asia and Japanese domination of Asian peoples.

Within Japan, there were no longer any forces capable of blocking or discouraging the aggression against Asia pushed through while juggling these two approaches. Independent mass movements opposing Japanese aggression and aimed at national liberation and independence organized by Asian peoples in general and by the peoples of Vietnam and Indochina in particular could have created a true alternative to Japan's brand of "liberation of the peoples of East Asia," discouraged Japan's ambitious plans, and finally brought about an end to the war Japan was prosecuting. Had the peoples of Asia succeeded in organizing themselves to oppose Japan, what would have been the effect on the social conditions and attitudes of the mass of Japanese people, and how would they have reacted? These are questions we cannot avoid.

In this connection, I would like to note that to this day, apologists for the war frequently claim that Japan was defeated only by America's overwhelming military and economic might and that the "Greater East Asia War" heightened national awareness and stimulated independence movements among the peoples of Asia. Can anyone deny that this is merely the postwar version of the wartime line extolling "liberation of the peoples of East Asia"? How truly independent nationalist movements would have developed had the peoples of Asia stood up to Japan is a question not only of historical interest but also one that all Japanese today should ponder in examining their own attitudes toward Japan's recent history.

The first version of this paper was published under the title "Hanoi ni okeru Nishihara kikan: 1940 nen 7 gatsu" [The Nishihara Mission in Hanoi: July 1940], in *Jimbun gakuhō* [Journal of social sciences and humanities], no. 167 (March 1984): 75–130. A revised version of that paper was included as the first chapter of my *Sensō kakudai no kōzu: Nihongun no "Futsuin shinchū"* [The pattern of war expansion: The Japanese army's occupation of French Indochina] (Tokyo: Aoki Shoten, 1986). The present paper is a revised version of the introduction, first chapter, and final chapter of that book.

------

[114] Document 51.

LIST OF DOCUMENTS

The documents cited in this paper are listed below in chronological order and identified by number. The location or source of each document is indicated by a capital letter in parentheses, according to the following key: A—Foreign Ministry Archives, B—the library of the Defense Agency's Institute for Defense Studies, C— the library of the Ajia Keizai Kenkyūjo [Institute of Developing Economies], D—the National Diet Library, and E—Jun Tsunoda, ed., *Nitchū sensō 3* [The Sino-Japanese War 3], vol. 10 of *Gendaishi shiryō* [Sources of contemporary history, 1925–1945] (Tokyo: Misuzu Shobō, 1964). The dates given are those on which the documents were sent except in the case of documents 21 and 34, for which the dates on which they were received are given.

1. *Unnan oyobi Annan no shuzoku to sono Shūkyō narabini shūkan* [The peoples of Yunnan and Annam and their religion and customs], Army General Staff, August 26, 1938 (D)

2. "Shina jihen ni taisuru Futsukoku no dōkō" [French opinion on the China Incident], Third Department, Naval General Staff, December 10, 1938 (B)

3. "Arita gaimu daijin hatsu zai Doku Kurusu taishi ate no dempō, betsuden: Futsuin mondai ni kansuru tai Doku mōshiire no ken" [Telegram from Foreign Minister Arita to Ambassador Kurusu in Germany, separate dispatch: Proposal to Germany concerning the French Indochina issue], June 18, 1940 (C)

4. "Futsuin keiyu gunjuhin yusō mondai ni kansuru Tani jikan Anrī taishi kaidan roku" [Record of discussions between Vice-Minister Tani and Ambassador Henry concerning the shipping of military supplies through French Indochina], June 19, 1940 (B)

5. "Shisatsuin haken ni kansuru tai Futsu mōshiire" [Proposal to France concerning the dispatch of a surveillance group], hand-delivered by Vice-Minister Tani to the French ambassador, June 22, 1940 (B)

6. "Hanoi kimitsu dai ni gō" [Hanoi secret message 2], letter from Toshiyo Yamada to the head of the Third Department, Naval General Staff, June 22, 1940 (B)

7. "Daikaibaku kimitsu dai 381 gō" [Imperial Headquarters Navy Section secret message 381], June 24, 1940 (B)

8. "Daihon'ei kaigunbu Futsuin haken iin hensei" [Imperial Headquarters Navy Section members of the group dispatched to French Indochina], June 24, 1940 (B)

9. "Daihon'ei rikugunbu Futsuin haken iin hensei" [Imperial Headquarters Army Department members of the group dispatched to French Indochina], June 24, 1940 (B)

10. "(Shijō dai 9 gō) Teki no gunjuhin yunyū jōkyō: Futsuin no busshi fūsa no tekigun hokyū ni oyobosu eikyō" [(Message 9 on the situation in China) The situation with regard to enemy imports of materiel: The effects of French Indochina's blockade of goods on supplies to enemy forces], Imperial Headquarters Army Department, June 25, 1940 (B)

11. "Futsuryō Indoshina ni taisuru kinkyū shochian" [Proposal on emergency measures toward French Indochina], Yasukichi Nagata, June 26, 1940 (A)

12. "Ippan jōkyō no ken hōkoku: Hanoi kimitsu dai san gō" [Report on the general situation: Hanoi secret message 3], from Toshiyo Yamada to the head of the Third Department, Naval General Staff, June 29, 1940 (B)

13. "Futsuin oyobi Biruma keiyu no en Shō busshi yunyū no genjō" [Current status of imports of supplies for Chiang via French Indochina and Burma], Third Department, Naval General Staff, June 1940 (B)

14. "Futsuingawa ni taisuru mōshiire" [Proposal to the French Indochina authorities], July 1, 1940 (B, E)

15. "Futsuin ni okeru teikoku guntai oyobi shichō no tsūka mondai" [The problem of the transit of imperial troops and military supplies in French Indochina], First Department, Naval General Staff, July 1, 1940 (B)

16. "Futsuin kaiha shoshin kimitsu dai ichi gō" [Secret message 1 from the navy contingent dispatched to French Indochina], from Captain Kuranosuke Yanagisawa, head of the navy contingent dispatched to French Indochina, to Captain Takeji Ono, head of the First Department, Naval General Staff, July 2, 1940 (B, E)

17. "Futsuin kaiha shoshin kimitsu dai ni gō" [Secret message 2 from the navy contingent dispatched to French Indochina], July 4, 1940 (B, E)

18. "Hanoi, Suzuki sōryōji hatsu Arita gaimu daijin ate dempō" [Telegram from Consul General Suzuki in Hanoi to Foreign Minister Arita], July 5, 1940 (A)

19. "Rondon, Shigemitsu taishi hatsu Arita gaimu daijin ate dempō" [Telegram from Ambassador Shigemitsu in London to Foreign Minister Arita], July 5, 1940 (A)

20. "Futsuin sōtoku no oboegaki (taika mondai ni kansuru kaitō)" [Memorandum from the governor general of French Indochina (reply concerning the accumulated-cargo issue)], July 6, 1940 (B)

21. "Nishihara kikan hatsu dempō" [Telegram from the Nishihara Mission], July 6, 1940 (A)

22. "Futsuin kai[ha shoshin] kimitsu dai san gō" [Secret message 3 from the navy contingent dispatched to French Indochina], July 7, 1940 (B, E)

23. "Nishihara kikan hatsu jichō ate dempō, dai 62 gō" [Telegram 62 from the Nishihara Mission to the assistant chiefs], July 8, 1940 (B)

24. "Hanoi, Suzuki sōryōji hatsu Arita gaimu daijin ate dempō" [Telegram from Consul General Suzuki in Hanoi to Foreign Minister Arita], July 9, 1940 (A)

25. "Futsuin kai[ha shoshin] kimitsu dai yon gō" [Secret message 4 from the navy contingent dispatched to French Indochina], July 9, 1940 (B, E)

26. "Jichō hatsu Nishihara kikan ate dempō" [Telegram from the assistant chiefs to the Nishihara Mission], July 9, 1940 (B)

27. "Suzuki sōryōji hatsu Arita gaimu daijin ate dempō" [Telegram from Consul General Suzuki to Foreign Minister Arita], July 10, 1940 (A)

28. "Nishihara kikan hatsu jichō ate dempō dai 92 gō" [Telegram 92 from the Nishihara Mission to the assistant chiefs], July 11, 1940 (B)

29. "Washūdan sambōchō hatsu jichō ate dempō, Washū san den 996 gō" [Telegram from the Nanning Army chief of staff to the assistant chief, Nanning Army staff telegram 996], July 11, 1940 (B)

30. "Satō taisa no mōshiire" [Proposal by Colonel Satō], July 12, 1940 (A)

31. "Nichi Futsuin kyōtei yōkō" [Outline of the agreement between Japan and French Indochina], July 12, 1940 (A)

32. "Arita gaimu daijin hatsu Suzuki sōryōji ate dempō, dai 123 gō den" [Telegram from Foreign Minister Arita to Consul General Suzuki, telegram 123], July 13, 1940 (A)

33. "Suzuki sōryōji hatsu Arita gaimu daijin ate dempō, dai 134 gō den" [Telegram from Consul General Suzuki to Foreign Minister Arita, telegram 134], July 14, 1940 (A)

34. "Nishihara kikan hatsu dempō" [Telegram from the Nishihara Mission], July 14, 1940 (A)

35. "Yosano shokikan hōkoku (ichi)" [Report 1 from Secretary Yosano], July 15, 1940 (A)

36. "Teikoku kantai no Futsuin oyobi Kōshū wan nyūkō keii ni kansuru oboe" [Memorandum on circumstances leading up to the Imperial Fleet's port calls at French Indochina and Gwangzhou Bay], July 15, 1940 (B)

37. "Nishihara kikan hatsu jichō ate dempō" [Telegram from the Nishihara Mission to the assistant chiefs], July 16, 1940 (B)

38. "Namishūdan sambōchō hatsu jichō ate dempō, Namishū san den dai 669 gō" [Telegram from the Kwantung Army chief of staff to the assistant chief, Kwantung Army staff telegram 669], July 19, 1940 (B)

39. "Arita daijin hatsu zai Nankin, zai Kanton, zai Shanhai, zai Junēbu taishi arui wa sōryōji ate dempō, dai 1607 gō" [Telegram 1,607 from Minister Arita to the ambassadors or consuls general in Nanjing, Guangdong, Shanghai, and Geneva], July 22, 1940 (A)

40. "Futsuin kaiha shoshin [kimitsu] dai roku gō" [Secret message 6 from the navy contingent dispatched to French Indochina], July 27, 1940 (B, E)

41. "Washūdan sambōchō hatsu jichō ate dempō, Washū san den dai 138 gō" [Telegram from the Nanning Army chief of staff to the assistant chief, Nanning Army staff telegram 138], July 29, 1940 (B)

42. "Futsuin kaiha shoshin kimitsu dai hachi gō" [Secret message 8 from the navy contingent dispatched to French Indochina], August 3, 1940 (B, E)

43. "[Nishihara kikan to Futsuingawa to no] genchi sesshō (6 gatsu 30 nichi-8 gatsu yokka)" [Local negotiations between the Nishihara Mission and the French Indochina authorities (June 30-August 4)], drafted by Captain Takeji Ōno, directly assigned to the head of the First Department, Naval General Staff, August 1940 (B, E)

44. "Futsuin shinchū kyōkō ni ōzuru hōdō senden yōryō" [Summary of information and propaganda to be disseminated in the event of the forcible occupation of French Indochina], Imperial Headquarters Army Department and Navy Section, September 15, 1940 (B)

45. "Nichi Futsuin kan zemmenteki buryoku shōtotsu jakki ni taiō suru hōdō senden yōryō" [Summary of information and propaganda to be disseminated in the event of the provocation of a general military conflict between Japan and French Indochina], Imperial Headquarters Army Department and Navy Section, September 15, 1940 (B)

46. "Nishihara hatsu rikugun jikan, sambō jichō ate dempō, Hanoi den 515 gō" [Telegram from Nishihara to the vice-minister of war and the assistant chief of the Army General Staff, Hanoi telegram 515], September 25, 1940 (B)

47. "Hanoi Haga jimukan Ō-A kyoku dai san ka Miyake jimukan ate shokan" [Letter from Attaché Haga in Hanoi to Secretary Miyake in the Third European and Oceanic Affairs Bureau], October 3, 1940 (A)

48. "Nihongun Futsuin shinchū ni kansuru Nichi Futsu kyōtei shūketsu kōshō keii (Shōwa 15 nen 7 gatsu-9 gatsu)" [Details of negotiations on the conclusion of an agreement between Japan and France concerning the occupation of French Indochina by the Japanese army (July-September 1940)], Second Division, South Seas Bureau, Ministry of Foreign Affairs, October 1940 (A)

49. "Futsuin hakengun shiyō shihei ni kansuru ken" [Item concerning scrip for troops dispatched to French Indochina], July 3, 1941 (A)

50. "Saigon Minoda sōryōji hatsu Toyoda gaimu daijin ate dempō, dai 259 gō" [Telegram 259 from Hanoi Consul General Minoda to Foreign Minister Toyoda], July 21, 1941 (A)

51. "Futsuin ni kansuru kyōdō bōei kyōtei seiritsu ni tomonau yoron shidō hōshin" [Policy for guiding public opinion upon the conclusion of a joint defense agreement concerning French Indochina], Information Bureau, Ministry of Foreign Affairs, July 26, 1941 (A)

52. "Futsuin haken iin jōmu buntan hyō" [Table of assignments of members dispatched to French Indochina], undated (B)

2

Two Features of Japan's Indochina Policy During the Pacific War

Masaya Shiraishi and Motoo Furuta

Introduction

Two features definitively distinguished Japan's policy toward Indochina during World War II from its policies toward other parts of Southeast Asia. One feature was that French Indochina was the only area under Japanese military influence in which a Western colonial regime was allowed to remain in place. Japan occupied northern Indochina in September 1940 but left the colonial regime intact until March 9, 1945—almost the end of the Pacific War. The other feature was that when the Japanese army carried out what it called *Futsuin shori* (disposition of French Indochina, or the settlement of the French Indochina question), staging a coup d'état and overthrowing the French colonial regime on March 9, 1945, it did not impose military rule, as it had in other parts of Southeast Asia, but instead granted the three nations of Indochina immediate, if nominal, independence.

These two features of Japan's policy toward Indochina had a significant effect on the development of the Vietnamese nationalist movement at the time. Nonetheless, there has been little study of their derivation. By analyzing the process through which Japan's Indochina policy was formulated and implemented, this paper tries to answer two questions: Why did Japan continue to follow the policy of preserving the French colonial regime for such an extended period after the outbreak of the Pacific War? And why did Japan adopt the policy of granting independence to the three countries of Indochina immediately after overthrowing the French colonial government?[1]

---

[1] Two important studies of relevance are available in Japan: Defense Agency, War History office, ed., *Shittan, Meigō sakusen: Biruma sensen no hōkai to Tai, Futsuin no bōei* [The Sittang and Meigō operations: The collapse of the Burma front and the defense of Thailand and French Indochina] (Tokyo: Asagumo Shimbunsha, 1969) and Kajima Heiwa Kenkyūsho [Kajima Institute of International Peace], ed., *Nihon gaikōshi* [Diplomatic history of Japan], vol. 24, *Dai Tōa sensō senji gaikō* [Diplomacy during the Greater East Asia War], ed. Ichirō Ota (Tokyo: Kajima Kenkyūsho Shuppankai, 1971). The first book is a collection of military documents on two military operations, while the second elucidates the diplomatic process that led to the "disposition of French Indochina" on the basis of Ministry of Foreign Affairs documents. Both are invaluable, and are the sources of many of the documents cited in this paper. The significance of the paper is twofold: first, we have scrutinized these documents from the standpoint of answering the questions at hand, and have pointed out some issues hitherto unaddressed. Second, we have supplemented the known sources with some newly discovered documents and with in-

In dealing with the first question, it is extremely important to take into account the fact that the framework of Japanese policy toward Indochina, whereby the Japanese military would use French Indochina to its advantage by keeping the French colonial regime intact—or exercise what the Vietnamese call "joint control by Japan and France"[2]—had already been formulated before the outbreak of the Pacific War, on the basis of the experience gained after the Japanese occupation of northern Indochina in September 1940 and of southern Indochina in July 1941. This paper does not dwell on this aspect, however, but limits itself to clarifying the reasons the colonial regime was allowed to remain in power for an extended period after the outbreak of the Pacific War, while in other parts of Southeast Asia the Japanese dismantled one colonial regime after another, establishing their own military administrations in the occupied territories.

A number of factors must be examined if the two questions posed above are to be answered fully and satisfactorily: the international political and economic environment at the time, the situation in France, the attitude of the French colonial regime, and French Indochina's military and economic value to Japan. However, these factors will be referred to only briefly, insofar as they had a significant bearing upon Japan's policy-making process. This paper addresses the two questions from the perspective of the decision-making process. Our analysis, based on identification of the characteristics of the Japanese policy-making process at the time as manifested in policy toward Indochina, concentrates on the following factors.

---

terviews with some of the military and diplomatic officials involved in the formulation of policy toward Indochina during the relevant period.

Available studies having a direct bearing upon this paper's theme list three factors that contributed to the prolongation of Japan's policy of keeping the French colonial regime in power: the fact that France was governed by an Axis-affiliated government in Vichy; the fact that there were contradictory policies among the Allied powers, especially the fact that the Roosevelt administration in the United States was reluctant to restore France to power in Indochina; and the fact that the French colonial government had no choice but to collaborate with Japan in order to safeguard French colonial interests in Indochina. The first factor is emphasized by all the studies. The second factor is emphasized by Bernard B. Fall, *The Two Vietnams: A Political and Military Analysis* (New York: Praeger, 1963) and Ellen J. Hammer, *The Struggle for Indochina* (Stanford: Stanford University Press, 1954). The third aspect is emphasized by Jean A. Decoux, *À la Barre de l'Indochine* (Paris: Plon, 1949); Haruyasu Katō, "1945 nen Vetonamu hachi gatsu kakumei to Furansu" [The Vietnamese August 1945 Revolution and France], *Rekishigaku kenkyū* [Journal of historical studies], no. 305 (October 1965); Jun'ichirō Shimbo, "Tōnan Ajia ni okeru minzoku undō" [Nationalist movements in Southeast Asia], in Matsuo Ara et al., eds., *Iwanami kōza: Sekai rekishi* [Iwanami history of the world], vol. 29 (Tokyo: Iwanami Shoten, 1971). *Shittan, Meigō sakusen* and *Nihon gaikōshi* 24 also attach importance to the French colonial government's cooperative attitude toward Japan. Little inquiry into the policy of granting immediate independence to the three countries of Indochina has been undertaken. That the Foreign Ministry conceived of such a policy prior to the coup is mentioned only briefly in *Shittan, Meigō sakusen, Nihon gaikōshi* 24, and Shizuo Maruyama, *Ushinawaretaru kiroku: Tai Ka, nampō seiryaku shi* [Lost records: The secret history of political tactics toward China and the south] (Tokyo: Kōraku Shobō, 1950). For an analysis of the relationship between Japanese policy during World War II and the Vietnamese nationalist movement, see Kenneth E. Colton, "The Influence of Japanese Wartime Policy on the Independent Political Movement in Vietnam after March 1945" (unpublished MS).

[2] This expression is used by contemporary Vietnamese scholars. A leading Vietnamese study of Japan's wartime policy toward Indochina is Tran Huy Lieu, Nguyen Luong Bich, and Nguyen Khac Dam, eds., *Tai Lieu Tham Khao Su Cach Mang Can Dai Viet Nam tap 8–9: Xa Hoi Viet Nam Trong Thoi Ky Phap Nhat*, vols. 1, 2 (Hanoi: Nha Xuat Ban Van Su, 1957).

First, although it is not at all unusual for conflicts of opinion among policy makers to emerge, reflecting differences in assessment of a given situation, there was a disproportionate degree of conflict among Japanese policy makers during World War II, because they failed to form among themselves a clear consensus about the very purpose of the war, even though such a consensus should have been fundamental in assessing the war situation. Second, conflict among policy makers made the Japanese policy-making process very haphazard: when policy makers decided on a certain policy, they tended to be much more concerned about making bargains and compromises with one another than about whether that particular policy was consistent with a fixed policy ideal. Third, and partly consequent upon the first two factors, the key words of a certain policy were often given different meanings under different circumstances, and by different policy makers. The extremely vague definition of key words was a cause as well as a result of conflict among the policy makers. At the same time, it acted as a "shock absorber," allowing policies to be changed tacitly and in a piecemeal manner to suit new developments in the war situation and enabling policy makers to make vague and noncommittal compromises with one another on many issues.

In the following pages, references to the central policy makers indicate the prime minister, the Ministries of Foreign Affairs and of Greater East Asia (especially the minister of foreign affairs), army headquarters (which consisted, unless otherwise specified, of the chief and the assistant chief of the Army General Staff and the War Plans Unit of the Army General Staff), and navy headquarters. Local authorities, meaning those in Indochina, included the Japanese embassy in Indochina, the Southern Army, and the Japanese garrison army in Indochina (later the Thirty-eighth Army). Furthermore, it is assumed that top decisions at the center were made by Imperial Headquarters-government liaison conferences (later the Supreme War Plans Council).

This paper considers that the will of army headquarters was represented by the War Plans Unit of the Army General Staff, and thus attaches special importance to the attitude of this unit. Established on October 10, 1940, as the twentieth unit under the direct control of the assistant chief of the Army General Staff, it was charged with the task of seeing to it that "war planning [is] not oriented excessively toward campaigns and operations." Although the unit was reorganized into the Fifteenth Section of the First (Operations) Department of the Army General Staff in February 1942, it was again put under the direct control of the assistant chief of the Army General Staff as the twentieth unit in October 1943.[3]

It is often pointed out that the policy-making process of the Japanese military during World War II was always preoccupied with planning for campaigns and operations in the immediate future and gave little serious thought to war planning suited to the execution of a "total war."[4] It is true, therefore, that the will of the Army General Staff was influenced by the Second (Operations) Section of the First Department, the opinions of the War Plans Unit often being brushed aside.

---

[3] For further information on the War Plans Unit, see Suketaka Tanemura, *Daihon'ei kimitsu nisshi* [Imperial Headquarters secret war diaries] (Tokyo: Daiyamondosha, 1952).

[4] See, for example, Akira Fujiwara, "Sensō shidōsha no seishin kōzō" [The mentality of the war leaders], in Bunzō Hashikawa and Sannosuke Matsumoto, eds., *Kindai Nihon seiji shisōshi* [History of modern Japanese political thought], vol. 2 (Tokyo: Yūhikaku, 1970).

Nonetheless, this paper attaches more importance to the War Plans Unit's role in the formulation of Indochina policy for the following reasons. It was not until immediately before the use of force against French Indochina, toward the end of the war, that the region became a focus of military operations in the narrow sense; this means that from the beginning of the Pacific War in December 1941 to the coup in March 1945, a period during which no battles took place in the region, Indochinese affairs called for diplomatic and political, rather than military, decisions, and it is plausible to assume that the War Plans Unit played a more active role in these decisions than it would have under other circumstances. Furthermore, judging from the "Daihon'ei kimitsu sensō nisshi" [Imperial Headquarters secret war history diaries] and other contemporary documents, the War Plans Unit conceived of policy toward Indochina from a standpoint that put operations and campaigns above all else, and in this sense its approach can be regarded as representing the army's intent.

With these factors in mind, this paper explicitly takes into account the conflicts of opinion and the gaps in perception between the military's top echelons and their overseas representatives, and between the Foreign Ministry and its embassy in Indochina, though we have been unable to probe deeply into conflicts within central headquarters.

I. Retention of the French Colonial Government

The Imperial Headquarters-government liaison conference of November 15, 1941, officially approved a "Plan for Facilitating the Conclusion of the War against the United States, Britain, the Netherlands, and Chiang [Kai-shek's regime in China],"[5] which proposed that Japanese policy toward Indochina should not be changed upon the commencement of the Pacific War; the French colonial government there should be retained, as it had been since the Japanese occupation of northern Indochina in September 1940.

Given the fact that this policy had already been announced in Imperial Headquarters Army Department Directive 991, dated November 6, 1941,[6] it seems clear that even prior to the November 15 decision there was a consensus among Japanese policy makers that the French colonial government in Indochina should be retained after Japan initiated war against the United States, Britain, and the Netherlands.

On December 9, immediately after the commencement of the Pacific War, the government of French Indochina agreed to accede to the military demands that Japan had made in line with Directive 991. Military agreements between Japan and France concerning the joint defense of French Indochina assured the French colonial government of continued existence during the war. To the French authorities in Indochina, cooperation with Japan appeared to be the only viable means of safeguarding their sovereignty over Indochina. Their home country was under siege by Nazi Germany; the United States and Britain were preoccupied with the European front, and in Southeast Asia they were already too busy defending their own colonial possessions to spare any thought for the French colony. Isolated and helpless, the French colonial authorities chose not to resist the Japanese but instead to maintain their sovereignty in Indochina, even if in name alone, by accepting the terms presented by the Japanese.

---

[5] Defense Agency, War History Office, *Daihon'ei rikugunbu* [Imperial Headquarters Army Department], vol. 2 (Tokyo: Asagumo Shimbunsha, 1968), p. 643.

[6] Ibid., p. 610.

In Japan, meanwhile, even though army headquarters and the Foreign Ministry were in agreement on the immediate policy of keeping the French colonial regime intact, they did not necessarily view this policy's purpose and intent in the same way.

From a standpoint that regarded Japan's self-preservation and self-defense *(jison jiei)* as the purpose of the war, control of Southeast Asia was to be aimed primarily at securing the supplies of natural resources indispensable for national defense and also at ensuring the conditions necessary for this, that is, the maintenance of public peace and order, or "the maintenance of tranquillity" *(seihitsu hoji)*, in the occupied territories.[7] The top priority of policy in French Indochina was thus to be placed on the maintenance of tranquillity, that is, on seeing to it that French Indochina was well defended, public peace and order were properly maintained, the local authorities cooperated with Japan satisfactorily, and French Indochina proved useful to the smooth execution of Japan's operations in the rest of Southeast Asia.

In the light of these priorities, Japan's policy toward French Indochina was quite "rational." Wishing to avoid the waste that would probably occur if it tried forcibly to oust the existing administrative structure and military forces, Japan adopted the highly "rational" policy of attaching itself parasitically to the existing system, securing the area as a relay point and rear base for supplying the military and acquiring access to local resources while retaining the French administrative apparatus. To put it bluntly, the policy of keeping the colonial regime intact was not an exception to but a model case of Japanese policy for the administration of the southern territories under its occupation, which stipulated that "in implementing military administration, every effort should be made to use the existing administrative machinery."[8]

From a standpoint that regarded "the liberation of Greater East Asia" as the primary purpose of the war, however, allowing the French colonial government to remain in power in Indochina, a region intended to be an integral part of the Greater East Asia Co-Prosperity Sphere, was an unacceptable contradiction.[9]

Put simplistically, army headquarters was inclined to the former view, while the Foreign Ministry favored the latter.[10] This is not to say that army headquarters was

---

[7] This is evident in the ideas expressed in "Nampō senryōchi gyōsei jisshi yōryō" [Summary of the implementation of administration in the occupied territories of the south], approved by the Imperial Headquarters-government liaison conference of November 20, 1941 (Defense Agency, *Daihon'ei rikugunbu* 2, p. 648), and "Nampō sakusen ni tomonau senryōchi tōchi yōkō" [Outline of the administration of occupied territories in connection with operations in the south], issued by the Imperial Headquarters Army Department on November 25, 1941.

[8] Defense Agency, *Daihon'ei rikugunbu* 2, p. 648.

[9] Makoto Ōiwa, a civilian, argued in an essay titled "Futsuin no seiritsu katei to minzoku kaihō undō no hatten" [The process of the formation of French Indochina and the development of the national liberation movement] that if France were willing to cooperate with the establishment of the Greater East Asia Co-Prosperity Sphere, it should recognize "the independence of the Vietnamese people," and that otherwise the French colonial regime would be overthrown. See Makoto Ōiwa, *Minami Ajia minzoku seiji ron* [The politics of South Asian peoples] (Tokyo: Banrikaku, 1942), pp. 190–91.

[10] It is well known that at the beginning of the Pacific War, Japanese policy makers decided first to declare war and only then deliberated on the pretext by which to justify the war. It is also well known that in the course of deliberations on the most plausible pretext, which lasted from the Imperial Headquarters-government liaison conference of November 15, 1941, to the issuing on December 6 of the imperial rescript declaring war, there was a conflict between those arguing that the purpose of the war was to ensure Japan's "continued self-preservation and self-defense" alone and those maintaining that "establishment of the Greater East Asia Co-Prosperity Sphere" should also constitute a war objective, with the former group finally

totally opposed to the latter view, with its emphasis on "autonomous cooperation and unity among the countries of Greater East Asia."[11] Rather, it regarded the French colonial government as essentially a "middle force"[12] that was only superficially obedient to Japan and would eventually have to be "dealt with decisively."[13] Nonetheless, army headquarters countered the argument for "the liberation of Greater East Asia" by stressing the need to "avoid racial war"[14] and by arguing that keeping the French colonial government intact would be the most rational means of maintaining tranquillity in Indochina for the time being.

The Foreign Ministry, meanwhile, was concerned that Japan's diplomatic stance toward French Indochina, a colony of the pro-German Vichy government, be consistent with its diplomatic stance toward Germany. Moreover, it was impossible for the ministry to deny the military's point that Japan could not afford to disturb law and order in French Indochina, which was to be an important rear base for Japan's operations in Southeast Asia. In the circumstances, the ministry was compelled for the time being to go along with the army and pursue the policy of keeping the French colonial regime in power despite its belief that this policy ran counter to the purpose of the war.

Because of the two opposing policy ideals underlying it, Japan's policy toward French Indochina during the Pacific War was highly susceptible to changes in the external situation. Of the various developments that frustrated this policy, three seem to have been of particular importance.

One was developments in the war in the European theater, including France, the Middle East, and North Africa—developments that affected Japanese policy toward French Indochina in two ways. One important factor was that France was under de facto German occupation, the Vichy-based government sustaining its precarious existence by virtue of being a pro-German regime. While this made it possible for Japan

---

prevailing. See Rekishigaku Kenkyūkai [Historical Science Society of Japan], ed., *Taiheiyō sensōshi* [History of the Pacific War], vol. 4 (Tokyo: Aoki Shoten, 1972), pp. 133–35. Some argued that Japan should proclaim its intent to "liberate Greater East Asia," in opposition to the Atlantic Charter of the United States and Britain. With regard to Japanese policy toward Indochina, it was Foreign Ministry officials who first questioned the policy of keeping the French colonial regime intact, citing the local independence movement. See the entry for March 16, 1942, in Army General Staff, War Plans Unit, "Daihon'ei kimitsu sensō nisshi" [Imperial Headquarters secret war diaries], War History Office, Defense Agency.

[11] This was asserted by Foreign Minister Mamoru Shigemitsu in 1943. See Kajima Heiwa Kenkyūsho, ed., *Nihon gaikōshi* 24, p. 461.

[12] For example, the French colonial regime was criticized as "pink" in Army General Staff, "Daihon'ei kimitsu," November 9, 1942.

[13] In February 1942 Captain Shingo Ishikawa of the Naval General Staff stated that "French Indochina should be dealt with as quickly as possible." Army General Staff, "Daihon'ei kimitsu," February 9, 1942.

[14] Lieutenant Colonel Chō Katō of the Military Affairs Section of the War Ministry stated in a speech delivered on April 11, 1942, "Nampō kensetsu no hōshin to genkyō" [The policy behind and present status of the construction of the south]: "We should treat nationals of the Axis countries in a friendly manner. Since the present war is not a racial war between the white race and colored races, it is essential that we refrain from denouncing nationals of the Axis countries en masse as whites, and thus from reducing this war to the kind of racial war the United States and Britain are planning." Kikakuin Kenkyūkai [Cabinet Planning Board Research Group], *Dai Tōa kensetsu no kihon kōryō* [Basic Program for the construction of Greater East Asia] (Tokyo: Dōmei Tsūshinsha, 1943), p. 345. In the army's view, French Indochina was the only region that proved that the Greater East Asia War was not a racial war.

to conclude with the Vichy government a series of agreements guaranteeing Japan's status in French Indochina,[15] it also led Japanese policy makers to worry, in the initial stage of the war, that Germany might intervene in French Indochina,[16] and made them feel obliged to link their policy toward French Indochina with that toward the Axis powers, especially Germany. Another factor of importance was that, as the war situation in Europe grew increasingly unfavorable to the Axis powers, the French colonial authorities dissociated themselves from the Vichyites, while in France the Vichy government grew increasingly unstable and finally collapsed. In the eyes of Japanese policy makers, this meant that the pro-Japanese stance of the French colonial government in Indochina, formerly affiliated with the Vichyites, was also weakened. Furthermore, the collapse of the Vichy government in France meant that the series of Franco-Japanese agreements that had been the basis for "joint control by Japan and France" became worthless.

The second development of importance was that the French colonial government's collaborative stance toward Japan weakened or, seen from the Japanese side, that French Indochina became openly hostile toward Japan. This development had two aspects: on the one hand, the Gaullists within French Indochina stepped up their resistance activities; on the other hand, the colonial government became increasingly reluctant to cooperate with Japan. What is important to note here is that the Vichyites and the Gaullists in French Indochina were united in defense of French colonial interests, and that therefore even the Gaullists collaborated with Japan, if only on the surface, as long as this was deemed necessary to protect such interests.[17] In other words, the change in the balance of power between the Vichyites and the Gaullists did not manifest itself straightforwardly in French Indochina as a sudden switch from collaboration to resistance. This is why the question of the French colonial government's collaboration with Japan ought to be viewed independently from the change in the balance of power in France itself.

The third development of importance was that the war in East Asia turned against Japan, giving rise to the possibility that Allied assaults would turn Indochina into a battleground. This possibility was extremely troubling to Japan, partly because the French colonial government was collaborating with Japan only halfheartedly, as a means of protecting French colonial interests, and partly because, if the military balance in Indochina changed as a result of Allied assaults, Japan would not be able to count on collaboration from the French colonial government or from the French troops stationed in Indochina.[18]

---

[15] These agreements included the notes exchanged between Yōsuke Matsuoka and Charles Arsène Henry on August 30, 1940 (Matsuoka was the Japanese foreign minister and Henry the French ambassador to Japan at the time); the agreement between Japan and French Indochina on details of local military affairs of September 22, 1940; the trade agreement between Japan and French Indochina of May 6, 1941; the agreement between Japan and French Indochina on joint defense of July 23, 1941; the protocol between Japan and French Indochina on joint defense of July 29, 1941; and the agreement between Japan and France on military affairs in French Indochina of December 9, 1941.

[16] Kajima Heiwa Kenkyūsho, ed., *Nihon gaikōshi* 24, pp. 193–94.

[17] This point is discussed in detail in Katō, "1945 nen Vetonamu hachi gatsu kakumei."

[18] The way in which Indochina's strategic significance to Japan changed over time may be summarized as follows. September 1940–July 1941: A component of the blockade of China. July–December 1941: A means of breaking the military, political, and economic links joining the United States, Britain, China, and the Netherlands, and a base for Southern Army operational preparations. December 1941–May 1942: With the establishment of the Southern Army

II. THE POLICY OF SEVERING FRENCH INDOCHINA FROM FRANCE

Thus, the policy of keeping the French colonial government intact, supported mainly by an army headquarters preoccupied with military operations, was burdened with a number of destabilizing factors. One important reason this policy could be maintained for so long despite such factors is that Japanese policy makers regarded it as one and the same thing as the policy of severing the French colony from France.

The policy of cutting off French Indochina from France was defined by the War Plans Unit of the Army General Staff as that of "separating French possessions in East Asia from France and incorporating them under the guidance of the [Japanese] Empire in the future."[19] More specifically, this policy was designed to retain the French colonial government in Indochina, enable the French governor general there to secure a considerable degree of independence from his home government, and have him turn this region into a stable part of the Greater East Asia Co-Prosperity Sphere.

Originally formulated out of anxiety that Germany might lay claim to French Indochina as part of its sphere of influence as the French government in Vichy became increasingly pro-German, this policy had been agreed upon by the army, the navy, and the Foreign Ministry at the administrative level in the immediate aftermath of the start of the Pacific War.[20] Japan interpreted the appointment of Pierre Laval as prime minister of France in April 1942 as representing the Vichy government's increased affinity with Germany,[21] and the Imperial Headquarters-government liaison conference of April 24 adopted a "Decision on Immediate Measures Toward France."[22] On that occasion, army headquarters proposed that Japan explicitly pronounce a national policy of severing French Indochina from France. This proposal was met by opposition from Prime Minister Hideki Tōjō, who argued that "this question should be deferred until such time as the situation of the war between Germany and the Soviet Union takes a turn for the better for Germany, with the result that Germany will become unconcerned about a stronger Japanese policy toward France."[23] Consequently, the liaison conference agreed that no change should be made in the legal status of French Indochina for the time being; the army had to be content with the prime minister's statement that "Though we know in our hearts that

---

General Headquarters, development into an operational base and a command center. May 1942–November 1944: A supply base for the Southern Army and a maritime relay base linking the Southern Army and Japan. November 1944–August 1945: The center for the self-sustaining, self-sufficient defense of the south and for liaison between Japanese forces in the south and in China. See Daiichi Fukuinkyoku [First Demobilization Bureau], "Futsuryō Indoshina hōmen sakusen kiroku" [Records of operations in and around French Indochina], 1946, Ministry of Health and Welfare. Although Japanese policy makers remained apprehensive throughout this period about the possibility that the Chungking army would advance into Indochina, only in November 1944 did the Japanese army begin seriously to consider turning Indochina into a battlefield.

[19] Army General Staff, "Daihon'ei kimitsu," April 23, 1942.

[20] Ibid., March 16, 1942.

[21] Ibid., April 17, 1942.

[22] "Tōmen no tai Futsu sochi ni kansuru ken," in Army General Staff, ed., *Sugiyama memo* [Memoranda of General Hajime Sugiyama], vol. 2 (Tokyo: Hara Shobō, 1967), pp. 115–16.

[23] Army General Staff, "Daihon'ei kimitsu," April 23, 1942.

it is right to detach French Indochina [from France] in the future, we cannot afford to put it down in the record."[24]

Subsequently, however, the policy of separating the colony from its suzerain began to be pursued, not in its "extreme" form of having French Indochina sever itself legally from France[25] but in the form of a policy intended to make the colonial government relatively independent of the home government and to induce the governor general to collaborate more closely with Japan at his own discretion. Moreover, this policy was pursued not in the context of preventing the spread of German influence to French Indochina but with the manifest purpose of isolating French Indochina as much as possible from the setbacks and instability being suffered by the Vichyites in both France and Indochina.

On November 8, 1942, Allied troops landed in Algeria. Learning of the fall of this important French colony,[26] on November 12 General Shunroku Hata, assistant chief of the Army General Staff, informed the chief of staff of the Southern Army General Headquarters of Tokyo headquarters policy in a telegram that read in part: "Under all circumstances, and as long as this war is being fought, it is essential that we see to it that public peace and order are maintained in French Indochina and that Japan never has its military power checked in that region."[27] The Imperial Headquarters-government liaison conference of November 21 approved this policy.[28] It was to maintain law and order in French Indochina that Japan found it imperative to prevent the "vicious effects" of the European theater from spreading there. The policy

---

[24] Ibid., April 24, 1942.

[25] Prime Minister Tōjō used the term "extreme" when voicing his opinion at the imperial conference of May 31, 1943. Army General Staff, ed., *Sugiyama memo* 2, p. 413.

[26] Upon learning of the fall of Algeria to the Allies, Japanese policy makers were concerned over the possibility that "French colonies will begin breaking away from the French homeland, either joining the de Gaulle camp or establishing themselves as quasi-independent states." See the description of the Imperial Headquarters-government liaison conference of November 21, 1942, in Army General Staff, ed., *Sugiyama memo* 2, p. 178. Prior to this, the Japanese military forces in French Indochina, which had been charged primarily with the task of maintaining law and order in the occupied territory upon completion of Southern Army operations on May 18, 1942, submitted a proposal to Imperial Headquarters on September 26 in the name of Iwaichi Fujiwara, a Southern Army staff officer. This document, "Futsuin no tekisei senjo yōryōan" [Draft proposal on cutting off hostile elements in French Indochina], argued that Japan should take measures to quash maneuvers conducted by Gaullists within the French Indochina government. In response to this proposal, on October 14 army and navy headquarters and the Foreign Ministry jointly drafted a directive titled "Futsuin no tekisei senjo ni kansuru ken" [On the question of cutting off hostile elements in French Indochina] and sent it to the garrison army in Indochina. Emphasizing the importance of remaining true to "the policy of not raising a storm when all is calm," the directive advised the local army forces to try to deal with the question of "hostile elements in French Indochina" within the bounds of the policy of retaining the colonial regime, by having the local army and navy forces and the embassy work more closely with one another in putting greater pressure on and keeping closer surveillance over the colonial regime. Army General Staff, "Daihon'ei kimitsu," September 26, October 3, and October 14, 1942.

[27] "Nampōgun (reika butai) kankei dempō tsuzuri" [File of telegrams concerning the Southern Army (subordinate troops)], War History Office, Defense Agency. Meanwhile, the order to set up a garrison army headquarters, with Lieutenant General Kazumoto Machijiri as commander, was issued on November 9, and the headquarters was established in Saigon on December 5. Defense Agency, ed., *Shittan, Meigō sakusen*, p. 542.

[28] Army General Staff, ed., *Sugiyama memo* 2, pp. 178–79.

implemented to this end was that of *effectively* cutting off French Indochina from France.

As the first concrete step toward implementation of this policy, negotiations were held between the Japanese embassy in French Indochina and the French authorities there. In their meetings with Governor General Admiral Jean A. Decoux in December 1942 and January 1943, Ambassador Kenkichi Yoshizawa and Secretary General Shigeru Kuriyama demanded that the governor general take steps to make his colonial government collaborate more closely with Japan—and that he do so on his own authority as governor general, without consulting his home government. The steps demanded of him consisted of de facto revision of the existing treaties between Japan and France and the purging of anti-Japanese and pro–Anglo-American elements from the colonial government.[29]

It was in the process of the negotiations preceding the Japanese occupation in February 1943 of Guangzhou Bay, a territory leased by France and incorporated into French Indochina, that Japan began full-scale application of the policy of effectively severing Indochina from France proper. In January 1943, when Japan conceived of occupying Guangzhou Bay as a means of facilitating the Wang Zhaoming government's entry into the war, it asked France to relinquish its holdings in China to the Wang government and abandon its extraterritorial rights in China. At the same time, Japan considered that if France declared that it was relinquishing Guangzhou Bay, the Chungking army would probably advance into the area. To prepare itself for that likelihood, Japan talked the French government and the French Indochina government into agreeing to joint Japanese-French defense of Guangzhou Bay and Japanese military occupation of the area. Occupation proceeded smoothly and was completed on February 22.[30]

What is worthy of attention here is the way in which the negotiations were carried out. In order to implement its military occupation of Guangzhou Bay, Japan negotiated not only with the French home government but also, separately, with the governor general of French Indochina, which had jurisdiction over the bay. Japan managed to persuade the governor general to give de facto approval to the Japanese advance into the area at his own discretion, without consulting the home government. The War Plans Unit of the Army General Staff lauded this as a successful application of the policy of effectively severing French Indochina from France: "This [accomplishment] is gratifying to the Empire, and is expected to set a precedent that will benefit our policy toward France on many occasions in the future."[31]

---

[29] See "Dai Tōa sensō kankei ikken: Jōsei no henka ni ōzuru Futsuin shori mondai" [Items on the Greater East Asia War: The problem of the disposition of French Indochina to deal with changes in the situation], a file of telegrams in the Foreign Ministry Archives. See especially "Tai Futsuin seisaku ni kansuru Kuriyama Dokū kaidan" [Conference between Kuriyama and Decoux concerning policies toward French Indochina], a telegram from Rokurō Suzuki, deputy consul general in Saigon, to Greater East Asia Minister Kazuo Aoki dated January 13, 1943.

[30] For details of the Japanese military occupation of Guangzhou Bay, see Kajima Heiwa Kenkyūsho, ed., *Nihon gaikōshi* 24, pp. 201–6. For the Imperial Headquarters-government liaison conference decisions of January 14 and 30, 1943, on the occupation, "Tōmen no tai Futsu sochi ni kansuru ken" [Decision on immediate measures toward France] and "Tai Futsu sochi ni kansuru ken" [Decision on measures toward France], respectively, see Army General Staff, ed., *Sugiyama memo* 2, pp. 352, 362.

[31] Army General Staff, "Daihon'ei kimitsu," February 21, 1943.

It is generally believed that the army and the Foreign Ministry acted in concert in carrying out the negotiations concerning the Japanese occupation of Guangzhou Bay. When it came to assessing the policy of effectively separating French Indochina from France as it was actually implemented on that occasion, however, there was a considerable difference of opinion between the army and the Foreign Ministry.

Within the Army General Staff, the War Plans Unit and the Second (Intelligence) Department disagreed. In its draft policy on French Indochina, completed on January 22, 1943, the Second Department proposed that French Indochina be made an independent nation, not simply in effect but legally, and that a "movement to enlighten the natives" be launched. The War Plans Unit rejected this proposal on the grounds that "the maintenance of tranquillity in French Indochina is our national policy at present; therefore, if the Second Department immediately launches covert actions on the basis of this plan, the result will be 'a thousand evils and no good.'"[32] The War Plans Unit was of the opinion that effectively severing French Indochina from France would suffice for the time being, and did not wish to have this basic policy disturbed by activities of a different orientation. That position prevailed in army headquarters at the time.[33]

The reason the Foreign Ministry and the embassy in French Indochina chose at that juncture actively to support the policy of effectively separating the French colony from its home government seems to be that they regarded this policy as the first step toward implementing the ideal of "the liberation of Greater East Asia" in French Indochina.[34] By the beginning of 1943 the embassy had begun to undertake two maneuvers: one to equip the governor general with the authority to discipline, mete out reward and punishment to, and appoint and discharge personnel of, the French Indochina army; and the other to raise the political consciousness of "the Annamese" (the Vietnamese).[35] The latter was frowned upon by the War Plans Unit. This means that the embassy, while siding with the army for the time being on the question of effectively separating the French colony from its homeland, was also trying to find ways to implement the policy of "the liberation of Greater East Asia." The Foreign Ministry and the embassy began advocating active pursuit of this ideal explicitly in

---

[32] Ibid., January 22, 1943.

[33] At the time, the chief of the Army General Staff and his operations officers leaned strongly toward the view that "given the present situation of overall troop operations, it is imperative to try as far as possible to avoid the possibility that the Imperial Army will engage the Chungking army in battle in French Indochina or elsewhere." See the draft plan for the occupation of Guangzhou Bay drawn up by the Second Section of the Army General Staff, recorded in Army General Staff, "Daihon'ei kimitsu," January 12, 1943. See also the assertion by Army General Hajime Sugiyama, chief of the Army General Staff, at the Imperial Headquarters-government liaison conference of January 11, recorded in Army General Staff, ed., *Sugiyama memo* 2, p. 348.

[34] Opinion was also divided within the Foreign Ministry, however. Telegrams exchanged between Foreign Minister Masayuki Tani and Ambassador to Germany Hiroshi Ōshima on the question of the reversion of French settlements and leased territories in China reveal that the foreign minister thought it important to "maintain tranquillity in French Indochina" for the time being because, he believed, French Indochina was becoming more cooperative with Japan following the fall of Algeria, while the ambassador urged that Japan proceed with the construction of the Greater East Asia Co-Prosperity Sphere by having Wang Zhaoming participate in the war, by forcing France to abandon its settlements and leased territories in China and break off diplomatic relations with the Chungking government, and by adopting a "firm policy" toward French Indochina. See "Zai Shi Futsu sokai, soshakuchi ikken" [On the French settlements and leased territories in China], Foreign Ministry Archives.

[35] Army General Staff, "Daihon'ei kimitsu," March 3, 1943.

1944, insisting on the need to carry out "a policy in French Indochina that is consistent with the Greater East Asia Declaration."[36]

III. Preparations for Operation Ma

Following Japan's retreat from Guadalcanal in February 1943, its military hegemony in East Asia began to crumble rapidly. On the European front, Italy surrendered on September 8, and defeat for the Axis powers appeared increasingly certain. Under these circumstances, the Imperial Headquarters-government liaison conference of September 25 decided to demarcate a "sphere of absolute national defense." Spurred by this decision, policy makers began to reexamine Japan's policy toward French Indochina. At the liaison conference the preceding day, which had discussed a draft "Assessment of the World Situation," Prime Minister Tōjō had stated: "[The United States and Britain] will intensify their machinations vis-à-vis French Indochina, Thailand, and Burma, planning to pick them off one by one. Since there is a strong possibility that they will try to accomplish this by enticing these countries with terms more favorable than those offered by the Empire, it is necessary to study concrete ways of counteracting this strategy."[37]

In addition to the general turning of the war against Japan, two factors encouraged policy makers to reconsider their policy toward French Indochina. One was that the Gaullists were beginning to gather momentum in French Indochina at long last: the Gaullist resistance organization, the Comité National Français, declared in October that it would take part in liberation of the West Pacific region and French Indochina; in December the Comité announced its policy on Indochina; and at about the same time, a Free France military mission was established in Kunming.[38] The other factor was that in Thailand, which Japan had regarded as a region similar to French Indochina, an incident took place that could endanger the country's stance of cooperation with Japan: Prime Minister Luang Phibun Songkhram did not attend the Greater East Asia Conference, convened in Tokyo in November. Japan took his absence from the conference as indicating that he was "influenced as significantly as ordinary Thai people by the war situation, which has recently been unfavorable to the Axis powers, and by the propaganda the enemy is directing toward Thailand to take advantage of this situation."[39]

Under the pressure of these circumstances, Japan's policy makers came to share the view that policy toward French Indochina ought to be reexamined. It was in the course of such reexamination that a plan to deal with French Indochina by force (military code name "Operation Ma") was studied as one possible course.

---

[36] Shigemitsu's assumption of office as foreign minister on April 20, 1943, seems to have been instrumental in inducing the ministry to take an increasingly assertive stance. See Mamoru Shigemitsu, *Shōwa no dōran* [The upheavals of the Shōwa era], vol. 2 (Tokyo: Chūō Kōronsha, 1952).

[37] Army General Staff, ed., *Sugiyama memo* 2, p. 465.

[38] See Katō, "1945 nen Vetonamu hachi gatsu kakumei."

[39] This assessment was made by Ambassador to Thailand Teiji Tsubogami. Kajima Heiwa kenkyūsho, ed., *Nihon gaikōshi*, 24, p. 470. Commenting on this incident, General Sugiyama, chief of the Army General Staff, also expressed concern at an Imperial Headquarters-government liaison conference that Thailand could become "the Italy of the Orient." Army General Staff, ed., *Sugiyama memo* 2, p. 501.

The idea of using force against French Indochina was proposed most urgently by two groups. One was the garrison army in French Indochina. On August 11, 1943, Colonel Masao Kushida, a senior staff officer in the Southern Army, strongly requested troop reinforcements in French Indochina of Major General Jōichirō Sanada, chief of the Second Section of the Army General Staff, on the grounds that to cope with the aftermath of the political change in Italy (the fall of the Mussolini government on July 25), Japan might have to take measures toward French Indochina on its own authority, that is, use force against the French colonial regime.[40] Furthermore, on January 6, 1944, Lieutenant General Kitsuju Ayabe, assistant chief of staff of the Southern Army, and Major General Saburō Kawamura, chief of staff of the garrison army in French Indochina, during an official visit to Tokyo submitted an opinion to army headquarters on behalf of the local army, arguing that, in view of developments in the war in East Asia, the situation in French Indochina was bound to be disturbed sooner or later, and that dealing with French Indochina by force soon should be made an explicit national policy.[41]

The local army's primary objective in arguing strongly for the use of force against the French Indochina regime was to impress upon Tokyo headquarters the need to reinforce the Japanese troops in French Indochina, which, despite the worsening war situation, consisted of only a small headquarters charged mainly with diplomatic negotiations and a garrison army roughly the size of a division.[42] It is inconceivable that the regional forces actually regarded military action against French Indochina as an urgent issue.[43] It is more plausible to assume that when the local military authorities submitted their view of the unavoidability of the use of force against French Indochina in the near future to Tokyo headquarters, which was beginning to consider changing its policy toward French Indochina, they did so in the hope of accomplishing their immediate purpose of having their troops reinforced.[44]

The other group that advocated the use of force against Indochina consisted of the Foreign Ministry and the embassy in French Indochina, both of which made the following assertions: Allied machinations would inevitably disturb the situation in Thailand and French Indochina; the Decoux faction in French Indochina had been infiltrated by elements antagonistic to the Axis powers; therefore Japan should take decisive steps to deal with French Indochina by force; and in so doing, Japan should grant Annam (central Vietnam), Tonkin (northern Vietnam), and Laos independence. In other words, the Foreign Ministry and the embassy judged that, with the war situation on the European front worsening, Japan could now act without deference toward Germany and should implement as quickly as possible a policy of dealing with French Indochina militarily and granting the native populations independence,

---

[40] Defense Agency, ed., *Shittan, Meigō sakusen*, p. 578.

[41] Army General Staff, "Daihon'ei kimitsu," January 6, 1944.

[42] The Japanese troops stationed in Indochina at the time consisted of a headquarters, the Twenty-first Division, the First Military Police Unit of the Southern Army, the Thirty-fourth Independent Motor Transport Company, and the Second and Fourth Southern Army Hospitals.

[43] Defense Agency, ed., *Shittan, Meigō sakusen*, p. 579.

[44] This desire was partially satisfied; the headquarters of the garrison army was reinforced following a military tactical command issued on January 6, 1944, and the Thirty-fourth Independent Mixed Brigade arrived in Indochina in March. Ibid., pp. 551–52.

thereby defining its policy toward French Indochina more explicitly as part of its pursuit of "the liberation of Greater East Asia."[45]

It was army headquarters in Tokyo that reacted most negatively to these arguments favoring decisive action. The position of army headquarters, represented by the Second Section and the War Plans Unit of the Army General Staff, was made clear in the course of consultations with Colonel Kushida conducted on December 16 and 26, 1943, to hear his views on the Army General Staff's "Plan of Measures Toward France and French Indochina," similar consultations with Generals Ayabe and Kawamura conducted on January 6, 1944, and the presentation on January 8 of the unified opinion of the War Ministry and the Army General Staff in response to the opinions expressed by those local army leaders.[46] Army headquarters' attitude, as expressed on these occasions, boiled down to the following set of assertions: there was no immediate need to change policy toward French Indochina significantly; when France ceased in effect to be a pro-Axis nation, Japan should let French Indochina effectively dissociate itself from the home country; in accomplishing this Japan should exercise force if necessary; and even if Japan exercised force, it should subsequently govern Indochina by making use of the existing administrative machinery.[47] In other words, army headquarters was of the opinion that to cope with the changed situation it would be sufficient to reconfirm the present national policy of de facto separation of French Indochina from France.

This stance also differed from that of the garrison army, which maintained that the use of force against French Indochina should be established as the basic Japanese policy toward the region; that once military might was exercised, it would become impossible to use the existing administrative machinery; and that therefore military rule should be established, dangling before the indigenous population "the bait of independence" and thus mobilizing it to collaborate with Japanese military rule.[48]

The army headquarters' view prevailed at the Imperial Headquarters-government liaison conference of January 24, 1944, which approved a "Plan of Measures Toward French Indochina to Deal with Changes in the Situation."[49] The document began by emphasizing the need to "adhere to the existing policy of maintaining tranquillity" and to "avoid anything that might instigate native nationalist movements," thus rejecting the approach advocated by the Foreign Ministry and the garrison army. The plan also supported the army headquarters' position by asserting that Japan should deal with "changes in the situation" by forcing French Indochina to dissociate itself from the home country but should not have recourse to military action except in an "unavoidable situation."

By that time, the war situation in East Asia had become so unfavorable to Japan that policy makers—especially Prime Minister Tōjō and the central military author-

---

[45] See the statement by Shigemitsu at the Imperial Headquarters-government liaison conference of January 24, 1944, and the statement by Ambassador Yoshizawa during talks with the War Ministry on January 29. Army General Staff, "Daihon'ei kimitsu," January 24 and 29, 1944.

[46] Ibid., December 16 and 26, 1943; January 6 and 8, 1944.

[47] Defense Agency, ed., *Shittan, Meigō sakusen*, pp. 579–81.

[48] The entry for January 6, 1944, in Army General Staff, "Daihon'ei kimitsu," notes that "there is a considerable gap in thinking between the center [central headquarters] and those on the scene in regard to the disposition of French Indochina."

[49] "Jōsei no henka ni ōzuru tai Futsuin sochi fukuan," in Army General Staff, ed., *Sugiyama memo* 2, p. 530.

ities—were strongly inclined to prevent the expansion of the war as much as possible. This is evident in the prime minister's statement at the January 24 liaison conference: "It is necessary to reduce as far as possible the costs to be borne by the Empire in maintaining law and order in French Indochina."[50] It was at the same conference that a decision was made to cope with the imminent crisis as far as possible by upholding the policy of retaining the French colonial government in Indochina as a reliable framework of administration and by having French Indochina dissociate itself from the home country.[51]

Thus, the January 24 decision had the intent of limiting the exercise of force in French Indochina to situations in which it was "unavoidable," in direct opposition to the opinion expressed by the Foreign Ministry and the embassy in French Indochina. It should be borne in mind, however, that as the war situation subsequently grew still more unfavorable to Japan, this same decision, by having recognized, if only in a limited way, the necessity of dealing with French Indochina militarily, came to be used as a convenient pretext for rationalizing efforts to change Japanese policy toward the region in a piecemeal manner.

IV. The Process Leading to the "Measures toward French Indochina" Decision

It was not until the war situation grew tenser in June to August 1944 that Japan was forced to change its policy toward French Indochina.[52] Two developments prompted the shift: the opening of a second front in Europe by the Allied powers and the collapse of the Vichy government in France.

On June 6, 1944, Allied troops landed in Normandy, France. On August 20 the French government moved from Vichy to Belfort, signaling its de facto collapse. August 29 saw the fall of Paris and the establishment of a provisional government headed by General Charles de Gaulle.

The Japanese authorities in French Indochina responded swiftly to these developments. On June 9 Ambassador Yoshizawa cabled the Greater East Asia Ministry inquiring how the government would react if the Vichy government stopped functioning.[53] Similarly, in a June 16 document, "Assessment of the Situation in the Southwestern Region in the Light of the Recent War Situation," the Southern Army stated that "if the situation on the second front takes a turn favorable to the United States and Britain with intensification of Anglo-American political offensives and air raids, we cannot deny the possibility that, regardless of how the war situation in East Asia develops, Thailand and French Indochina will drop out as early as this autumn."[54] Also, during a simulation analysis undertaken by the Southern Army beginning on August 6, staff officers of the garrison army expressed their wish to ask

---

[50] Ibid., p. 531.

[51] The plan stated that "in the event that France ceases in effect to be a pro-Axis nation, French Indochina is to be substantively separated from the homeland." Ibid., p. 530.

[52] In the first half of 1944 Japan considered the French Indochina regime's collaboration to be "good." See the report of firsthand observation of the situation in the south by Tōru Hagiwara of the Southern Affairs Bureau of the Greater East Asia Ministry in Army General Staff, "Daihon'ei kimitsu," April 4, 1944. See also a communication submitted to General Hata, assistant chief of the Army General Staff, by General Machijiri, commander of the garrison army, during Hata's tour of the south. Ibid., May 16, 1944.

[53] Telegram dated June 9, 1944, "Dai Tōa sensō."

[54] "Nampōgun kankei dempō."

Imperial Headquarters for instructions concerning Operation Ma by the end of September.[55]

The war in the Pacific was also taking a turn for the worse. The "sphere of absolute national defense" was rapidly crumbling, with Japan sustaining a series of major setbacks beginning in June 1944, including defeat in the battle of the Marianas, the fall of Saipan, and the failure of the Imphal campaign in Burma.[56] These setbacks resulted in the resignation of the Tōjō cabinet and the establishment in July of a new cabinet headed by Kuniaki Koiso. An imperial conference on August 19, the first held under the new cabinet, assessed the situation pessimistically:

> Given the current world situation, the nations of Greater East Asia, with the exception of Manchukuo, are already showing signs of becoming reluctant to collaborate with Japan. It is expected that a further turn of the tide of the war against the Axis powers in Greater East Asia as well as in Europe and further escalation of enemy political intrigue will combine to produce the effect of gradually making the governments and peoples of these nations more restless and of worsening law and order in these nations.[57]

It was in this state of mind that Japanese policy makers faced the de facto collapse of the Vichy government in France.[58]

At a Supreme War Plans Council meeting on September 5, Foreign Minister Shigemitsu referred to an opinion expressed by the French ambassador to China, Henri Cosme. According to this opinion, Cosme and the leaders of the French Indochina government considered the Vichy government to have already ceased to exist and were planning to ask for instructions from the new and legitimate government as soon as it was established. This suggested that, if the worst came to the worst, French Indochina might cease to be friendly toward Japan. In the light of this possibility, the council agreed on the "urgent need to study the measures to be taken toward French Indochina."[59] Meeting again on September 14, the council decided on "Measures Toward French Indochina to Deal with Changes in the Situation."

That decision asserted that "although the policy of maintaining the status quo should be pursued with regard to French Indochina for the time being, necessary preparations for dealing with a sudden change in the situation should also be made." The "sudden change" alluded to here was "the establishment of a unified government" in France. (At the time, Japan did not regard de Gaulle's provisional government in Paris as such a regime.) If this sort of "sudden change" took place, Japan was to act in accordance with one of three scenarios, depending on the attitude of the French colonial government in Indochina. Under the first scenario, which assumed

---

[55] Ibid.

[56] The Imphal campaign was suspended on July 4, 1944.

[57] Army General Staff, *Haisen no kiroku* [Record of the defeat] (Tokyo: Hara Shobō, 1967), p. 151.

[58] The issue was taken up as early as August 26 by the Supreme War Plans Council, where Foreign Minister Shigemitsu asked about the "attitude of the high command with regard to the new developments in French Indochina consequent upon the changes in the European situation." General Umezu, chief of the Army General Staff, said in response that "it is absolutely necessary to adhere to the policy of maintaining tranquillity." Army General Staff, "Daihon'ei kimitsu," August 26, 1944.

[59] Ibid., September 5, 1944.

that the colonial government would "continue to collaborate with Japan," Japan too would continue to pursue its existing policy of having French Indochina dissociate itself from France. The second scenario was based on the assumption that the leaders of the colonial government would "tender their resignations peacefully, on the grounds that they can no longer continue collaborating with Japan." In that event, it was proposed, Japan would put French Indochina under its own military control, utilizing the existing administrative machinery as far as possible. The third, worst-case, scenario assumed that "either the French Indochinese authorities or the French troops in Indochina openly break away from Japan and mount resistance against Japan." In such an "unavoidable situation," Japan would liquidate the French colonial regime by force.[60]

During the deliberations culminating in this decision, the foreign minister proposed that Japan "make French Indochina independent by the hands of the natives." In other words, he advocated that the exercise of military power not be limited to the circumstances posited by the third scenario but that Japan take advantage of the opportunity to sweep away the colonial regime. This proposal was rejected by the army, which claimed that it had "neither the capability nor the confidence" to execute such a military operation.[61] Even at that point, army headquarters felt that it was most urgent to concentrate its troop strength on the battles in and around the Philippines and thus wished to avoid stirring up French Indochina, which was an indispensable supply base for operations in the Philippines.

On the surface, therefore, the decision of September 14 differed little from that of January 24. Both prescribed the maintenance of the status quo for the time being, and in both cases the army showed reluctance to take military action in French Indochina, at least in the near future. But closer examination reveals that the decision of September 14 differed decisively from that of January 24 in one respect: the army no longer objected to the exercise of armed force in French Indochina as a matter of principle. The military situation had become so grave by that time that even army headquarters had to recognize that the military disposition of French Indochina was one of the few realistic choices. The possibility of dealing with French Indochina militarily was no longer conceived to be only ancillary to the policy of separating the French colony from France, as in the January 24 decision, but was regarded as a policy toward French Indochina in its own right, and in a completely different context.

As a consequence, the decision of September 14, unlike that of January 24, specified the requirements that needed to be met to justify the use of force. For those who saw no possibility of the first two scenarios, such as the garrison army in French Indochina, the decision essentially meant that a policy of dealing with French Indochina militarily had now been officially adopted. Moreover, because the issue of the military disposition of French Indochina had been removed from the context of the policy of maintaining the French colonial government intact, pains were taken to reach a compromise between the positions of army headquarters and the Foreign Ministry with regard to the question of how to administer the region once military action was carried out. Specifically, the decision offered two parallel answers to the

---

[60] "Jōsei no henka ni ōzuru tai Futsuin sochi ni kansuru ken," in Army General Staff, *Haisen no kiroku*, pp. 182–83.

[61] Army General Staff, "Daihon'ei kimitsu," September 14, 1944. Commenting on the foreign minister's statement, this account asserts that the statement was "extremely infantile, both as an assessment of the situation and in terms of the Empire's policies as a whole, especially strategic policy."

question, one stating that "of the French residing in French Indochina, those cooperative with us should be used as much as possible," and the other stating that "political participation by the native population should be encouraged."

Thus, the September 14 decision put the question of the military disposition of French Indochina in a context completely different from that of the January 24 decision. In theory, the latter decision was an extension and a concretization of the former. In effect, however, the September decision radically modified the January decision's definition of "military disposition."

V. The Decision to Take Military Action

The Philippine campaign began on October 18, 1944. Army headquarters in Tokyo considered this operation so important that it even proposed suspending the "operation to cut through China" in order to concentrate its forces on the Philippine front. It is no wonder that the measures to be taken toward French Indochina were eclipsed by the Philippine campaign.[62]

In Europe, meanwhile, the United States, Britain, and the Soviet Union recognized de Gaulle's new government in Paris on October 23. The Foreign Ministry determined that this recognition constituted the kind of "sudden change in the situation"—"the establishment of a unified government" in France—anticipated by the Supreme War Plans Council decision of September 14. On November 2 the ministry issued a document titled "The French Indochina Problem,"[63] which stated bluntly that since "French Indochina is being administered simply at the discretion of Decoux," the question of "the disposition of French Indochina has become an urgent matter demanding the Imperial Government's consideration."

The document presented a pessimistic assessment of the political situation in French Indochina and of the colonial government's further collaboration with Japan. "Because it is anticipating the victory of the United States and Britain," the document stated, French Indochina "may change its attitude of collaboration with the Japanese military at any moment and cater to the wishes of the United States and Britain so as to turn the situation to its own advantage." Moreover, "the covert activities of Annam independence activists based in Chungking and Kunming and affiliated with the Communist Party or the Nationalist Party are reaching increasingly dangerous proportions." By that time, the Foreign Ministry had obtained information that General Eugène Mordant, former commander of the French colonial army in Indochina and still residing there, had become the de Gaulle government's representative in French Indochina and that preparations were under way within the Decoux government to switch allegiance to de Gaulle.[64]

On the basis of its assessment of the Indochinese situation, the Foreign Ministry urged that Japan, "resolving to restore independence to Annam," use force against Indochina to end French rule, in accordance with the spirit of the Greater East Asia

---

[62] The War Plans Unit of the Army General Staff urged that the China operation be postponed to allow the army to concentrate on the Philippines. It was next to impossible for the War Plans Unit, so deeply preoccupied with the Philippine campaign, to think about mounting a military operation in French Indochina. Ibid.

[63] "Futsuin mondai," in Army General Staff, *Haisen no kiroku*, pp. 209–11.

[64] See telegram from Shanghai Consul General Seiki Yano to Shigemitsu dated August 30, 1944, in the file "Dainiji Ōshū taisen kankei ikken" [Items on the Second European War], Foreign Ministry Archives.

Declaration.[65] In other words, the Foreign Ministry, from a foreign-policy standpoint, regarded the Indochina problem with a strong sense of urgency, while the military was so preoccupied with the Philippine campaign that it attached only secondary or even tertiary importance to Indochina.

The difference of opinion between the Foreign Ministry and the army was exposed at the October 28 meeting of the Supreme War Plans Council. In response to Foreign Minister Shigemitsu's expression of "the urgency of resolving the French Indochina problem," General Yoshijirō Umezu, chief of the Army General Staff, asserted that, although he agreed with this opinion in principle, "in view of the fact that the military preparations are not yet complete, the question calls for careful study."[66] Consequently, both the Supreme War Plans Council steering committee, meeting on October 31, and the full council, meeting on November 2, supported the army's judgment that it was "still too early for a decision on the French Indochina problem" and decided that "the two supreme-command bodies [army and navy headquarters] should further study the question."[67]

The failure of the Philippine campaign, however, made it impossible for army headquarters to continue deferring a decision on military action in Indochina, a policy with which it claimed to agree in principle. On December 19 the Japanese forces abandoned Leyte. With this the Philippine campaign, Japan's last-ditch effort to turn the tide of the war in its favor once again, ended in unmitigated failure.[68]

Mention must be made here of a new factor that began to weigh heavily in Japanese policy makers' deliberations on Indochina policy. It is generally accepted that with the establishment of the Koiso cabinet Japan's top policy makers began to explore in earnest the possibility of a negotiated peace.[69] Their wish to avoid offending Chungking and the Soviet Union, the two main targets of maneuvers for a negotiated peace, began to produce subtle effects on policy toward French Indochina.

Prime Minister Koiso, for instance, planned to offer Tonkin to Chungking to entice the Chiang Kai-shek government into making peace with Japan.[70] Because of this he was an ardent advocate of the use of force against French Indochina. At the Supreme War Plans Council meeting of December 7, when the army still showed reluctance to commit itself on the issue, he suggested that Japan "deal with Indochina by a speedy exercise of force."[71]

This was how matters stood when an event occurred that had serious implications for Japanese policy toward French Indochina: on December 10 the Soviet Union

---

[65] "Futsuin mondai," in Army General Staff, *Haisen no kiroku*, p. 211.

[66] Army General Staff, "Daihon'ei kimitsu," October 28, 1944.

[67] Ibid., October 31 and November 2, 1944.

[68] On December 18 Takushirō Hattori, chief of the Second Section of the Army General Staff, explained to the assistant chief of the Army General Staff the decision to "switch from a philosophy emphasizing a showdown to one emphasizing a holding defense" in the battle of Leyte.

[69] On this point, see Masaji Inada, "Shūsen to tennō, jūshin, seifu oyobi gumbu no enjita yakuwari" [The conclusion of the war and the roles played by the emperor, senior statesmen, the government, and the military], in Nihon Gaikō Gakkai [Society for the Study of Japanese Diplomacy], ed., *Taiheiyō sensō shūketsu ron* [On the conclusion of the Pacific War] (Tokyo: Tokyo Daigaku Shuppankai, 1958); Rekishigaku Kenkyūkai, ed., *Taiheiyō sensōshi* 5, pp. 317–18, etc..

[70] Maruyama, *Ushinawaretaru kiroku*.

[71] Army General Staff, "Daihon'ei kimitsu," December 7, 1944.

and France signed a treaty of alliance and mutual assistance. As far as was known, the treaty applied only to Europe; but Japanese policy makers were afraid that, if it were applied to Asia as well, Japanese military action against French Indochina could cause the Soviet Union to take a harsher stance toward Japan or, worse still, induce it to declare war against Japan. Since Japan considered it imperative to negotiate peace with the Soviet Union or at least persuade it to remain neutral, apprehension that Japanese military action in French Indochina might offend the Soviet Union had a significant effect on Japan's policy toward French Indochina.

On December 23 Suketaka Tanemura, head of the War Plans Unit of the Army General Staff, asked Shigemitsu: "Considering the changes in the situation, including [the formation of] the French-Soviet alliance, is there no room for reconsidering Japanese policy toward French Indochina?"[72] Somewhat earlier, on December 12, Shigemitsu had instructed Ambassador Naotake Satō, in Moscow, to sound out the Soviet government on this point.[73] After receiving Satō's report of his meetings with Soviet Foreign Minister Vyacheslav M. Molotov and Deputy Foreign Minister Alexander Lozovsky,[74] Shigemitsu told the Supreme War Plans Council on January 11, 1945, that in his judgment the French-Soviet alliance would not affect the French Indochina question.[75] Consequently, it was decided that for the time being no change would be made in the policy of military action against French Indochina. Nevertheless, it should be borne in mind that, as will be pointed out later, Japan's policy toward French Indochina would be significantly affected by considerations about the possible effects of such action on Japanese-Soviet relations.

After the failure of the Philippine campaign, it became more urgent than ever for Japan to make a final decision on its policy toward French Indochina. The Philippine failure meant that an Allied landing in French Indochina was suddenly a strong probability, not a mere possibility. By January 1945 the Second Section of the Army General Staff and the Southern Army General Headquarters had concluded that American troops would probably land on the shores of southeastern China and French Indochina in February or March.[76] The intensive bombing of French Indochina and the South China Sea by a US task force on January 11 and 12 made this assessment seem all the more realistic.[77] Meanwhile, on the Burmese front, British troops occupied Akyab on January 2, giving rise to the possibility that Allied forces might launch assaults on French Indochina from Burma, as well. And if Allied troops did surge into French Indochina, the Japanese troops there could expect absolutely no collaboration from the French colonial regime and its army.[78] Under the com-

---

[72] Ibid., December 23, 1944.

[73] Telegram from Shigemitsu to Satō dated December 12, 1944, in the file "Sensō shūketsu ni kansuru Nisso kōshō kankei" [Documents on Japanese-Soviet negotiations on the conclusion of the war], Foreign Ministry Archives.

[74] Telegrams from Satō to Shigemitsu dated December 22, 1944, and January 5, 1945. Ibid.

[75] Army General Staff, "Daihon'ei kimitsu," January 11, 1945.

[76] See the assessment of the situation submitted by the Second Section of the Army General Staff on January 16 and the opinion of the local army submitted by Major Tsuneishi on January 26. Ibid., January 16 and 26, 1945.

[77] Defense Agency, ed., *Shittan, Meigō sakusen*, p. 598.

[78] At the time, the Thirty-eighth Army was in possession of information about infiltration by Gaullist clandestine units airdropped into Indochina and their activities to recruit anti-Japanese resistance fighters; speeches by Decoux criticizing Japan and praising de Gaulle; and the French colonial army's efforts to recruit indigenous soldiers, disperse units in the suburbs

bined effects of all these factors, army headquarters in Tokyo was under strong pressure to decide finally to initiate military action against the French Indochina regime.

Meanwhile, the failure of the Philippine campaign also changed the strategic importance of French Indochina. Overland communications with Japanese troops in China having been established as a result of Joint Operation No. 1 at the end of 1944, French Indochina was now regarded, along with Thailand, Malaya, and Sumatra, as a "southern region core area," that is, a stronghold for protracted resistance to be waged in Southeast Asia in concert with the decisive battle for the home islands.[79] In short, French Indochina was no longer a rear base but a front line of defense. With this change in the region's strategic importance, the Japanese garrison army in French Indochina was reinforced. On December 20, 1944, the garrison army was reorganized into the Thirty-eighth Army, a field combat army, incorporating the Twenty-second and Thirty-seventh divisions from China and the Second Division from Burma.[80]

Only when the probability of an Allied assault on French Indochina loomed so large that all other alternatives appeared impossible and a considerable troop force had been concentrated there did army headquarters in Tokyo begin to take steps in earnest to deal with French Indochina by force. On December 30 the Supreme War Plans Council agreed to the foreign minister's proposal that a decision on military action in French Indochina be made by mid-January, following closer study of the French-Soviet alliance and other pertinent factors.[81]

As already pointed out, on January 11, 1945, the council determined that the French-Soviet alliance presented little cause for worry, at least for the time being. A blueprint for military operations drawn up by the Second Section of the Army General Staff and presented on January 16, titled "Comprehensive Plan of Future Operations," anticipated that Allied forces would attack southeastern China and neighboring areas in February or March and recommended the "timely use of force" against French Indochina. Thus army headquarters in Tokyo finally came to the conclusion that military action would be unavoidable.[82]

On January 17 an "Agreement Between the Army and Navy Central Headquarters on the Military Disposition and Subsequent Defense of French Indochina" was concluded and relayed to the Southern Army. The policy of dealing with French Indochina by force was now determined, with the purpose, in the words of the agreement, of "overthrowing the existing French Indochina regime and its military forces and forcing them to surrender, thus stabilizing and securing French Indochina and strengthening our ability to defend it."[83] The surprise-attack operation for this

---

and the countryside, and construct defensive fortifications. See Daiichi Fukuinkyoku, "Futsuryō Indoshina." It should also be pointed out that negotiations between Japanese authorities and the French colonial regime on the military budget for fiscal 1945 had come to a standstill. See Kajima Heiwa Kenkyūsho, ed., *Nihon gaikōshi* 24, p. 209.

[79] An Imperial Headquarters Army Department directive to that effect was issued to the commander in chief of the Southern Army on January 27, 1945, in accordance with "Teikoku rikukaigun sakusen keikaku taikō" [Outline of the plan of operations of the Imperial Army and Navy], adopted by the Imperial Headquarters on January 20. Defense Agency, ed., *Shittan, Meigō sakusen*, p. 568.

[80] Ibid., p. 593.

[81] Army General Staff, "Daihon'ei kimitsu," December 30, 1944.

[82] Ibid., January 16, 1945.

[83] Defense Agency, ed., *Shittan, Meigō sakusen*, pp. 598–99.

assault was given the code name "Operation Meigō," and the military began preparations.

VI. Plans for Governing Post-Coup Indochina Proposed by Japanese Authorities in Indochina

Following the September 14, 1944, decision of the Supreme War Plans Council, the Japanese authorities in Indochina began to prepare themselves in earnest for military action. Below we will discuss the plans drawn up by the Japanese military and diplomatic leaders in Indochina regarding its administration after the overthrow of the French.

During a visit to Tokyo in early October 1944 Major General Kawamura, chief of staff of the Japanese garrison army in Indochina, gathered that military action to overthrow the French regime would be executed sooner or later.[84] On October 31, shortly after his return to his post, he ordered a staff officer, Lieutenant Colonel Hidezumi Hayashi, to draw up a plan for the subsequent administration of Indochina.[85]

By mid-December Hayashi had completed a draft plan that envisioned granting independence to the three countries of Indochina (Vietnam, Cambodia, and Laos) immediately after the *coup de force* rather than placing the area under Japanese military rule, and also putting Ngo Dinh Diem and other pro-Japanese Vietnamese in charge of the Vietnamese government after independence. However, Hayashi's plan also proposed that Japan take over the powers of the French government general, since it would be impossible to divide these powers and delegate them among the three Indochinese countries immediately.[86] Hayashi believed that the Japanese occupation forces in continental Southeast Asia would ultimately have to entrench themselves in the Laotian highlands and resist the Allies there. This was why he opposed the idea of placing Indochina under Japanese military rule, which would require stationing large numbers of troops and administrative officials in the lowlands.[87]

At first Hayashi's plan met with strong opposition from leaders of the Southern Army and the garrison army in Indochina, who found his plan radically different from their long-held assumption that Indochina would be placed under Japanese military rule just like other occupied areas of Southeast Asia. One Southern Army staff officer criticized Hayashi's plan on two counts: for one thing, he maintained, the peoples of the three Indochinese countries were incompetent to rule themselves, and therefore it would be risky to grant them independence immediately; for another, if Japan did not establish military rule, it would encounter tremendous difficulties mobilizing local labor and maintaining law and order.[88]

Despite these and other criticisms, Hayashi's plan was approved by the supreme council of the Thirty-eighth Army on December 28 as the local army's official plan,

---

[84] Ibid., pp. 594–95.

[85] This information is based on interviews with Hayashi.

[86] Ibid. The contacts between pro-Japanese Vietnamese, including Ngo Dinh Diem, and Japanese authorities deserve to be discussed at length in a separate study.

[87] Ibid. Earlier, the garrison army had requested central headquarters, through the Southern Army, to supply several hundred administrative officials to enable the imposition of military rule in French Indochina as in other occupied territories of Southeast Asia.

[88] Ibid.

because Lieutenant General Tadakazu Wakamatsu, assistant chief of staff of the Southern Army General Headquarters, who knew Hayashi personally, strongly backed the plan, saying, "Leave the government plan to Hayashi and you won't have to worry."[89] However, partly because of the process by which the plan had been formulated and partly because Lieutenant General Yūichi Tsuchihashi, the recently appointed commander of the Thirty-eighth Army,[90] had played no part in this process, the local army apparently failed to build a strong consensus within its own ranks about how Indochina should be administered after the coup.[91]

At around the same time, the Japanese embassy was preparing its own plan for the administration of post-coup Indochina. Completed under the auspices of Ambassador Shun'ichi Matsumoto, who took office on November 24, 1944, the embassy plan consisted of four documents drawn up at the end of 1944 and the beginning of 1945: "Draft Outline of the Disposition of French Indochina," "Draft Outline of the Joint Statement by Three Countries [Annam, Cambodia, and Laos] on the Formation of a Federation of Vietnam," "Japan-Annam Alliance Draft Treaty," and "Main Points of the Protocol Attached to the Japan-Annam Alliance Treaty."[92]

The embassy plan had four major characteristics. First, the purpose of the military action was "the independence of Annam," in keeping with "the spirit of the Greater East Asia Declaration." Second, upon the granting of independence to the three Indochinese countries, a "Federation of Vietnam" would be formed and the French Indochina government general's powers transferred to a "committee for the administration of the federation" composed of representatives of the kings of the three countries. Third, in Annam (Vietnam) a pro-Japanese regime would be brought to power, and to accomplish this "the independence of Annam [would be realized by] carrying out a political coup d'état under the present dynasty and setting up a pro-independence government." Finally, the embassy and its affiliated organs would provide "internal direction" to the "Federation of Vietnam" (that is, Indochina).

In short, the embassy plan, with its emphasis on a military coup as a means of granting independence in keeping with the Greater East Asia Declaration, was a faithful recapitulation of the Foreign Ministry's position. Also, given the basic agreement between its own plan and Hayashi's plan on the need to grant immediate independence to the three Indochinese countries, the embassy, at least at the beginning of 1945, was optimistic about the possibility of ironing out its differences with the military.[93]

At that juncture, however, something happened that upset the calculations of the local authorities, especially the military leaders: large-scale bombing raids by a US task force on January 11 and 12. Driven by the strong apprehension that these her-

---

[89] Ibid.

[90] Machijiri was transferred to a post at central headquarters on November 22; Tsuchihashi, appointed as his successor by the emperor, took over on December 14. See Defense Agency, ed., *Shittan, Meigō sakusen*, p. 596.

[91] Judging from the telegrams exchanged between the Foreign Ministry and the embassy during January and February 1945, opinions within the local army varied considerably.

[92] These documents are mentioned in telegrams from Saigon Consul General Takeshi Tsukamoto to Shigemitsu dated January 16, 23, and 24, 1945. "Dai Tōa sensō."

[93] In a telegram to Shigemitsu dated January 16, 1945, Tsukamoto reported that the embassy was holding discussions with the local army on the question of the administration of Indochina after the coup, "with the expectation that an agreement can be reached if the embassy further explains its plan" to the army. Ibid.

alded an imminent landing by US troops in Indochina, the Thirty-eighth Army, now under Tsuchihashi's leadership, began to revise its plan for administering Indochina after the coup to adapt it better to the exigencies of countering the anticipated US offensive.[94]

Tsuchihashi initiated this reworking of the administrative plan by arguing that the army would have to devote itself totally to combat and to the maintenance of law and order and therefore could not afford to occupy itself with politics; that for this reason, while the army did not object to the idea of granting independence to the three Indochinese countries, it could not implement "independence policy measures" immediately; that the army was even more opposed to any measures that could only cause "confusion," such as bringing Prince Cuong De of the Vietnamese royal family back from his exile in Japan or reorganizing the local regime into a pro-Japanese one; and that the best way of administering Indochina for the time being would be to keep the existing government general's administrative machinery functioning, with the commander taking over the governor general's duties and embassy personnel replacing high-ranking colonial officials.[95]

Tsuchihashi's blueprint differed greatly from the plan drawn up by Hayashi. Commenting on the commander's plan at the end of February, Hayashi said: "Based on the belief that granting independence would lead to an undesirable state of confusion, this is a plan for Japan to take over the French Indochina government as completely as possible without impairing its present administrative apparatus."[96] The commander ordered Hayashi's plan scrapped and instructed him to draft a new one. This was submitted to Tokyo headquarters as the Southern Army draft plan on January 27 by Southern Army Chief of Staff Takezō Numata.[97]

The new plan's primary purpose was "to restore rule as quickly as possible, while preventing confusion and instability." Its major points were as follows: 1. The existing administrative offices and their staffs would be ordered to continue to perform their duties, though officials holding the post of bureau director or higher would be subject to suspension of their duties, which would be taken over by embassy personnel. 2. Administrative offices and procedures would be kept intact. 3. The three countries of Annam, Cambodia, and Luang Prabang [Laos] would be guided to gain independence autonomously. 4. Emperor Bao Dai of Annam would not be dethroned.[98]

In short, the local army's new plan, while agreeing in principle with the granting of independence to the three Indochinese countries, proposed that this be deferred until law and order had been restored and that the Japanese army rule Indochina after the coup by taking control of and making use of the existing apparatus of the French Indochina government general. This plan differed significantly from that formulated by the embassy, with the result that the army and the embassy found themselves sharply opposed over the question of how Indochina should be governed after the military coup.

---

[94] The US bombings led Tsuchihashi to conclude finally that the use of force against French Indochina was unavoidable. See "Tsuchihashi Yūichi chūjō no sengo no kaisō" [Postwar recollections of Lieutenant General Yūichi Tsuchihashi], War History Office, Defense Agency.
[95] Ibid.
[96] Telegram from Matsumoto to Shigemitsu dated February 25, 1945. "Dai Tōa sensō."
[97] Interviews with Hayashi.
[98] Defense Agency, ed., *Shittan, Meigō sakusen*, p. 600.

VII. Formation of the Policy of Granting Immediate Independence

In late January 1945, when policy makers in Tokyo were preparing to implement the *coup de force,* they received two conflicting reports, one from the embassy and one from the local army.

From the embassy, Ambassador Matsumoto submitted to Foreign Minister Shigemitsu a report critical of the local army's plan for ruling post-coup Indochina. In a telegram to the foreign minister dated January 26, the ambassador warned that within the army in Indochina "the voices of those . . . who hitherto called for Annamese independence . . . have become muted," while "those who anticipate that French Indochina will become a battleground" were urging that "to ensure our hold" it was necessary to impose "military rule pure and simple."[99]

Meanwhile, a report on the local army's views arrived on January 26 from Major Shigetsugu Tsuneishi, who had been sent to French Indochina by Imperial Headquarters. The report made two major points: in the local army's view, strengthening defenses should be the sole purpose of the military operation, and the handling of the question of Annam's independence should be left to the local army.[100] The following day, as already mentioned, Southern Army Chief of Staff Numata arrived in Tokyo and presented the Southern Army's new plan to army headquarters.[101]

On January 26 Tanemura, head of the Army General Staff War Plans Unit, called on Foreign Minister Shigemitsu to inform him of the two points stressed in Tsuneishi's report and of the army headquarters' view that the military action in French Indochina should be executed as soon as possible, after which the region should be placed under de facto military rule.[102]

Both the February 1 "Decision Regarding the Disposition of French Indochina to Deal with Changes in the Situation" and the February 26 "Outline of the Political Disposition of Indochina" of the Supreme War Plans Council were the outcome of a decision-making process that assumed that execution of a military coup in Indochina was established policy. In other words, the decision-making process was a process of bargaining between the military establishment and the Foreign Ministry over the questions of what the justification of the coup should be and how Indochina should be governed afterward.

The February 1 decision confirmed that the coup was official policy, declaring that "the Empire, in view of both the trend of the war and developments in French Indochina, and because of the absolute necessity of self-preservation and self-defense, at an appropriate time will execute the military disposition of French Indochina on its own initiative."[103] In the course of drafting this decision, the army argued that given the probability of a US landing, French Indochina would have to be dealt with by force, but to ensure that this would not adversely affect Japan's relations with the Soviet Union, Japan should refrain from taking steps that would negate French sovereignty over French Indochina, that is, should not grant independence to the three Indochinese countries. In short, the operation should be the minimum action necessary to maintain military self-preservation and self-defense;

---

[99] "Dai Tōa sensō."

[100] Army General Staff, "Daihon'ei kimitsu," January 26, 1945.

[101] Ibid., January 27, 1945.

[102] Ibid., January 26, 1945.

[103] For the February 1 decision, see Army General Staff, *Haisen no kiroku,* pp. 227–28.

once the operation was over, it should be Japan's policy to place French Indochina temporarily under the administration of the Japanese army, while continuing to respect French sovereignty.[104]

The Foreign Ministry countered that, as long as Japan intended to deal with French Indochina by force, it was meaningless to claim that Japan had no intention of denying French sovereignty over Indochina. Rather, Japan should strive to realize fully its ideal of "the liberation of Greater East Asia." Since the Soviet Union could not oppose national liberation, this would be the best way to prevent the deterioration of Japanese-Soviet relations. Therefore, support for independence of the region should be explicitly included among the objectives of the military action.[105]

Even at the February 1 meeting of the Supreme War Plans Council, the military and the foreign minister clashed over the question of whether the justification of the military disposition of French Indochina should be limited to the need for self-preservation and self-defense or should also include support for independence.

The foreign minister insisted that, if Japan carried out the coup under the sole pretext of safeguarding its self-preservation and self-defense and "[placed] the occupied territory under military rule *[gunsei]*," it would offend the Soviet Union and other neutral countries. "If, however," he added,

> the Empire takes steps, concurrently with and immediately following the exercise of force, to abolish the treaties of protection in Annam and elsewhere, to announce its intention of granting independence to them, and to protect them under the Empire's patronage, the fact that our intention is not one of aggression but is in accordance with the spirit of the Greater East Asia Declaration should be self-evident, and there should be no danger of offending any third party.[106]

This met with a rebuttal from Major General Sanada, now head of the Military Affairs Bureau of the War Ministry and coordinator of the Supreme War Plans Council, who asserted "that the pretext of national liberation could easily degenerate into racial war and that since at the moment there were no independence leaders in Annam, nor were any being trained, it was highly likely that independence would be empty of content; therefore, it would be best to leave the independence question to those on the scene."[107]

Ultimately, as is evident from the wording of the council's decision, "because of the absolute necessity of self-preservation and self-defense," the military's position prevailed with regard to the justification of the operation. However, on the question of how Indochina should be administered after the coup, the decision stated both parties' positions: "For the time being [Indochina] shall be placed under the administration of the army *[gun no kanri]*," and "the local army shall take appropriate measures to improve and support the independent status of Annam and the other countries [of Indochina] and to ensure [their] active collaboration with us." The army

---

[104] Telegram from Hagiwara to Moriyama, a minister in the embassy in Indochina, dated January 30, 1945. "Dai Tōa sensō."

[105] Ibid.

[106] Telegram from Shigemitsu to Matsumoto dated February 7, 1945. Ibid.

[107] Army General Staff, "Daihon'ei kimitsu," February 1, 1945.

placed emphasis on the expression "administration of the army"[108] and did not consider the question of independence to be an urgent matter, believing that the council had entrusted the handling of this issue to the local army.[109] The Foreign Ministry was also content that its insistence upon the need "to improve and support the independent status" of the Indochinese countries had been accepted.[110]

The ambiguity of the February 1 decision exacerbated the hostility between the local army and the embassy, then at loggerheads over the questions of whether independence should be granted immediately after the coup or only after law and order had been restored, whether the staff of the government general should be reinforced by embassy personnel, and whether the embassy itself should be retained. Worried over this conflict, on February 15 Ambassador Matsumoto asked Foreign Minister Shigemitsu to see to it that a policy for post-coup rule of Indochina be formulated in Tokyo, to "prevent army headquarters from making wild claims that the task of working out the details of the matter has already been entrusted to the local army."[111]

Acting on this request, Shigemitsu proposed to the military that an "Outline of the Political Disposition of Indochina" be worked out. By February 22 a working group had completed a draft, which the Supreme War Plans Council granted preliminary approval on February 22 and final approval on February 26.[112] The army's very agreement to these guidelines represented a concession. Moreover, in the course of drafting the document the army changed its policy with regard to the granting of immediate independence, switching from opposition to agreement.

---

[108] The term used in the original draft, "military rule" *(gunsei)*, was changed to "the administration of the army" *(gun no kanri)* out of concern for "third countries," meaning the Soviet Union.

[109] The entry for February 1, 1945, in Army General Staff, "Daihon'ei kimitsu," states that it was explained that "it would be best to leave the independence question to those on the scene. The original draft [of the February 1 decision] prevailed."

[110] In his telegram to Matsumoto dated February 7, 1945, Shigemitsu explained that the February 1 decision was made because "in view of the spirit of the Greater East Asia Declaration, it is natural for us to start working now for the independence of French Indochina."

[111] In a telegram to Shigemitsu dated February 15, 1945, Matsumoto stated: "[Commander Tsuchihashi's] primary concern, in anticipation of the possibility that French Indochina will become a battleground, is to maintain the present administrative machinery of the government general for the time being; to keep the administrative setup more or less as is by having embassy personnel take over the major posts in the government general, such as director general, bureau director, and governor; and to use this administrative setup for the benefit of military operations. He has no intention of abolishing the present status of Annam, Cambodia, and the other countries [of Indochina] and absolutely no intention of preparing them for future complete independence. When I informed the military leaders of Your Excellency's explanation at the Supreme War Plans Council, both the commander and the chief of staff asserted that the local military had not received any information to that effect, that there is no prospect whatsoever of independence for Annam until there is an improvement in the war situation, and that therefore it is meaningless to start taking measures now to enhance the prestige of these countries, such as dispatching ministers extraordinary. Although I have tried to persuade them that in carrying out the [planned] measures we must advance the cause of national liberation as a justification because otherwise we will not be able to defend ourselves if accused of being an aggressor nation, they have shown not the slightest inclination to change their minds on this point." Ibid.

[112] Army General Staff, "Daihon'ei kimitsu," February 22 and 26, 1945.

The army changed its position not because it now shared the Foreign Ministry's thinking but because of concern over the Soviet Union, that is, because it came around to the view that granting independence would be the best way to prevent the coup from worsening Japan's relations with the Soviet Union. This is eloquently revealed by a telegram from army headquarters in Tokyo to the local army on February 23, which read in part:

> In regard to the instructions recently cabled . . . , that 'the local army shall take appropriate measures to improve and support the independent status of Annam and the other countries,' central headquarters will respond to the local army's implementation [of the February 1 decision] by utilizing [these measures] to make clear to foreign countries, particularly the Soviet Union, the nonaggressive nature of this exercise of force. . . . Let us add, for your consideration, that this matter was reconfirmed at the Supreme War Plans Council meeting on the twenty-second.[113]

The provisions of the "Outline of the Political Disposition of Indochina" were as follows: 1. The coup should not be interpreted as meaning that Japan has entered into a state of war with France. 2. Even though Japan is to exercise military rule *(gunsei)* in the areas under direct French control, that is, Cochinchina, Hanoi, Haiphong, and Tourane, its official stance vis-à-vis the outside world should be that these areas are to be under the administration *(kanri)* of the Japanese army only temporarily. 3. Japanese administration *(kanri)* of all of Indochina should be effected by staffing the higher posts in the government general with Japanese officials. 4. Japan should speedily[114] have the three countries of Indochina spontaneously abrogate their treaties of protection with France, thus clarifying the restoration of independence.[115]

The compromise between army headquarters and the Foreign Ministry led to the adoption of the policy of granting immediate, if only nominal, independence to the three countries of Indochina. Understandably, however, army headquarters had absolutely no intention of granting true independence. All that mattered was ensuring that the three countries abrogated their treaties of protection and declared their independence as soon after the coup as possible so that the military action would not aggravate Japan's relations with the Soviet Union.[116] In keeping with the position of Tokyo headquarters, the army in Indochina abandoned its policy of devoting several months after the coup to restoring law and order before even beginning to think about independence measures, and adopted a new policy of "having each country,

---

[113] Secret army telegram from the vice-minister of war and the assistant chief of the Army General Staff to the chiefs of staff of the Southern Army and the Thirty-eighth Army dated February 23, 1945. "Dai Tōa sensō."

[114] In the original draft, the expression "as speedily as possible" *(narubeku sumiyaka ni)* was used, but this was changed to "speedily" *(sumiyaka ni)*. Telegram from Shigemitsu to Matsumoto dated February 27, 1945. "Dai Tōa sensō."

[115] "Indoshina seimu shori yōkō," in Army General Staff, *Haisen no kiroku*, pp. 232–34.

[116] The secret army telegram of February 23, 1945, emphasized the point with the following explanatory note: "We will declare that, having thrown off the yoke of French Indochina, the treaties of protection concluded between French Indochina and Annam and the other countries have died a natural death, and therefore we do not intend to force through specific independence measures in any particular hurry."

with the help of our internal direction, spontaneously declare independence as speedily as possible after the exercise of force."[117]

As for the questions of what the status of the embassy staff would be and whether the embassy itself would survive or be dismantled after the coup, on March 1 the directors general of the Political Affairs Bureau of the Foreign Ministry, the General Affairs Bureau of the Greater East Asia Ministry, and the Military Affairs Bureau of the War Ministry reached an agreement whereby the Foreign Ministry and its embassy in Indochina gave ground.[118]

After the tortuous process described above, the military coup in French Indochina was finally carried out on March 9, 1945. The most decisive factor influencing the decision to act was the anticipation of an imminent landing by US troops in Indochina. And it was considerations of Japanese-Soviet relations that led Japanese policy makers to adopt the unusual policy of granting independence to the three Indochinese nations immediately after the coup.[119] But by the time of the coup Japanese troops on Iwojima were on the verge of annihilation, and US forces were preparing to attack Okinawa and then the main islands of Japan. Moreover, at the Yalta Conference on February 4–14, 1945 the Soviet Union had already promised to join the war against Japan.

CONCLUSION

The answer to the first of the two questions posed at the outset of this paper—Why did Japan allow the French colonial regime in Indochina to remain intact for so long?—can be found in the leadership role played by army headquarters in the formulation of policy toward French Indochina. Army headquarters regarded the policy of retaining the French colonial regime as the most effective way of ensuring "the maintenance of tranquillity," which was the prerequisite for the smooth execution of military operations. Headquarters was also unwilling to expand the war front to French Indochina because it saw this as detrimental to the smooth execution of military operations elsewhere in East and Southeast Asia. Moreover, it opposed taking firm steps in French Indochina to realize the ideal of "the liberation of Greater East Asia," and countered proponents of that policy by stressing the need to avoid "racial war." That an army headquarters with such views played the leading role in the formulation and implementation of Japan's policy toward French Indochina explains why the French colonial regime was allowed to remain in power for such an extended period.

It can also be pointed out that the policy of keeping the French colonial regime in power was able to last as long as it did because it was not a rigid policy of maintaining the status quo. Rather, its combination with the policy of separating French Indochina from France gave it the flexibility needed to cope with developments in the European theater. This paper has made clear that the policy of separating French

---

[117] Telegram from the chief of staff of the Southern Army to the vice-minister of war and the assistant chief of the Army General Staff dated March 18, 1945. "Dai Tōa sensō."

[118] According to this agreement, embassy officials would be "utilized by the army in their present status as civilian employees" and the embassy would, in effect, cease functioning. These terms signified real concessions by the Foreign Ministry and the embassy, but the army also made the nominal concession of allowing diplomatic officials to retain their "present status." Telegram from Shigemitsu to Matsumoto dated March 1, 1945. Ibid.

[119] Vietnam declared independence on March 11, Cambodia on March 13, and Laos on April 8.

Indochina from France was first conceptualized in the context of Japan's relations with Germany, was revived in the context of responding to developments on the European front, and finally, after the fall of the Vichy government, took on yet another meaning, that of extending ex post facto approval of the situation in French Indochina. It should also be pointed out that this shrewd ability to adapt policies to fit new situations was responsible for the flexibility of the Japanese decision-making process.

The second question posed at the outset was, Why did Japan adopt the policy of granting independence to the three Indochinese countries immediately after over-throwing the French colonial government? One important reason advanced by many is that, because Japan retained an embassy in French Indochina even after the start of the Pacific War, the Foreign Ministry and the embassy were able to have some say in the formulation and implementation of policy toward French Indochina, and they urged the granting of immediate independence. Ironically, however, they were able to have some say in Indochinese affairs precisely because Japan followed the policy of retaining the French colonial regime. Thus, that the Foreign Ministry and its embassy were given a say in Indochinese affairs does not in itself answer the question satisfactorily. As we have pointed out, the granting of immediate independence to the three Indochinese countries became Japan's official policy only when army headquarters, for considerations having to do with Japanese-Soviet relations, decided to go along with the Foreign Ministry and the embassy.

The most outstanding feature of Japanese decision making in regard to policy toward French Indochina during the Pacific War was its inconsistent, haphazard nature. The army, preoccupied with successful implementation of its military opera-tions elsewhere in Southeast Asia, and thus stubbornly insisting that the policy objective in French Indochina should be "the maintenance of tranquillity," and the Foreign Ministry, upholding "the liberation of Greater East Asia" as the primary policy objective, were pitted against each other. Unable to resolve their ideological differences, they made one ad hoc decision after another to deal with "changes in the situation." In the absence of a consensus on the principles underlying policy, they had to deal with a series of factors of potentially great impact on Japanese policy toward French Indochina, such as possible German reaction to Japan's policy, war developments in Europe and the Pacific, the French Indochina regime's hostility toward Japan, and possible Soviet reaction to Japan's policy. All these issues were dealt with in a haphazard manner.

To view the problem from a different perspective, it has often been pointed out that Japan's plan to establish a Greater East Asia Co-Prosperity Sphere through the Pacific War counted from the start upon Axis victories in the European theater. The contradictions inherent in the plan to construct a Greater East Asia Co-Prosperity Sphere also manifested themselves in Japan's policy toward French Indochina, in the form of conflict or contradiction between the argument for "the liberation of Greater East Asia" and that emphasizing the need to avoid "racial war." This conflict or contradiction was bound to remain unresolved, because there was no consistency in Japan's policy toward French Indochina.

The lack of a basic principle to guide Japan's war effort in general, and its policy toward French Indochina in particular, was reflected in lack of confidence on the part of policy makers, as is eloquently revealed by the following entry in "Daihon'ei kimitsu sensō nisshi" dated March 9, 1945, the very day the coup was carried out:

French Indochina, which remained a neutral area in the Greater East Asia region until the last, has finally been toppled immediately before landings by American and British troops. Seen as a military operation, the disposition of French Indochina should be regarded as a great success; but in terms of war planning it is open to criticism by future historians, even though there were unavoidable reasons [for the action taken]. If the war is further protracted, and especially after the conclusion of the German war, racial war is highly likely to break out, inevitably placing a major obstacle in the way of the Empire's efforts to end the war.

After the coup in French Indochina and the granting of immediate independence to the three Indochinese countries—both actions carried out as a result of haphazard decision making and based on two unfounded beliefs, that a US landing was imminent and that granting independence would deter the Soviet Union from entering the war against Japan—Japan was no longer in a position to affect the fate of Indochina in any significant way. The future of Indochina was now being determined by an indigenous nationalist movement, of which the Vietnamese August Revolution of 1945 under the leadership of the Viet Minh was the dramatic manifestation.

ACKNOWLEDGMENTS

This paper is the product of a joint research project awarded a grant by the Ajia Seikei Gakkai [Society for the Study of Asian Politics and Economics] in fiscal 1975. The authors would like to express their gratitude to the staff of the Defense Agency's War History Office and of the Foreign Ministry Archives, as well as to many former Imperial Army officers and embassy personnel who served in French Indochina, for their invaluable help.

This paper was originally published under the title "Taiheiyō sensō ki no Nihon no tai Indoshina seisaku: Sono futatsu no tokuisei o megutte" [Two features of Japan's Indochina policy during the Pacific War], in *Ajia kenkyū* [Asian studies] 23, no. 3 (1976): 1–37.

3

Indochina's Role in Japan's Greater East Asia Co-Prosperity Sphere: A Food-Procurement Strategy

Yukichika Tabuchi

I. Introduction

Japan employed every possible colonization policy in French Indochina after advancing into the region in September 1940. These policies, like the advance itself, were based on extremely "rational" considerations. "Wishing to avoid the waste that would probably occur if it tried forcibly to oust the existing administrative structure and military forces, Japan adopted the highly 'rational' policy of attaching itself parasitically to the existing system, securing the area as a relay point and rear base for supplying the military and acquiring access to local resources while retaining the French administrative apparatus."[1] This scheme underlies the development of my argument in this paper.

In terms of international trade theory, the exchange clearing system that Japan devised for trade with Indochina can be seen to be one of the most important components of the plan, and therefore must be elucidated, though the process by which Japan introduced the exchange clearing system requires a lengthy explanation. We must also examine Indochina's position in the Greater East Asia Co-Prosperity Sphere, that is, the role that Japan envisioned for Indochina, if we wish to understand how Japan came to adopt that system and why it was the most "rational" method of settling trade accounts from Japan's point of view.

Japan made use of the same type of clearing agreement that Germany had concluded with southern and eastern European nations, and for the same reason: to ensure a "rational" means of acquiring vital goods. This paper will explore the background and describe the strategy—the exchange clearing system—adopted by Japan to secure food supplies.

II. Trade between Japan and Indochina

A brief review of the relatively long history of trade between Japan and Indochina will help clarify their overall relationship. Figure 1 shows changes in the value of Japanese imports from Indochina from 1913 through 1945.[2] Except for the 1918–1920 and 1940–1943 periods, which best illustrate the nature of the relationship, trade between the two showed no striking features.

For footnotes to this chapter, see pp. 105–12.

Figure 1. Changes in the Total Value of Japan's Imports from Indochina, 1913–1945

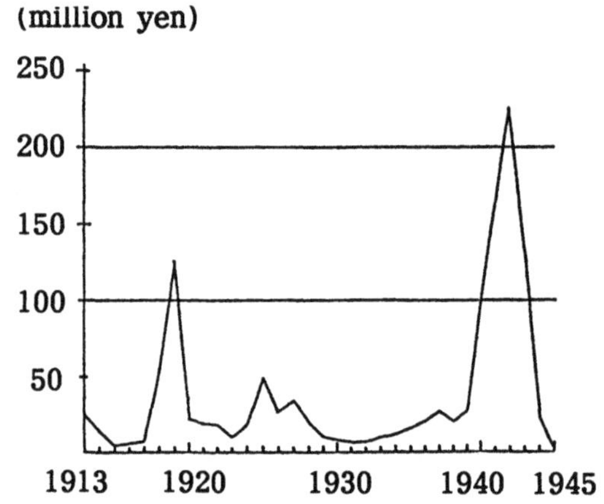

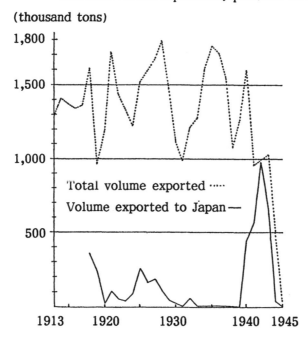

Source: Prime Minister's Office, Statistics Bureau, *Dai ikkai Nippon tōkei nenkan* [First yearbook of Japanese statistics] (Tokyo: Mainichi Shimbunsha, 1949), p. 477.

Figure 2. Changes in the Total Volume of Rice Exported from Indochina (1913–1945) and in the Volume Exported to Japan (1918–1945)

Sources: For total volume exported and volume exported to Japan, 1913–1930: Yves Henry, *Futsuryō Indoshina no nōgyō keizai* [Economie agricole de l'Indochine], trans. Tōa Kenkyūjo [Institute for East Asian Studies], vol. 2 (Tokyo: Tōa Kenkyūjo, 1941), pp. 188, 189, 213. For total volume exported and volume exported to Japan, 1931–1939: Shigeo Hemmi, *Futsuryō Indoshina kenkyū* [A study of French Indochina] (Tokyo: Nippon Hyōronsha, 1941), pp. 131–32. For total volume exported, 1940–1945: La chambre de commerce chinois du Sud vietnam, *Annuaire du commerce chinois du Sud vietnam* (Saigon: La chambre de commerce chinois du Sud vietnam, 1953), p. J-29. For volume exported to Japan, 1941–1945: U.S. Strategic Bombing Survey, *Nippon sensō keizai no hōkai* [The effects of strategic bombing on Japan's war economy], trans. Chifuyu Masaki, 2d ed. [Tokyo: Nippon Hyōronsha, 1972; orig. pub. Washington, D.C.: Government Printing Office, 1946), table C–121.

In 1919, Japanese imports from Indochina shot up to ¥124 million, a twelvefold increase over the usual figure of around ¥10 million. Japan was in the throes of a rice famine at the time. Rice riots in Toyama Prefecture, which spread to virtually the entire country, had erupted in August 1918. Rice prices had spiraled, and Japan had had to increase its imports of Southeast Asian rice to avoid a critical shortage. Examination of the volume of Indochinese rice exported to Japan in 1919 reveals clearly that increased exports by Indochina corresponded to substantially higher imports of rice by Japan (fig. 2). Japan considered Indochina a food source in emergencies even then.

Trade between Japan and Indochina followed a fairly even course from 1920 to 1940. The relationship was low-key, and Japan showed a trade deficit, as usual. This passive relationship was transformed into an active one when Japan's national ambitions were revealed during the Pacific War and Japan suddenly began manifesting a keen interest in Indochina.

As table 1 indicates, imports from Indochina peaked in 1942 at ¥224 million, or 12.8 percent of the total value of Japanese imports. This was a phenomenal increase, considering that imports from Indochina had represented only 0.5 percent of all Japanese imports in 1930 and had remained below 1 percent until 1940. Except for China, Korea, and Taiwan, Indochina was the only Asian country whose share of Japanese imports accounted for over 10 percent of the total that year. Imports from Thailand, by comparison, accounted for 9.5 percent of all Japanese imports in 1942.[3]

Table 1. Indochina's Share of the Total Value of
Japan's Imports, 1930–1945

(million yen)

Year	All imports	Imports from Indochina	%
1930	1,546	8	0.5
1931	1,236	6	0.5
1932	1,431	6	0.4
1933	1,917	10	0.5
1934	2,283	11	0.5
1935	2,472	15	0.6
1936	2,764	20	0.7
1937	3,783	27	0.7
1938	2,663	20	0.8
1939	2,918	27	0.9
1940	3,453	98	2.8
1941	2,889	161	5.6
1942	1,752	224	12.8
1943	1,924	132	6.9
1944	1,947	22	1.1
1945	957	0	0.0

Source: Prime Minister's Office, *Dai ikkai Nippon tōkei nenkan*, pp. 474, 477.

To gain a more precise idea of Indochina's share of trade with Japan, we must consider it in the context of other Asian countries' shares. As we see in table 2, except for China, British India was Japan's largest Asian trade partner before the Pacific War, followed in descending order by the Netherlands East Indies, the Philippines, Indochina, and Thailand. After the Pacific War broke out, however, imports from Indochina and Thailand rose, reaching a level comparable to that for trade with India before the war. In terms of figures, Indochina and Thailand replaced India as trade partners. Moreover, they were two of the region's three major rice exporters.

Table 2. Shares of Various Asian Countries[a] of Japan's Trade,[b] 1930–1945

(%)

Year	China[c]	British India	Netherlands East Indies	Indochina	Philippines	Thailand	Other	Total
1930	44.9	28.5	9.5	1.3	1.7	3.0	11.2	100.0
1931	47.9	26.9	9.3	1.2	1.8	1.4	11.3	100.0
1932	45.9	25.9	8.9	1.3	2.2	2.4	13.3	100.0
1933	42.9	31.1	8.5	1.5	2.1	1.8	11.8	100.0
1934	38.5	35.7	7.8	1.4	2.3	0.2	14.2	100.0
1935	40.7	35.2	9.0	1.7	2.8	0.6	10.2	100.0
1936	37.5	35.1	10.8	1.9	3.4	0.8	10.6	100.0
1937	15.1	34.7	11.8	2.1	3.5	1.1	31.7	100.0
1938	55.2	16.8	8.6	2.0	3.5	0.5	13.4	100.0
1939	57.9	15.4	6.1	2.3	4.1	0.5	13.7	100.0
1940	50.1	11.7	8.3	6.5	4.0	3.5	15.9	100.0
1941	51.1	7.0	9.2	9.6	3.3	10.9	8.9	100.0
1942	73.5	0.1	0.8	13.5	0.4	10.0	1.7	100.0
1943	74.2	0.0	5.6	7.4	3.1	2.7	6.9	100.0
1944	87.4	0.3	3.4	1.1	0.9	0.5	6.3	100.0
1945	93.9	0.6	0.1	0.0	0.1	0.0	5.3	100.0

[a]Korea and Taiwan excluded.

[b]Based on total value of Japanese imports from the Asian region only.

[c]Hong Kong and Guandong included.

Source: Prime Minister's Office, *Dai ikkai Nippon tōkei nenkan*, pp. 476–77.

These facts indicate the importance of Indochina and Thailand in the Greater East Asia Co-Prosperity Sphere. Indochina occupied an especially important position, because it was losing its sovereignty, making it an easier target for Japan than Thailand, an independent nation. In addition, neither country experienced much direct fighting during the war. For that reason, exports to Japan from Thailand and Indochina rose from 1940 to 1942, the peak year. This demonstrates the "rational" basis of Japan's advance into Indochina.

Changes in the volume of rice exported from Indochina to Japan are charted in figure 2. From 1930, the year that Japan established a system of self-sufficiency in rice, until 1940, the year the Pacific War began, imports of rice from Indochina were negligible. Reflecting the food shortages in Japan in 1939, however, about 30 percent of all Indochinese rice exported went to Japan in 1940. This grew to 60 percent in 1941, and in 1942 almost all the rice that Indochina exported went to Japan.[4] Indochina's economy, which until then had been subjugated to French interests, was forced into a close linkage with Japan's. The relationship was short-lived, however; imports of Indochinese rice plummeted after 1943, due to Japanese defeats on various fronts and the accompanying shortage of transport ships. Nevertheless, Japan controlled Indochina's economy from 1941 through 1943 as a de facto Japanese colony, though there certainly remained conflicts between Japan and the Indochinese French authorities.

However, while the statistics showing increasing exports of rice from Indochina to Japan are understandable, those indicating a drop in overall export volume raise certain questions. The total volume of Indochinese rice exports in 1942 was about the same as in 1931, when the effects of the Great Depression were being felt. The volume rose somewhat in 1943 but was still low. Thus, total export volume was at Depression levels when Japan controlled Indochina.

Harvests had been more or less normal since Japan's advance into Indochina.[5] Why, then, were rice exports from Indochina so low while Japan was in control despite the Japanese authorities' forcing Indochinese farmers to grow more rice? A number of local factors can be suggested: the refusal of the ethnic Chinese population to cooperate with the Japanese authorities; poor organization of the system for exporting to Japan;[6] localized crop failures; increased rice consumption in Indochina; and market disruption due to inflation. Resistance on the part of Indochinese farmers was an additional factor. However, because of the scarcity of source materials, the exact causes are impossible to determine.

An interesting point is noted when figures 1 and 2 are compared: the curves described by the changes in the total value of Japanese imports from Indochina and in the volume of rice imported from Indochina correspond almost exactly. This again demonstrates that rice was the basis of the relationship between Japan and Indochina.

At any rate, it is clear that Indochina under Japanese rule (technically, Franco-Japanese administration) was an important component in establishing the autarky of the Greater East Asia Co-Prosperity Sphere. Indochina was made to serve as a food source, thus becoming a key factor in Japan's prosecution of the war.

III. Southern Expansion and Domestic Food Shortages

The extraordinarily close relationship between Japan and Indochina in connection with rice reflected food shortages in Japan. These shortages provided the immediate motivation for Japan's advance into Indochina, an objective that also promoted the strategic goal of southern expansion that had already been under way. To examine this, we must go back a bit, to the invasion of Hainan Island.

Japan invaded Hainan on February 10, 1939. Five months earlier, the colonial government of Taiwan had issued a document titled "Policy for Dealing with Hainan,"[7] which included fairly specific plans for developing the island. Item 3 of the document revealed Japan's intent to use Hainan as a springboard for strong domination over the southern region. Hainan was regarded as "an advance base of the Empire's southern policy."

Around the same time, the Taiwanese colonial administration issued another document, "Policies for Expanding and Strengthening Organs of Control in the Southern Colonies."[8] The first point made was the significance of the invasion of Hainan, though the relevant passage was written in the past tense, probably on the assumption that a structure for control would be established after the invasion: "The Empire's southern policy assumed increasing importance with the growth of Japan's power. Naturally, *the kinds of actions taken with regard to southern China and the South Seas have an important bearing on the execution of national policy* and a significant influence on the establishment of peace in East Asia. In particular, our *southern policy entered a new phase* with the recent incident [the invasion of Hainan]" (emphasis added).

Since "the kinds of actions taken with regard to southern China and the South Seas have an important bearing on the execution of national policy" and were seen as causing "southern policy [to enter] a new phase," the invasion of Hainan was undertaken as the first step in implementing the southern expansion policy. "The historical distortion of the southward expansion in the Shōwa era"[9] had begun. In fact, Hainan later became "a major relay point for southern expansion because of its excellent strategic location in relation to French Indochina, the Philippines, and the Netherlands East Indies."[10] The occupation of Hainan brought Indochina within range of Japan's southward push. Indochina was most conveniently placed, in terms of both distance and fabrication of the Greater East Asia Co-Prosperity Sphere. For that reason, Japanese expansion into Indochina was the second step in the execution of the policy of southern expansion.[11]

As the momentum of southern expansion grew, the Naval General Staff issued a document titled "A Study on Policies Toward Indochina" on August 1, 1940,[12] less than two months before the Japanese advance into Indochina. This document summed up three advantages to advancing into (invading) Indochina: its value as a base for advancing into Burma and Malaya; Cam Ranh Bay's value as a military port;[13] and the value of improved access to coal, rubber, rice, and iron ore. Because Indochina offered these advantages, the document concluded, an advance (invasion) was essential.

However, there were a number of reasons for trying to avoid an armed invasion: first, the United States might impose an embargo on exports to Japan; second, "taking losses in French Indochina would be detrimental in the present situation when the Japanese government has to prepare for war against Britain and the United States"; third, an armed invasion would require large amounts of personnel, materiel, and money; fourth, it might "provoke discriminatory economic measures" by Britain; and fifth, diverting forces from the Chinese front might have the effect of helping the Chiang Kai-shek regime. Because of this, "the Empire should avoid making a hasty decision on military action in French Indochina, but should first determine its intentions and make preparations."

The most pressing matter was completing war preparations. Japan believed that even if the United States banned exports to Japan as a result of a Japanese advance into Indochina, it would not immediately declare war on Japan. However, a US embargo would still be a vexing problem. To avoid provoking the United States, Japan felt that it was necessary to use diplomatic negotiations to reach agreement with the colonial administration in Indochina so that expansion could take place under cover of peace. Doing so would avert needless waste and disruption, as well as devastation of the land. Indochinese resources would be accessible immediately, and the area could be used as a relay point and supply base for expansion farther south.

If military action proved necessary despite all the advantages of avoiding it, the military thought it should take place after the beginning of November 1940, since war preparations were expected to be complete by then. In either case, it is evident that those who drew up the policy study considered rice a "national defense resource."

Attempts to take over Indochina, whether by diplomatic or by military means, had begun in 1938. However, Japan began actually to need Indochina only around July 1939, when domestic food shortages became an issue. Poor rice harvests in Korea and western Japan in 1939 caused a decline in domestic stockpiles. Table 3 clearly shows the decline in imports (transfers) of Korean rice. Shipments of Korean rice dropped sharply in July 1939, when the volume shipped was only 28 percent of that for the same month of the previous year. Domestic food shortages continued throughout the Pacific War.

Table 3. Decrease in the Volume of Korean Rice Shipped to Japan, January 1938–
October 1940

(thousand *koku*)[a]

Year/month		Volume	Year/month		Volume	Year/month		Volume
1938	Jan	1,262	1939	Jan	688	1940	Jan	131
	Feb	721		Feb	574		Feb	12
	Mar	1,079		Mar	583		Mar	23
	Apr	1,055		Apr	611		Apr	12
	May	1,052		May	716		May	14
	Jun	748		Jun	318		Jun	11
	Jul	656		Jul	184		Jul	—
	Aug	478		Aug	178		Aug	1
	Sep	317		Sep	139		Sep	—
	Oct	251		Oct	59		Oct	—
	Nov	671		Nov	133			
	Dec	966		Dec	45			

[a]One *koku* equals 5.12 US bushels.

Source: Shinkichi Katayanagi, *Nippon senji shokuryō seisaku* [Japan's wartime food
policy] (Tokyo: Itō Shoten, 1942), p. 73.

Concern over food supplies began to spread just as the nation was becoming
impatient with the protracted and inconclusive war in China. At the same time,
because Japan was trying to shift to a policy of southern expansion, it was eager to
obtain the strategic supplies needed to conduct a lengthy war. Nothing could erase
the fear from uncertainty over food supplies. It is no exaggeration to say that when it
is necessary to mobilize popular opinion to support escalation of a war, food
problems are the major cause of anxiety among the populace. In fact, it is impossible
to prosecute a war unless such problems are solved.

The minutes of a meeting of district public prosecutors investigating violations of
economic controls, held May 29–31, 1940,[14] reveal vividly the pervasive anxiety over
food supplies at the time. A few of the prosecutors' reports are summarized below. A
Nagoya prosecutor discussed the normal rice supply and demand in Nagoya and
described how the rice shortage had developed there. "At present, Nagoya rice
dealers have only two days' stock," he said. "People have only a two-day supply; no
one knows today where rice will come from after that."[15] A prosecutor from Tokyo
said that rice supplies had begun to shrink around July 1939 and that the shortage
had reached a peak around December that year. The shortage had eased somewhat
around the beginning of 1940, because every possible measure had been taken, but he
added that "the situation regarding shipments of rice and stocks on hand does not
warrant optimism,"[16] indicating in an understated way that every conceivable
avenue had already been explored. An Osaka prosecutor criticized the lack of any
government policy, complaining that supplies in his area "depend entirely on rice
sold by the government" and that *"the government has been very tardy in releasing rice
for sale. The situation has not improved, rice dealers have exhausted their stocks, and
supplies are becoming tighter than ever"* (emphasis added).[17]

As figure 3 shows, Japan's stocks of rice peaked in 1934 and declined steadily
thereafter. In 1939 supplies dropped to one-fourth the peak level. This illustrates
clearly the severity of the rice shortage in 1939 and 1940. The situation improved
considerably in 1941, thanks to imports of rice, but after that stockpiles were almost
nonexistent until Japan's defeat.

Figure 3. Changes in Japan's Rice Stocks, 1931–1945

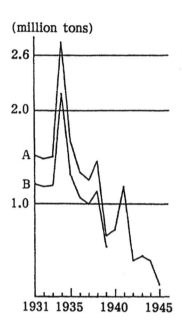

Sources: For A: US Strategic Bombing Survey, *Nippon sensō keizai no hōkai*, table C–202. For B: V. D. Wickizer and M. K. Bennett, *Monsūn Ajia no beikoku keizai* [The rice economy of monsoon Asia], trans. Torao Tamai and Yoshio Hirota (Tokyo: Nippon Hyōron Shinsha, 1958; orig. pub. Stanford: Stanford University Press, 1941), p. 327.

Japan had always had difficulty attaining and maintaining self-sufficiency in rice. Increased shipments of rice from its Taiwanese and Korean colonies in 1930 finally permitted Japan to achieve self-sufficiency,[18] thanks to the success of plans to increase rice production in the colonies. Rice shipments grew rapidly because of "the implementation of large-scale plans to increase rice production in Taiwan and Korea," which thus "became indispensable elements in Japan's rice-economy bloc."[19] Taiwanese and Korean rice "not only took the place of foreign rice but also made domestic self-sufficiency possible."[20] Having achieved self-sufficiency in 1930, Japan eventually withdrew from the world rice market. In regard to self-sufficiency, the 1930–1939 period was a good one for Japan. On the other hand, cheap Taiwanese and Korean rice flowing into Japan posed a potential threat to domestic rice producers, as indicated by the fact that from 1930 onward minimum price was the major determinant of rice policy.[21]

Thus, rice stockpiles appeared more or less satisfactory until 1939. But the dependence of Japan's system of self-sufficiency on Korea and Taiwan was also its weak point. This weakness was revealed by the poor Korean rice harvest of 1939, which, combined with poor harvests in western Japan, led to a severe food shortage. Needless to say, "the importance of food supplies in prosecuting the war cannot be overstated";[22] "securing food is the first priority in wartime."[23] Thus, poor harvests in Korea and western Japan not only disrupted the food supply but also affected the course of the war, driving Japan into a crisis.

The sudden drop in rice shipments from Korea and Taiwan worsened the food situation in Japan. One reason for decreased rice production in Korea was that "industrialization and agricultural diversification had begun to spread"[24] there. The combination of decreased agricultural output due to industrialization and a bad harvest caused a dramatic reduction in the amount of rice shipped to Japan. In Japan, too, the proliferation of heavy industry for war production took workers away from farms, thus contributing to the food shortage, in addition to which the influx of workers into the cities increased demand for food. Food naturally became a major concern as the economy was put on a war footing. Although "nothing must be allowed to cause anxiety over food, the most important aspect of people's daily lives,"[25] the sharp drop in rice shipments had precisely that effect.

Until that time, food supplies had not been a major concern. According to the "1938 Comparison of Supply and Demand in Major Goods and Measures to Fill Deficiencies," issued by the Cabinet Planning Board in May 1938,[26] there was an estimated 4.23 million *koku* (829,412–bushel) surplus of rice.[27] This was equivalent to about 610,000 tons of unhulled rice. The "1938 Tables Comparing Supply and Demand in Major Goods and Measures to Fill Deficiencies" issued by the Cabinet Planning Board on June 21[28] showed a rice surplus of 4.55 million *koku* (892,157 bushels, or about 660,000 tons of unhulled rice). The authorities appeared to feel that the rice supply was satisfactory. However, the "Tables Comparing Supply and Demand" dated December 26[29] for some reason showed only 2.02 million *koku* of rice (396,078 bushels, or about 290,000 tons of unhulled rice), though there was still a surplus.

Despite this, shortages were registered from July 1939 onward. "On the Outline of the Results of and Outlook for Programs for Commodity Flow, Productivity Improvement, Labor Mobilization, and others," a summary of a report made by Kakichi Takeuchi, head of the Cabinet Planning Board, at a meeting of cabinet advisers on February 28, 1940,[30] acknowledged that performance of the fiscal 1939 commodity flow program was unsatisfactory, due mainly to drought in Korea and western Japan and floods in Taiwan and northern China, and that "about ¥100 million worth of imported rice is needed." And according to "The Present Condition of and Outlook for the War Economy, Centered on the Commodity Flow Program," issued by the Cabinet Planning Board in March 1940,[31] the drought had caused "a decrease of 10 million *koku* [about 1.45 million tons] of Korean rice," disrupting the balance between supply and demand in Japan and necessitating "large-scale imports of foreign rice to make up the shortfall."

Domestic measures to ease the situation included lowering the polishing ratio for rice, restricting the amount of rice used for *sake* production, and encouraging the use of substitute staples (*daiyōshoku*) or rice mixed with other cereals. Though "everthing possible was done to ensure the volume needed by importing rice," however, "the supply of rice in fiscal 1940 was not plentiful to begin with." The "Tables Comparing Supply and Demand" of July 10, 1940,[32] estimated that 4.21 million *koku* (825,490 bushels, or about 610,000 tons) of rice would have to be imported; but the actual amount imported that year, excluding rice from Korea and Taiwan, was about 1.25 million tons,[33] twice the projected amount. This indicates that the rice shortfall was even more severe than expected. From the standpoint of domestic food supplies, the situation was ripe for a Japanese advance into Indochina.[34]

IV. Japan's Strategy for Acquiring Food Supplies

Indochina as a Source of Food

Indochina as discussed in major documents

Before advancing into northern Indochina, Japan was interested in Indochina mainly because it wanted to cut off Chiang Kai-shek's supply route. Rice was still a minor issue. Japan estimated that in June 1940 about half the supplies for Chiang's forces were funneled through Indochina.[35] Thus, Japan was most interested in cutting off this route, but was unable to do so forcibly for fear of further provoking anti-Japanese sentiment on the part of the United States. If this could not be avoided, Japan had two alternatives. One was to import essential goods from the United States ahead of schedule for stockpiling; the other was to secure resources from the south. Since any sudden move to the south was sure to incense the United States, the authorities decided that the best course was to stockpile imported American raw materials rapidly and then move to obtain resources from the south. Moreover, acquiring Indochinese resources and using that region as a base for advancing farther south to obtain essential goods would enable Japan to throw off its economic dependence on the United States.

In fact, the "Draft Outline of Southern Policy Measures" issued by the Cabinet Planning Board on July 23, 1940,[36] called for "departing from our present economic system, dependent on the United States and Britain, and establishing a supply region in Southeast Asia and the southern regions to acquire the resources we lack." The areas targeted included French Indochina, Thailand, Burma, the Netherlands East Indies, the Philippines, and British Malaya and Borneo. Japan intended to set up an East Asia Economic Sphere, an economic version of the Greater East Asian Co-Prosperity Sphere, with those areas as members, "to ensure a permanent supply of vital resources by gaining complete access to resources and leasing, corporate, and joint-venture rights."

Four items in the document outlined fairly specific policies: (1) achieve "close economic cooperation" and "secure military interests" because Indochina's geographical position was "extremely important to our southern expansion"; (2) formulate and execute measures to "draw French Indochina into Japan's political and economic sphere of influence" because of concern that Germany would reach out toward Asia if the war in Europe ended; (3) obtain Indochinese resources (rice was not mentioned specifically); and (4) "improve and expand the structure of trade with French Indochina, including import and export mechanisms, financial institutions, and transportation."

Aware that, unlike the Netherlands East Indies, French Indochina would "inevitably become an area of intense competition between the United States and Japan," Japan adhered to a "firm policy line" toward Indochina. However, because France fell to Germany (leading to the establishment of the pro-Japanese Vichy regime) and rice shortages at home worsened, Japan could not use armed force to implement its policies. It had to confine itself to implementing this "firm policy line" through diplomatic negotiations, concentrating on furthering its economic interests.

The military, charged with ensuring the success of Japan's "firm policy line," gave almost no thought to economic matters, particularly Indochinese resources. This was especially true of the army. The version of "Outline of Measures to Deal with Changes in the World Situation" issued by the Imperial Headquarters Army

Department on July 3, 1940,[37] did not even mention Indochinese resources, though the version issued by the Imperial Headquarters Navy Section on July 9, 1940,[38] included a brief reference, in regard to Indochina, to the need to "endeavor to acquire resources necessary to the Empire." The final version, adopted on July 27, 1940, by the Imperial Headquarters Government Liaison Council,[39] retained this reference. At that juncture, however, the military considered such considerations to be secondary. There was only a vague awareness of Indochina's importance as a source of resources—and that mainly because the food shortage in Japan had stirred mild interest.

On August 6, 1940, the Cabinet Planning Board issued an "Outline of Southern Economic Policy Measures."[40] This document, based on the "Draft Outline of Southern Policy Measures," regarded the "completion of a Greater East Asia Economic Sphere" led by Japan as the pivot of southern economic policy. Indochina was considered part of the "inner-sphere zone" as a potential source of goods for Japan. A basic policy of endeavoring to "use local capital and materials as far as possible" in acquiring goods from southern regions, including Indochina, was also set forth. Thus the Cabinet Planning Board's policy on acquiring resources compensated for the military authorities' limited perspective.

The agreement between Yōsuke Matsuoka and Charles Arsène Henry of August 30, 1940,[41] reflected that policy. This pact paved the way for Japan's incremental advance into Indochina, providing the rationale for the military to move into northern Indochina. It also contained the following passage referring to economic penetration: "In economic matters, France will promote trade between Indochina and Japan; [the two parties] will expeditiously discuss means to ensure that Japan and Japanese subjects are in the most advantageous position possible and that in all cases [Japan] is in a position superior to that of other third countries."

"Policy Measures for Economic Expansion in French Indochina," issued by the Cabinet Planning Board on September 3, 1940,[42] on the basis of the Matsuoka-Henry agreement, set forth economic policy toward Indochina more clearly. Indochina would form part of the Greater East Asia Co-Prosperity Sphere, in other words, the East Asia Economic Sphere, and Japan would "move quickly to establish a close economic relationship with French Indochina." Specifically, the document called for "demand[ing] guaranteed exports of rice, coal, apatite, manganese, industrial salt, tin, raw rubber, zinc, and silica" in order to "achieve independence from the United States and Britain in resources." Settlement of accounts was to involve "financial benefits" that the Bank of Indochina would be prevailed upon to offer, because Japan did "not intend to include [Indochina] in the yen bloc." In short, Japan planned to acquire Indochinese resources by arranging an advantageous payment method. (This system will be discussed at some length below.) The important point to note here is that for the first time specific Indochinese resources were enumerated. One of these, naturally, was rice.

The same day that this fundamental policy for the de facto colonization of Indochina was announced, the Cabinet Planning Board also issued a "Summary of Measures for the Acquisition of Goods and for Trade in French Indochina (A)."[43] This document listed "temporary measures" for acquiring Indochinese resources and established a basic policy for doing so. The measures outlined included the abolition of custom duties on exports to Japan, the establishment of a payment system, and the securing of shipping. Having thus established a scenario for acquiring Indochinese resources, Japan concluded the Japan-Indochina Military Agreement in Hanoi on

September 22, 1940.[44] The next day, on September 23, the Japanese Army advanced into northern Indochina. Two days after the agreement, on the 24th, the Cabinet Planning Board submitted the "Summary of Measures for the Acquisition of Goods and for Trade in French Indochina (B)"[45] to the cabinet. This document, specifying "permanent measures" for "developing Indochinese resources," complemented "Summary of Measures (A)." Clearly, fairly long-term domination over Indochina was envisioned.[46]

Indochina as a wartime source of food

Japan's maneuvers to seize control of Indochina were completed with the advance into southern Indochina, the main rice-exporting area, on July 28, 1941. This consolidated Indochina's position as a supplier of resources, and especially of food (rice), in the Greater East Asia Co-Prosperity Sphere, a self-sufficient bloc centered on Japan.

To recapitulate: before Japan advanced into northern Indochina, military considerations (cutting off the supply route to Chiang Kai-shek) predominated. The economic element was of only secondary importance. That the military and economic aspects came to assume equal importance, after which emphasis shifted to the economic aspect, was due mainly to the food shortage in Japan. Economic considerations finally became dominant with the advance into southern Indochina.

The "Fiscal 1941 Plan for the Mobilization of Goods," adopted on August 22, 1941,[47] less than a month after Japan's advance into southern Indochina, divided the areas supplying goods to Japan into four regions: the self-sufficiency region (Japan proper, its colonies, and the yen bloc), the primary supply region (Indochina and Thailand), the secondary supply region (the Philippines, Malaya, and the Netherlands East Indies), and the tertiary supply region (Australia, Burma, India, North and South America, and Africa). A foreign rice fund (the Y fund) was also established to pay for rice imports.

According to the "Outline of Economic Policy Measures in the South," issued by the Cabinet Planning Board in December that year,[48] economic policy in the south involved acquiring vital resources there, "establishing a self-sufficient system within the Greater East Asian Co-Prosperity Sphere to augment swiftly the economic power of the Empire." This policy extended to areas designated as region A (the Netherlands East Indies, British Malaya and Borneo, and the Philippines) and region B (French Indochina and Thailand). Regions A and B corresponded to the secondary and primary supply regions, respectively. Most of the "primary policy measures" had already been implemented in region B, that is, the primary supply region, by December 1941, and efforts were being made to "secure vital resources, especially foodstuffs," through "measures to achieve effective results on the basis of the established policy line." Thus, within the overall scheme of the Greater East Asia Co-Prosperity Sphere, Indochina and Thailand were considered primarily as food sources. Thai rice went mainly to Malaya and Singapore (because of the special milling process used, people in Malaya and Singapore preferred Thai and Burmese rice), while Indochinese rice was shipped to Japan and China.[49]

What role did Indochinese rice play in Japan, which had now begun to think of Indochina as a source of food? According to table 4, in 1940 almost as much rice was imported from Indochina (439,000 tons) as was shipped from Korea and Taiwan combined (445,000 tons), accounting for 26 percent of all rice imports. This was an astounding increase over the 8,000 tons of Indochinese rice imported in 1939.[50] Moreover, the volume of rice imported from the southern region as a whole in 1940 constituted almost 68 percent of all rice imports. In addition, the volume of Indochinese rice exported to Japan in 1940 was about the same as the 460,000 tons shipped to France in 1939,[51] a development presaging the reversal of the status of France and Japan in Indochina.

Table 4. Volume of Rice Imported from Various Asian Countries, 1940–1945

(thousand tons)

Country	1940	1941	1942	1943	1944	1945
Taiwan	385	272	262	207	150	9
	(22.7)	(12.2)	(10.0)	(18.2)	(19.2)	(6.0)
Korea	60	520	840	72	560	142
	(3.5)	(23.3)	(32.0)	(6.3)	(71.5)	(94.0)
Indochina	439	563	973	662	38	—
	(25.9)	(25.2)	(37.0)	(58.3)	(4.9)	—
Burma	421	438	47	18	—	—
	(24.9)	(19.6)	(1.8)	(1.6)	—	—
Thailand	284	435	508	177	36	—
	(16.8)	(19.5)	(19.3)	(15.6)	(4.6)	—
Other	105	5	—	—	—	—
	(6.2)	(0.2)	—	—	—	—
Total	1,694	2,233	2,629	1,136	783	151
	(100.0)	(100.0)	(100.0)	(100.0)	(100.0)	(100.0)

Figures in parentheses indicate percentages of total.

Source: US Strategic Bombing Survey, *Nippon sensō keizai no hōkai*, table C–121.

Of course, even 439,000 tons was not enough to satisfy Japan. In 1941 a 700,000-ton quota for rice from Indochina was set, though the amount actually imported was only 563,000 tons.[52] Even so, Indochinese rice made up the largest proportion of the rice imported that year. Imports of Indochinese rice peaked at 973,000 tons in 1942, declining from 1943 onward because the war was going badly for Japan and because transport ships were in short supply.

As indicated by table 5, Indochina also supplied larger quantities of other cereals than any other country. Japan imported 149,000 tons of cereals, a little over 55 percent of all cereal imports, from Indochina in 1940. The type of cereal imported from Indochina was probably corn.[53] While rice imports from Indochina peaked in 1942, imports of other cereals peaked in 1943 at 634,000 tons. A substantial volume of cereals was also imported in 1944, though the cause of this interesting phenomenon cannot be determined. The contemporary term "substitute staple" indicates that imported corn and other cereals were used to supplement rice, but it must be noted that this was done only after food supplies had become perilously low. Until then, corn was imported mainly as livestock feed.[54]

That Japan viewed Indochina primarily as a food source is clear from the above discussion. However, its value as a provider of other resources should also be noted. Japan wanted to obtain iron ore, as indicated by "Measures to Secure Resources Essential to the Empire Overseas, Especially in the Southern Regions," issued by the Cabinet Planning Board on October 2, 1939.[55] This document stated that "diplomatic and other means are necessary" to ensure supplies of iron ore and also noted a special need to increase imports of zinc, zinc ore, and industrial salt, taking into account the quantities Indochina could actually supply.

Table 5. Volume of Cereals Imported from Various Asian Countries, 1940–1945

(thousand tons)

Country	1940	1941	1942	1943	1944	1945
Taiwan	1	1	1	—	—	—
	(0.4)	(0.4)	(0.1)	—	—	—
Korea	3	1	600	25	25	15
	(1.1)	(0.4)	(72.9)	(3.3)	(4.9)	(6.5)
China	—	1	2	5	5	3
	—	(0.4)	(0.2)	(0.7)	(1.0)	(1.3)
Manchukuo	40	50	73	81	122	213
	(14.9)	(18.7)	(8.9)	(10.8)	(24.1)	(92.2)
Indochina	149	135	125	634	355	—
	(55.4)	(50.6)	(15.2)	(84.5)	(70.0)	—
Netherlands East Indies	77	79	22	5	—	—
	(28.6)	(29.6)	(2.7)	(0.7)	—	—
Total	269	267	823	750	507	231
	(100.0)	(100.0)	(100.0)	(100.0)	(100.0)	(100.0)

Figures in parentheses indicate percentages of total.

Source: US Strategic Bombing Survey, *Nippon sensō keizai no hōkai*, table C–122.

Once Japan moved into Indochina in 1940, it began to expect and demand a wide variety of resources. These included rice and corn, of course, but also coal, iron ore, manganese, zinc, industrial salt, and rubber. Indochina thus found itself obliged to supply industrial raw materials. Because coal, rubber,[56] and zinc in particular had valuable military applications, Japan went to considerable lengths to obtain them, though the pressure on Indochina lifted somewhat when Japan occupied the Netherlands East Indies and Malaya.

THE EXCHANGE CLEARING SYSTEM

Except for rice, the volume of raw materials that Japan expected from Indochina was small. For that reason, Japan thought that imports of raw materials other than rice could be offset by exports of textile goods. However, a shortage of foreign exchange made it difficult to pay for the huge quantities of rice being imported. Japan introduced an exchange clearing system to circumvent this problem.

The "Accord franco-japonais relatif au régime douanier, aux échanges commerciaux et à leur modalités de règlement entre l'Indochine et le Japon" (The Japan-France Trade Agreement on the Customs System, Trade, and Settlement of Accounts between Japan and Indochina) referred to hereafter as the Trade Agreement, was signed in Tokyo on May 6, 1941.[57] Instruments of ratification were exchanged on July 5, and the agreement went into force immediately. The Trade Agreement included thirty-one articles as well as lists of reduced-tariff and duty-free goods. The first half of the agreement dealt with Japan's request for most-favored-nation status in Indochina and Indochina's agreement to that request; the second half dealt with payment methods.

According to Articles 21 and 22, the Bank of Indochina, the only bank of issue in Indochina, was required to "provide the Yokohama Specie Bank with the amount of Indochinese piasters needed for payment in exchange for the equivalent amount of yen," with the Yokohama Specie Bank similarly providing the yen equivalent of piaster amounts. Both yen and piasters would be "converted to the same gold-convertible foreign currency" (mainly dollars), and accounts would be settled reciprocally.

The Bank of Indochina would open two accounts with the Yokohama Specie Bank, a general account (*compte* A) and a special account (*compte* B), while the Yokohama Specie Bank would open a single, general account (*compte* C) with the Bank of Indochina. Accounts were to be settled reciprocally on the last day of the month. If the balance remaining after settlement exceeded ¥5 million or its piaster equivalent, this balance would be settled "by payment in gold or a gold-convertible currency, at the request of the lending bank" (Art. 24).[58] Officials of the Japanese Ministries of Foreign Affairs and Finance were instructed to emphasize that such an exchange clearing system would be beneficial to both parties in that it would "eliminate the inconvenience of having to procure US dollars."[59] However, there were two exceptions to this system: rubber was to be paid for in US dollars,[60] and there would be one year's delay in settling accounts for rice purchases. Article 22 stated: "The Bank of Indochina shall provide in yen the equivalent of the amount in piasters that Japan will spend to buy rice, in the ratio of 100 percent for 1941, 70 percent for 1942, and 55 percent for 1943." In other words, the Bank of Indochina had to provide 100 percent of the amount Japan spent to buy rice in 1941, 70 percent of the amount spent in 1942, and 55 percent of the amount spent in 1943.

In addition, the funds in the Bank of Indochina's *compte* B could "not be used for any direct payments" (Art. 23). Because of this, rice payments deposited by the Yokohama Specie Bank in the Bank of Indochina could not be used to pay for other goods until one year had elapsed. After that, funds in the Bank of Indochina's *compte* B would be transferred to *compte* A; only then could the money be used to pay for imports from Japan. Naturally, the funds accumulating in *compte* A could be used only for reciprocal settlement of accounts with Japan.

Understandably, the Indochinese authorities were unhappy over an agreement that so blatantly favored Japan. Foreign Minister Yōsuke Matsuoka, in a report to the Privy Council, explained that "because rice is Japan's weak point, we reached agreement first [on the points regarding rice], after which we considered other important matters. In regard to rice, aside from price all that we have asked for has been granted, and in other matters it can be said that 80 percent of our objectives have been achieved. The French did not want this treaty and agreement [the Convention franco-japonais d'établissement et de navigation relative à l'Indochine française (the Japan-France Treaty on Residence and Navigation in French Indochina, or Futsuryō Indoshina ni kansuru Nichi-Futsu kyojū kōkai jōjaku), and the Trade Agreement]. They agreed to our demands only because they had no choice."[61] This comment expresses accurately the character of the Trade Agreement.

As Matsuoka noted, rice was Japan's weak point. Therefore, the need to import rice was urgent. But rice was also a weak point for Indochina, because it had lost its export markets. Japan was quick to spot this weakness and, backed by the threat of armed force, was able to make Indochina accept the Trade Agreement. Naturally, Indochina agreed to Japan's demands only because it had "no choice." Left to struggle on alone as France became enmeshed in the war in Europe, Indochina was impelled to accept those demands by the hope of reviving its economy through trade with Japan.

What were the advantages to Japan of the Trade Agreement's stipulation of payment in foreign exchange of balances of over ¥5 million after reciprocal settlement and of the Bank of Indochina's opening a special account for rice? Japan had always had a large trade deficit with Indochina. Nevertheless, it found itself having to import huge quantities of Indochinese rice. Japan was short of foreign exchange and faced growing problems in dealing with its swelling trade deficit. It hoped to increase exports to Indochina and use the money earned that way to offset payments for purchases of resources other than rice.

As table 6 indicates, in 1941 non-rice imports totaled ¥81 million, while exports to Indochina totaled ¥45 million, leaving a ¥36 million deficit. In 1942, however, Japan had a ¥38 million surplus. Thus, if rice was excluded, the ¥5 million ceiling was not such a problem for Japan. The special provisions dealing with rice, by enabling Japan to acquire all the rice needed, formally guaranteed Japan's free access to Indochinese rice.

Table 6. Advantages to Japan of the Trade Agreement

(million yen)

Year.	All exports (A)	All imports (B)	Rice imports (C)	B-C (D)	D-A	A-B	E	Major developments
1941	45	161	80 (49.7)	81	36	–116	80	Adoption of exchange clearing system (July 5, 1941)
1942	144	224	118 (52.7)	106	–38	–80	83	Shift to fixed exchange rate system (Dec. 28, 1941)
1943	97	132	86 (65.2)	46	–51	–35	47	Adoption of special yen system (Jan. 1, 1943)

A, B: Value of exports to and imports from Indochina.

C: Figures in parentheses indicate percentages of all imports accounted for by rice.

E: Sums of money the Bank of Indochina is thought to have provided for exports of rice to Japan.

Sources: For A, B: Prime Minister's Office, *Dai ikkai Nippon tōkei nenkan*, p. 477. For C: Ibid., p. 510. For E: Ibid., p. 477; Trade Agreement, Art. 22.

Nevertheless, the accumulating trade deficit was a burden for Japan, as was the retention of the system of settling accounts in foreign currency, though this was largely a formality. Japan thus devised a way of dealing with the increasing amount over ¥5 million in the balance it owed. In the "Lettres échangées concernant les modalités de règlement entre le Japon et l'Indochine française" (Official Exchange of Notes Concerning the Account Settlement between Japan and French Indochina) of January 20, 1943,[62] referred to hereafter as the Exchange of Notes, a "new method of settling accounts" using "special yen" (yen credits) was introduced. By this Japan tried to free itself completely from the need to secure foreign exchange. "Special yen" referred to yen currency that would be convertible to a gold-convertible foreign currency once conditions had returned to normal after the war. The ¥5 million ceiling was thus rendered meaningless, because the "special yen" did not need to be converted to gold. This method of payment gave Japan unlimited access to all Indochina's resources. But it was already too late, since the tide of the war began to turn against Japan that year.

It is worth noting that the system of settling accounts specified in the Trade Agreement was the first appearance of the "method of settling accounts [to be] adopted within the Greater East Asia Co-Prosperity Sphere."[63] By making use of the German exchange clearing system, Japan succeeded, if only briefly, in bringing Indochina into the Greater East Asia Co-Prosperity Sphere.[64]

The exchange clearing system was originally a trade strategy used by a politically stronger country to bring politically weaker countries into its own economic sphere. By means of the Trade Agreement, Japan drew Indochina into its own economic sphere, that is, the Greater East Asia Co-Prosperity Sphere. Moreover, just as the Japanese advance into Indochina was a political steppingstone to implementation of the southern expansion policy, so the Trade Agreement was a steppingstone to economic penetration of the south. In other words, the Trade Agreement was the first step in implanting Japan in the south, just as it was the first step in establishing the Greater East Asia Co-Prosperity Sphere, a bloc advantageous to Japan. The 1943 Exchange of Notes put the finishing touch on Japan's plan to secure Indochinese resources.

In effect, Japan made Indochina a colony while leaving the French colonial administration in place. This type of parasitic colonization was easiest to accomplish. The factors that made it possible were the weak and isolated state of the Indochinese economy, world political conditions at the time, and Japan's lack of resources and foreign exchange. The third factor provided the underlying motivation for colonization, while the first two made it easier than expected. Thus did Indochina become a major source of food for Japan and an indispensable component of the Greater East Asia Co-Prosperity Sphere.

V. Conclusion

Following its September 1940 advance into Indochina, Japan singlemindedly pursued a variety of policies to gain access to Indochinese resources. Securing these resources was necessary to the survival of the Japanese economy. There was no time to be lost in taking over the country, even though that meant violating the guiding principle of the Greater East Asia Co-Prosperity Sphere, "liberation of Asian peoples."

Japan brought Indochina into the Greater East Asia Co-Prosperity Sphere while leaving a European colonial administration in place and signing a trade agreement with it because of critical food shortages at home. It may be that the interests of Japan, which had to gain quick access to resources, especially food, coincided with those of the Indochinese colonial administration. But it is probably more accurate to say that the framework of an Indochina colonized for the purpose of supplying food was the product of a compromise among the Japanese military, the Japanese bureaucracy, Japanese companies moving into Indochina, Japanese trading companies that had been doing business there since before the war, and French trading companies.

A great many issues having to do with Japan's colonization of Indochina remain unaddressed, among them the impact of Japanese domination on Indochina's society and economy, the lender-borrower relationship between the Yokohama Specie Bank and the Bank of Indochina, and comparison of the colonization of Taiwan and of Indochina.[65] This period of history will not be fully elucidated until they are examined.

I would like to end by quoting a Japanese army officer executed in Vietnam after the war: "However we may justify our actions, there is no reason to expect [those who were on the receiving end] to agree."[66]

This paper was originally published under the title "'Dai Tōa Kyōeiken' to Indoshina: Shokuryō kakutoku no tame no senryaku" [The Greater East Asia Co-Prosperity Sphere and Indochina: A strategy for securing food supplies] in *Tōnan Ajia: Rekishi to bunka* [Southeast Asia: History and culture] 10 (1981): 39–67.

NOTES

[1] Masaya Shiraishi and Motoo Furuta, "Taiheiyō sensō ki no Nihon no tai Indoshina seisaku: Sono futatsu no tokuisei o megutte" [Two features of Japan's Indochina policy during the Pacific War], *Ajia kenkyū* [Asian studies] 23, no. 3 (1976): 5.

[2] The reason for considering only imports is that the value of Japan's exports was insignificant. Exports to Indochina were always very low. Many Japanese books and articles published around 1940 cited the elimination of this one-sided trade relationship as a justification for Japan's advance into Indochina. The thrust of their arguments was that Japan had put up with an unfavorable balance of trade since the Meiji era (1868–1912) because of France's protectionist trade policies and that the time had come to normalize trade relations between Japan and Indochina. See Seishū Yokoyama, *Futsuryō Indoshina ron* [French Indochina] (Tokyo: Nan'yō Kyōkai [South Seas Association], 1929), pp. 255–57; Taiheiyō Kyōkai [Pacific Association], ed., *Futsuryō Indoshina: Seiji, keizai* [French Indochina: Politics and economics] (Tokyo: Kawade Shobō, 1940), p. 384; Taiwan Development Co., Research Section, *Futsuin no seikaku to kankyō* [The character and environment of French Indochina] (Taipei: Taiwan Development Co., 1941), pp. 64–65, 97–102; Kokusai Keizai Gakkai [Association for International Economics], ed., *Tai, Futsuin no kenkyū: genchi chōsa hōkoku* [Studies of Thailand and French Indochina: Field reports], (Tokyo: Tōkō Shoin, 1942), p. 23; Tetsuo Kageyama, "Futsuryō Indoshina keizai jijō" [Economic conditions in French Indochina], in Nagoya City, Special East Asia Research Department, ed., *Nampō keizai jijō* [Economic conditions in the south] (Nagoya: Nagoya City, 1943), p. 53. Though the Yokoyama book is much older than the other works cited, I include it because the author was active in Indochina in 1940.

[3] Prime Minister's Office, Statistics Bureau, ed., *Dai ikkai Nippon tōkei nenkan* [First yearbook of Japanese statistics] (Tokyo: Mainichi Shimbunsha, 1949), p. 477.

[4] For further details, see table 6 (below) in Yukichika Tabuchi, "Nihon no tai Indoshina 'shokuminchi' ka puran to sono jittai" [Japan's plan for the colonization of Indochina and what actually happened], *Tōnan Ajia: Rekishi to bunka* [Southeast Asia: History and culture], 9 (1980): 125.

Changes in the Volume of Indochina's Rice Exports to Japan, 1918–1945

(thousand tons)

Year	All exports	Exports to Japan	%
1918–1920	1,258	206	16.4
1921–1925	1,450	107	7.4
1926	1,597	166	10.4
1927	1,665	181	10.9
1928	1,798	120	6.8
1929	1,471	48	3.3
1930	1,122	34	3.0
1931	983	0.5	0.1
1932	1,220	60	4.9
1933	1,277	1	0.1
1934	1,604	1	0.1
1935	1,759	3	0.2
1936	1,716	2	0.1
1937	1,548	1	0.1
1938	1,077	—	—
1939	1,251	—	—
1940	1,593	439	27.6
1941	954	563	59.0
1942	990	973	98.3
1943	1,023	662	64.7
1944	501	38	7.6
1945	44	—	—

The 1933 figure for all exports has been corrected from 1,227 in "Nihon no tai Indoshina 'shokuminchi' ka" to 1,277.—Au.

Sources: For 1913–1930: Henry, *Futsuryō Indoshina no nōgyō keizai*, vol. 2, pp. 188, 189, 213. For 1931–1939: Shigeo Hemmi, *Futsuryō Indoshina kenkyū*, pp. 131–32. For 1941–1945: La chambre de commerce chinois du Sud vietnam, *Annuaire du commerce chinois du Sud vietnam*, p. J–29.

[5] John R. Andrus and Katrine R. C. Green, "Recent Developments in Indo-China: 1939–43," supplement in Charles Robequain, *The Economic Development of French Indochina*, trans. Isabel A. Ward (New York: A.M.S. Press, 1974; orig. pub. Oxford: Oxford University Press, 1944), p. 382.

[6] Tabuchi, "Nihon no tai Indoshina 'shokuminchi' ka," pp. 118–26. This paper discusses the way in which the system was organized but does not examine the reasons for the drop in the supply of unhulled rice. Further research in this area is needed.

[7] "Kainantō shori hōshin," in Jun Tsunoda, ed., *Nit-Chū sensō 3* [The Sino-Japanese War 3], vol. 10 of *Gendaishi shiryō* [Sources of contemporary history, 1925–1945] (Tokyo: Misuzu Shobō, 1963), pp. 451–53.

[8] "Nampō gaichi tōchi soshiki kakujū kyōka hōsaku." Ibid., p. 464.

[9] Tōru Yano, *"Nanshin" no keifu* [The lineage of southern expansion] (Tokyo: Chūō Kōronsha, 1975), p. 168; Tōru Yano, *Tōnan Ajia sekai no ronri* [The logic of the world of Southeast Asia] (Tokyo: Chūō Kōronsha, 1980), p. 224.

[10] Japan Association of International Relations, Study Group on the Causes of the Pacific War, ed., *Nampō shinshutsu* [Southern expansion], vol. 6 of *Taiheiyō sensō e no michi* [The road to the Pacific War] (Tokyo: Asahi Shimbunsha, 1963), p. 149.

[11] Tsunoda, ed., *Nit-Chū sensō 3*, "Kaisetsu" [Commentary], p. 94.

[12] "Tai Futsuin hōsaku ni kansuru kenkyū," in Tsunoda, ed., *Nit-Chū sensō 3*, pp. 369–71.

[13] Cam Ranh Bay was of value as a military port because it "is about mid-point on a straight line from Singapore to Hongkong, and is about the same distance by sea from Bangkok, Manila and the ports of Sarawak and North Borneo," which made it useful as a staging area for assembling troops to dispatch to various fronts. (Andrus and Green, "Recent Developments," p. 352.)

[14] "Keizai jitsumuka kaidō gijiroku," in Takafusa Nakamura and Akira Hara, eds., *Kokka sōdōin 1* [National mobilization 1], vol. 43 of *Gendaishi shiryō* [Sources of contemporary history, 1925–1945] (Tokyo: Misuzu Shobō, 1970), pp. 720–75.

[15] Ibid., p. 772.

[16] Ibid., p. 733.

[17] Ibid., p. 739.

[18] See figure 3–1 (below) in Kazuo Saitō, *Beikoku keizai to keizai hatten: Ajia no beisakukoku no keizai hatten ni kansuru kenkyū* [Rice economies and economic growth: A study of economic development in Asian rice-producing countries] (Tokyo: Taimeidō, 1974), p. 88. This figure illustrates clearly that from 1930 onward imports of Southeast Asian rice dwindled to a negligible volume

Changes in the Volume of Rice Imported by Japan, 1900–1945

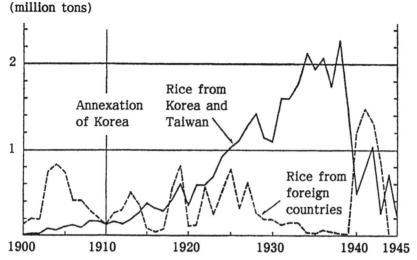

The unit has been changed from ten thousand tons in *Beikoku keizai* to one million tons.—Au.

Korean rice imported before Korea's annexation in 1910 is included in the category of rice from foreign countries. The rice-growing year extends from November through October.

Source: Ajia Keizai Kenkyūjo [Institute of Developing Economies], *One Hundred Years of Agricultural Statistics in Japan* (Tokyo: Ajia Keizai Kenkyūjo, 1969).

[19] Suehiro Ōgami, "Tōa keizaiken ni okeru kome seisan no hatten" [The development of rice production in the East Asia Economic Sphere], *Tōa keizai ronsō* [Papers on the East Asian economy] 1, no. 2 (1941): 205.

[20] Ibid., p. 207.

[21] One need only think of the Beikoku Tōsei Hō (Rice Control Law) of 1933 and the Beikoku Jichi Kanri Hō (Rice Autonomous Control Law) of 1936.

[22] Shinkichi Katayanagi, *Nippon senji shokuryō seisaku* [Japan's wartime food policy] (Tokyo: Itō Shoten, 1942), p. 1.

[23] Ibid., p. 14.

[24] Saitō, *Beikoku keizai*, p. 89.

[25] Katayanagi, *Nippon senji shokuryō seisaku*, p. 46.

[26] "Shōwa 13 nen jūyō busshi jukyū taishō oyobi hoten taisaku," in Nakamura and Hara, eds., *Kokka sōdōin 1*, pp. 283–94.

[27] The *koku*, a dry-measure unit used in Japan until the end of the war, was standardized at 5.12 US bushels in 1891.

[28] "Shōwa 13 nen jūyō busshi jukyū taishō oyobi hoten taisaku ichiranhyō," in Nakamura and Hara, eds., *Kokka sōdōin 1*, pp. 295–304.

[29] Ibid., pp. 342–57.

[30] "Butsudō keikaku, seisanryoku kakujū keikaku, rōmu dōin keikaku tō no jisseki oyobi kongo no mitōshi no gaiyō ni tsuite." Ibid., pp. 461–68.

[31] "Butsudō keikaku o chūkaku to suru waga senji keizai no genjō narabi ni kongo no mitōshi." Ibid., pp. 469–95.

[32] Ibid., pp. 504–23.

[33] This calculation is based on table C–121 in U.S. Strategic Bombing Survey, *Nippon sensō keizai no hōkai* [The effects of strategic bombing on Japan's war economy], trans. Chifuyu Masaki, 2d ed. (Tokyo: Nippon Hyōronsha, 1972; orig pub. Washington, D.C.: Government Printing Office, 1946).

[34] It may be rash to conclude that Japan became interested in Indochina only because it wanted rice. All raw materials obtained from Indochina, such as coal, rubber, iron ore, and industrial salt, were resources that Japan itself lacked. The military may have been more interested in coal and other minerals than in rice; but foodstuffs, and rice in particular, must be regarded as having been equally important for the Japanese government, in view of the three factors that bolstered the southern expansion doctrine: the sudden drop in Korean rice imports, the lower volume of rice produced in Japan proper, and the resulting food shortage. After invading Hainan, Japan advanced into northern Indochina in September 1940 and into southern Indochina in July 1941, whereupon Indochina became the strategic center of Japan's relentlessly expanding war front. An additional factor motivating Japan to approach Indochina was France's capitulation to Germany. With the fall of Paris on June 14, 1940, Indochina lost its largest export market. Since its closed economy had been dependent on France, Indochina was left totally isolated. Japan seized on this as a convenient excuse to "save" Indochina, a member of the Asian family of nations. The need to "save" Indochina was also one factor behind the ideal of a self-sufficient East Asia Economic Sphere (another name for the Greater East Asia Co-Prosperity Sphere). The advance into Indochina was thus the first step in the full-scale implementation of Japan's policy of southern expansion.

[35] Defense Agency, Institute for Defense Studies, Military History Department, *Daihon'ei rikugunbu: Dai Tōa sensō kaisen keii* [Imperial Headquarters Army Department documents on the circumstances leading to the Great East Asia War], vol. 1 (Tokyo: Asagumo Shimbunsha, 1973), p. 45.

[36] "Nampō shisaku yōkō (an)," in Nakamura and Hara, eds., *Kokka sōdōin 1*, "Kaisetsu," pp. 47–50.

[37] "Sekai jōsei no suii ni tomonau jikyoku shori yōkō," in Defense Agency, *Daihon'ei rikugunbu*, vol. 1, pp. 382–83.

[38] Ibid., pp. 517–18.

[39] Ministry of Foreign Affairs, ed., *Nippon gaikō nempyō narabi ni shuyō bunsho* [Chronology and major documents of Japanese diplomacy], vol. 2 (Tokyo: Hara Shobō, 1966), pp. 437–38.

[40] "Nampō keizai shisaku yōkō," in Nakamura and Hara, eds., *Kokka sōdōin 1*, pp. 177–78.

[41] Ministry of Foreign Affairs, ed., *Nippon gaikō nempyō*, vol. 2, pp. 446–48.

[42] "Tai Futsu Inshi keizai hatten no tame no shisaku," in Nakamura and Hara, eds., *Kokka sōdōin 1*, pp. 183–84.

[43] "Tai Futsu Indoshina busshi shutoku narabi ni bōeki hōsaku yōryō (A)." Ibid., pp. 185–86.

[44] "Nippon Indoshina gunji kyōtei," in Ministry of Foreign Affairs, ed., *Nippon gaikō nempyō*, vol. 2, pp. 454–56.

[45] "Tai Futsu Indoshina busshi shutoku narabi ni bōeki hōsaku yōryō (B)," in Nakamura and Hara, eds., *Kokka sōdōin 1*, pp. 187–89.

[46] "Summary of Measures (A)" (temporary measures) and "Summary of Measures (B)" (permanent measures) are the best expressions of Japan's plans for the colonization of Indochina. Seven temporary measures were listed: (1) preferential acquisition of vital resources, (2) abolition of Indochinese export duties, (3) acquisition of resources from the vicinity of Indochina, (4) introduction of an exchange clearing system, (5) control of Japanese trading companies doing business in Indochina, (6) securing of transport ships, and (7) effective use of goods, funds, and technical personnel to accomplish the above six objectives. A few of these measures require elaboration. In regard to item 1, priority was placed on acquiring minerals, rice, corn, rubber, and industrial salt. In regard to item 2, Japan wanted export duties on rice, corn, and

silica removed. Item 3 referred to the region south of Indochina, into which Japan would move after consolidating its hold on Indochina. This indicates Japan's intention of securing Indochina as a relay point or rear base from which to advance farther south. Because resources vital to Japan were "shipped to third countries after passing through Indochina," Japan intended to "obtain resources from the 'vicinity' using the same routes." Leaving the Indochinese colonial administration intact was also part of Japan's plan to secure Indochinese resources. (For further discussion, see Tabuchi, "Nihon no tai Indoshina 'shokuminchi' ka," pp. 115–26.) The most important measure was item 4:

"Funds to pay for goods acquired by Japan should come as far as possible from payments for goods exported by us. To that end, an export plan for domestic goods should be drawn up.

"Because Japan is short of foreign exchange and goods imported from French Indochina should be paid for as far as possible using funds earned by our exports, we must increase exports. To do this, we must endeavor to have import duties on Japanese goods lowered or removed and import quotas raised or removed. An export plan should be drawn up to try to ensure that the value of domestic goods exported is at least equal to the value of goods imported into Japan.

"While devising all [possible] means to conserve our foreign exchange—establishment of credit, payment in yen, barter arrangements, establishment of an exchange clearing system—measures must also be taken to avoid destroying the foundation of Indochina's currency and financial system."

This indicates that plans had already been made for an exchange clearing system (introduced ten months later, in July 1941) and for yen credits (introduced in January 1943). These measures were intended "to avoid destroying the foundation of Indochina's currency and financial system." However, the "Accord franco-japonais rélatif au régime douanier, aux échanges commerciaux et à leurs modalités de règlement entre l'Indochine et le Japon" and the "Lettres échangées concernant les modalités de règlement entre le Japon et l'Indochine française" (discussed later in this paper), which were extensions of this policy, accomplished precisely that result. In short, Japan, "needing to import many goods [from Indochina] but unable to provide much to export, . . . [found] onerous the one-sided trade generated by [Indochina's] trade surplus." Eigo Fukai, *Sūmitsuin jūyō giji oboegaki* [Memoranda on important Privy Council matters] (Tokyo: Iwanami Shoten, 1953), p. 160. This would obviously result in "destroying the foundation of Indochina's currency and financial system."

Permanent measures included general items and items on specific goods. The latter focused on such goods as coal, iron ore, salt, rice, and corn. In regard to rice and corn, for example, it was observed that "in the event of food shortages in Japan and Manchuria, Indochina will be an important supply source for rice and other provisions. We must therefore take steps to control dealings in rice and other foodstuffs in Indochina." In other words, Japan planned to control the rice trade to secure Indochina "permanently" as a food supply source. There were eight general items: (1) execution of specialized local surveys, (2) acquisition of supplies of vital goods, (3) removal of regulations restricting the operations of Japanese companies in Indochina, (4) provision of supplies and funds for a comprehensive development plan for Indochina, (5) control of the entry of new Japanese companies into Indochina to prevent competition, (6) provision of capital to local companies, (7) improvement of transportation, communication, and harbor facilities, and (8) establishment of experimental research facilities. We can see that it was planned to allow a small number of Japanese companies important for reasons of national policy to operate in Indochina and to provide capital to local companies in order to obtain Indochinese resources. The restrictive regulations referred to in item 3 were the following: third-country nationals were prohibited from obtaining mining rights; third-country nationals were prohibited from carrying out mineral resource surveys and from prospecting; government reservations were established in areas containing mineral resources; and ownership of land required for factories or offices was prohibited. These restrictions were removed by the "Convention franco-japonaise d'établissement et de navigation relative à l'Indochine française," signed on May 6, 1941, and implemented on July 5 that year, concluded under threat of Japanese military intervention. (The Japanese text of the treaty is found in Ministry of Foreign Affairs, ed., *Jōyakushū* [Collected treaties], collection 19, vol. 25, pp. 2–13.) The most important item was that pertaining to surveys of resources, necessary for more effective acquisition of resources. To carry out such surveys the Japanese government organized a 151–member Indochina Resource Survey Team. (The name by which it was known in Indochina, "La Mission Économique du Japon en Indochine," cleverly concealed its true intent.) For a detailed discussion of this team, see Tabuchi, "Nihon no tai Indoshina 'shoku-minchi' ka," pp. 104–14. Table 1 of that paper (p. 106; below) shows the team's makeup.

Makeup of the Indochina Resource Survey Team

Unit	No. members	No. assistants	No. interpreters	No. employees	Total
General Affairs Department	6	9	—	6 (3)[a]	21 (24)[b]
1st Agriculture and Forestry Unit (agriculture in general; rice, corn)	8	2	1	1	12
2d Agriculture and Forestry Unit (rubber)	4	2	1	—	7
3d Agriculture and Forestry Unit (cotton)	3	2	1	1	7
4th Agriculture and Forestry Unit (jute)	3	1	1	1	6
5th Agriculture and Forestry Unit (forest products)	5	1	1	1	8
6th Agriculture and Forestry Unit (leather, livestock)	2	2	1	—	5
Fisheries Unit (fisheries in general)	7	2	1	1	11
Salt Industry Unit (salt industry in general)	4	1	1	1	7
1st Mining Unit (mining resources in general)	7	4	1	—	12
2d Mining Unit (nonferrous metals)	10	6	1	1	18
3d Mining Unit (iron, manganese)	6	3	1	2	12
4th Mining Unit (coal)	5	4	1	—	10
5th Mining Unit (petroleum)	2	1	1	1	5
Hydroelectric Power Unit (hydro-electric power in general)	4	2	1	—	7
Total	76	42	14	16 (19)[b]	148 (151)[b]

[a]The figure in parentheses indicates personnel added in Indochina.

[b]Figures in parentheses are totals including personnel added in Indochina.

Source: Ministry of Foreign Affairs, *Futsuin shigen chōsadan jigyō kiroku* [Record of the Indochina Resource Survey Team project] (Tokyo: Ministry of Foreign Affairs, 1942); unpaginated.

[47] "Shōwa 16 nendo busshi dōin keikaku," in Nakamura and Hara, eds., *Kokka sōdōin 1*, "Kaisetsu," p. 65.

[48] "Nampō keizai taisaku yōkō," in ibid., pp. 195–98.

[49] Katayanagi, *Nippon senji shokuryō seisaku*, p. 264.

[50] Andrus and Green, "Recent Developments," p. 363. However, the source for this figure is unknown.

[51] Ibid. However, the source for this figure is unknown. According to Andrus and Green, 466,000 tons of Indochinese rice were exported to Japan in 1940, a figure that conflicts with the figure for that year in table 4 of this paper. The reason for the discrepancy is unknown.

[52] Ibid., p. 369.

[53] Ibid. Even considering that the 1941 quota for corn exports to Japan was 200,000 tons, in the case of Indochina cereals usually meant corn.

[54] Nobukazu Matsuda, *Futsuin nōgyōron* [Agriculture in French Indochina] (Tokyo: Asakura Shoten, 1944), p. 287. Matsuda traveled to Indochina as a member of the Japanese govern-

ment's Indochina Resource Survey Team (discussed in n. 46). He was in charge of studying corn. (For details, see Tabuchi, "Nihon no tai Indoshina 'shokuminchi' ka," p. 108.) The corn imported into Japan was used for animal feed, just as Indochinese rice shipped to France was used as animal feed there. Of the Indochinese rice shipped to France in 1937, 10 percent was for human consumption, 10 percent for industrial use, and 80 percent for livestock feed. These figures are from Shigeo Hemmi, *Futsuryō Indoshina kenkyū* [A study of French Indochina] (Tokyo: Nippon Hyōronsha, 1941), pp. 132–33.

55 "Teikoku hitsuyō shigen no kaigai toku ni nampō shochiiki ni okeru kakuho hōsaku," in Nakamura and Hara, eds., *Kokka sōdōin 1*, pp. 172–76.

56 Japan's thinking regarding rubber at the time of the advance into Indochina is clearly expressed in "Summary of Measures (B)":
"Of the approximately 70,000 tons of rubber produced in French Indochina, in the past most was exported to France. Recently, however, all the rubber produced there has been exported to the United States.
"If Japan could secure this amount [70,000 tons], it would suffice for our needs; therefore we must devise measures to ensure that Japan is supplied on a preferential basis.
"It is urgent that we acquire rubber plantations and arrange for Japanese rubber companies to operate in French Indochina."
Thus it is clear that Japan was planning to import rubber. What is noteworthy is that Japan believed that Indochina's rubber production would be sufficient to meet Japanese demand. Japan planned to import about 55,000 tons of rubber in 1939, according to the "Shōwa 14 nendo busshi dōin keikaku yōryō" [Summary of the fiscal 1939 plan for mobilization of goods], in Nakamura and Hara, eds., *Kokka sōdōin 1*, pp. 410–15. Rubber imports were to be paid for in US dollars. See Yokohama Specie Bank, Economic Research Division, *Dai Tōa kyōeiken shochiiki ni okeru kahei kin'yū kawase bōeki no gaiyō* [Outline of currency, financial, and exchange trade in the various regions of the Greater East Asia Co-Prosperity Sphere] (Yokohama: Yokohama Specie Bank, 1942), p. 35. See n. 60 for the reason Japan chose to pay in dollars.

57 "Nipponkoku Indoshina kan kanzei seido, bōeki oyobi sono kessai yōshiki ni kansuru Nichi-Futsu kyōtei," in Ministry of Foreign Affairs, *Jōyakushū*, collection 19, vol. 25, pp. 16–63.

58 A brief reference to the Trade Agreement is found in Jan Pluvier, *South-East Asia from Colonialism to Independence* (Kuala Lumpur: Oxford University Press, 1974), pp. 270–71. For the main points of the Trade Agreement, see "Nichi-Futsuin kan bōeki oyobi bōeki futai hiyō kessai hōhō ni kansuru ginkōkan kyōtei chōin no ken" [Matters concerning the signing of the interbank agreement between Japan and French Indochina relating to the method of settling accounts for trade and trade-related expenses], in Bank of Japan, Economic Research Department, ed., *Nippon kin'yūshi shiryō* [Sources of Japanese financial history], vol. 30 (Tokyo: Printing Bureau, Ministry of Finance, 1971), p. 217. For the agreement between the Yokohama Specie Bank and the Bank of Indochina, see Ministry of Finance, ed., *Shōwa zaiseishi* [History of finance in the Shōwa era], vol. 13 (Tokyo: Tōyō Keizai Shimpōsha, 1963), pp. 313–21.

59 Fukai, *Sūmitsuin*, p. 162.

60 Rubber was paid for in dollars because "rubber is a vital commodity for which there is strong international demand in the present circumstances, for which reason we have acceded to [Indochina's] wish [to be paid in dollars]." Ibid.

61 Ibid., p. 160.

62 "Nipponkoku Futsuryō Indoshina kan kessai no yōshiki ni kansuru kōkan kōbun," in Ministry of Foreign Affairs, ed., *Jōyakushū*, collection 21, vol. 9, pp. 1–5. A brief reference to the Exchange of Notes is found in Pluvier, *South-East Asia*, pp. 270–71.

63 Fukai, *Sūmitsuin*, p. 161.

64 Let us recall the series of trade agreements concluded between Germany and Hungary in the 1930s. The Trade Agreement of February 1934 and the Clearing Agreement of March 1934 were particularly important. The latter, "which made it possible for Germany to procure the strategic resources and food necessary for military expansion without having to pay for them

in foreign currency," was "the first step in establishing the large-scale economic bloc that was an extension of the Nazi policy of expansion into southeastern Europe." Tadashi Isayama, "Nachisu Doitsu no Tōnan Ō keizai seisaku: Tai Hangarii o chūshin ni" [Nazi Germany's economic policies toward southeastern Europe, principally Hungary], in *Nachisu keizai to Nyū Diiru* [The Nazi economy and the New Deal], vol. 3 of *Fashizumu ki no kokka to shakai* [State and society in the Fascist period], ed. Shakai Kagaku Kenkyūjo [Institute of Social Science] (Tokyo: Tokyo Daigaku Shuppankai, 1979), pp. 212–13. See also Takeshi Tsukamoto, *Nachisu keizai: Seiritsu to rekishi to ronri* [The Nazi economy: Origin, history, theory] (Tokyo: Tokyo Daigaku Shuppankai, 1978), pp. 214–34.

[65] If more were known about these issues, this paper would have more substance, but many points remain unclear. In regard to the impact of Japanese domination on Indochina's society and economy, the *cai* (intermediaries between French entrepreneurs and Indochinese laborers) played a role, but information about them during the period of Japanese control is unavailable. The following works are helpful, though the period they deal with differs from that of this paper: International Labour Office, *Indoshina rōdō chōsa* [Labour conditions in Indo-China], trans. Nan'yō Keizai Kenkyūjo [Institute of South Seas Economies] (Tokyo: Kurita Shoten, 1942; orig. pub. Geneva: International Labour Office, 1938), pp. 183–90; Shigeo Hemmi, *Indoshina no minzoku, seiji, keizai* [The people, politics, and economy of Indochina] (Tokyo: privately published, 1960), pp. 112–17; Ngo Van Hoa, "Furansu shokuminchi shihon no Betonamu rōdōsha kaikyū ni taisuru zenshihonshugiteki sakushu keitai ni tsuite" [The configuration of precapitalist exploitation of the Vietnamese working class by French colonial capital], trans. Yōko Takada, *Kokusai kankeigaku kenkyū* [The study of international relations] 4 (1978): 131–41. Ngo Van Hoa's paper, originally published under the title "Ban ve hinh thuc boc lot tien tu ban cha nghia cua tu ban thuc dan Phap doi voi giai cap cong nhan Viet-nam" in *Nghien Cuu Lich Su* 157 (1974), is incorporated in slightly abridged form in Ngo Van Hoa and Du'o'ng Kinh Quoc, *Giai cap cong nhan Viet Nam nhu'ng nam tru'o'c khi thanh lap dang* (Hanoi: Nha xuat ban khoa hoc xa hoi, 1978), pp. 236–46. I have not yet been able to elucidate the lender-borrower relationship between the Yokohama Specie Bank and the Bank of Indochina; collection of reference materials must begin immediately. In regard to comparison of the colonization of Taiwan and of Indochina, more research is now being done on Taiwan during the period of Japanese occupation. See, for example, Xu Shikai, *Nihon tōchika no Taiwan: Teikō to dan'atsu* [Taiwan under Japanese rule: Resistance and repression] (Tokyo: Tokyo Daigaku Shuppankai, 1972); Tu Shaoen, *Nihon teikokushugika no Taiwan* [Taiwan under Japanese imperialism] (Tokyo: Tokyo Daigaku Shuppankai, 1975).

[66] Fujio Sugimatsu, ed., *Saigon ni shisu—Yon sempan shikeishu no isho* [Death in Saigon: Writings of four war criminals condemned to death] (Tokyo: Kōwadō, 1972) p. 125. This book is a compilation of prison writings by four Japanese officers condemned to death as war criminals in Saigon after World War II. Sugimatsu was their chief defense counsel. The words quoted were written by Army Captain Junji Sakamoto.

4

THE BACKGROUND TO THE FORMATION OF THE TRAN TRONG KIM CABINET IN APRIL 1945: JAPANESE PLANS FOR GOVERNING VIETNAM

Masaya Shiraishi

INTRODUCTION

On the night of March 9, 1945, the Japanese army in Indochina carried out an anti-French coup d'état, bringing to an end three quarters of a century of French colonial rule. This coup is usually referred to in Japanese sources as the *Futsuin buryoku shori* (military disposition of French Indochina) or by its code name, "Operation Meigō." Two days later Bao Dai, the last emperor of the Nguyen dynasty, prompted by Japan, abrogated the treaty of protection concluded with France in 1884 and declared Vietnam's independence. On April 17 a cabinet headed by Tran Trong Kim was established in Hue.

The purpose of this paper is to contribute to an understanding of the nature of the Kim cabinet, established under Japanese military rule. Scholars have long held two divergent views on this question. One school of thought, that of Milton Sacks[1] and John T. McAlister,[2] holds that the Kim cabinet was composed of pro-Japanese politicians. Truong Buu Lam[3] and Kenneth Colton,[4] on the other hand, maintain that it was made up of nonpartisan technocrats. I support the latter view, though it would be hard to point to concrete or convincing evidence for either view in the research conducted so far. Filling the gaps in our knowledge of this period entails two tasks. The first is to examine the process that led up to the formation of the Kim cabinet in relation to the Japanese authorities' plans for governing Vietnam after removing the French; the second is to study the process by which the members of the Kim cabinet were selected and their backgrounds. This paper addresses the first of these tasks.

---

[1] [Milton Sacks], Department of State, *Political Alignments of Vietnamese Nationalists,* O.I.R. Report 3708 (Washington, D.C.: Office of Intelligence Research, 1949), p. 56.

[2] John T. McAlister, Jr., *Viet Nam: The Origins of Revolution* (New York: Knopf, 1969), pp. 168–70.

[3] Truong Buu Lam, "Japan and the Disruption of the Vietnamese Nationalist Movement," in *Aspects of Vietnamese History,* ed. W. F. Vella (Honolulu: University Press of Hawaii, 1973), p. 257.

[4] Kenneth Colton, "The Failure of the Independent Political Movement in Vietnam, 1945–1946" (Ph.D. diss., American University, 1969), pp. 34–35.

As is generally known, the five months from the armed overthrow of the French until the Japanese defeat was an extremely important period in terms of the subsequent fate of Vietnam. As it turned out, developments during this period contributed to the failure of the Bao Dai-Kim government to take the political initiative and led to the transfer of power to the Viet Minh under Ho Chi Minh. In considering the reasons for the Viet Minh's triumph in the August Revolution (*Cach Mang Thang Tam*), it is essential to study the factors behind the failure of the Bao Dai-Kim government as well as those behind the Viet Minh victory.[5] In this paper I seek to lay some of the groundwork for this task.[6]

I. Plans for Establishing a Pro-Japanese Regime

From the stationing of Japanese troops in northern Indochina in September 1940, through the beginning of the Pacific War in December 1941, right up to the overthrow of the French in Indochina in March 1945, Japanese policy consistently called for maintaining the French administration of Indochina, a policy referred to as *seihitsu hoji* (maintenance of tranquillity).[7] Indochina was the only area of Southeast Asia under Japanese military control in which a white colonial regime was allowed to remain in place. The elements in the Japanese army and government that most strongly advocated this policy were the First (Operations) Department and the War Plans Unit of the Imperial Army General Staff Headquarters and General Hideki Tōjō, prime minister from October 1941 to July 1944.[8] Eliminating the French regime would have meant deploying extra troops for that purpose, and Japan would have had to deal singlehandedly with the ensuing confusion and with the administration and defense of Indochina. This would have entailed waste and was to be avoided if

---

[5] This issue is also touched on in Masaya Shiraishi, "Dai ichiji Indoshina sensō: Sono mondai shikaku to sōkatsu" [The First Indochina War: A view of its major issues and an overview], in *Gendai Ajia shi no dammen* [A profile of modern Asian history], ed. Ajia Henshū Iinkai [Asian Editorial Committee] (Tokyo: Ajia Hyōronsha, 1982), vol. 1, pp. 255–57.

[6] This paper is part of my research on the process of political and social change within Vietnam as well as in relations between Japan and Vietnam and between Japan and French Indochina in the 1940–1945 period. Previously published papers include Masaya Shiraishi and Motoo Furuta, "Taiheiyō sensō ki no Nihon no tai Indoshina seisaku: Sono futatsu no tokuisei o megutte" [Two features of Japan's Indochina policy during the Pacific War], *Ajia kenkyū* [Asian studies] 23, no. 3 (1976); Shiraishi, "Betonamu Fukkoku Dōmeikai to 1940 nen fukkokugun hōki ni tsuite" [On the League for the National Restoration of Vietnam and the 1940 revolt by the restoration army], *Ajia keizai* [Asian economies] 23, no. 4 (1982); Shiraishi, "La Présence Japonaise en Indochine 1940–1945," in *L'Indochine Française: 1940–1945*, ed. Paul Isoart (Paris: Presses Universitaires de France, 1982). After writing the Japanese version of the present paper, I published "Vietnam under the Japanese presence and the August Revolution," *International Studies* 2 (1985) and "Dainiji taisen ki no Nihon no tai Indoshina keizai seisaku" [Japanese economic policy toward Indochina during World War II], *Tōnan Ajia: Rekishi to bunka* [Southeast Asia: History and culture] 15 (1986).

[7] Shizuo Maruyama, *Ushinawaretaru kiroku: Tai Ka, nampō seiryaku hishi* [Lost records: The secret history of political tactics toward China and the south] (Tokyo: Kōraku Shobō, 1950), pp. 271ff.; Defense Agency, War History Office, ed., *Shittan, Meigō sakusen: Biruma sensen no hōkai to Tai, Futsuin no bōei* [The Sittang and Meigō operations: The collapse of the Burma front and the defense of Thailand and French Indochina] (Tokyo: Asagumo Shimbunsha, 1969), p. 571.

[8] For details, see Shiraishi and Furuta, "Taiheiyō sensō ki"; Ralph B. Smith, "The Japanese Period in Indochina and the Coup of 9 March 1945," *Journal of Southeast Asian Studies* 9, no. 2 (1978).

at all possible. Retaining the French regime, promoting and strengthening its cooperation with Japan, was thus considered to be the most rational and efficient policy. It followed that Japan should avoid becoming involved in local anti-French movements.[9]

These views were reflected in Japan's official policy toward Indochina up until the armed overthrow of the French. This does not mean, however, that there were no differences of opinion within the Japanese military and government. There were two reasons for questioning the policy of retaining the French regime. One had to do with distrust of the regime's cooperativeness and loyalty, the other with dissatisfaction over the continued existence of a white colonial regime in contravention of the principle of "the liberation of Greater East Asia" *(Dai Tōa kaihō)*.[10] Such views seem to have been strongest within the Ministry of Foreign Affairs and its embassy in French Indochina (opened in October 1941) and in the Second (Intelligence) Department of the Army General Staff and that department's Eighth (Covert Activities) Section. They had long been urging the undertaking of "a movement to enlighten the native masses"[11] and operations aimed at educating and raising the political consciousness of the "Annamese."[12] Naturally, these organizations routinely gathered intelligence and carried out covert and propaganda activities, which meant that their personnel could not avoid involvement with anti-French movements. The Army General Staff's Eighth Section, for instance, had been in contact with Cuong De, a Vietnamese prince living in exile in Japan, since around 1939 and had helped him financially.[13] Meanwhile, the Japanese Kempeitai (military police) and the garrison army command carried out similar activities in Indochina.[14]

Apart from government and army links, a number of Japanese had a personal interest in Vietnamese political movements. For example, in Japan there were groups organized or inspired by General Iwane Matsui and the right-wing ideologue

---

[9] The position of the central authorities—maintenance of order and noninvolvement in nationalist movements—is expressed clearly in "Jōsei no henka ni ōzuru tai Futsuin sochi fukuan" [Plan of measures toward French Indochina to deal with changes in the situation], which emerged from the Imperial Headquarters-government liaison conference of January 24, 1944. This document stated that "in the present circumstances, the Empire should adhere to the existing plan for the maintenance of tranquillity in French Indochina and should avoid encouraging native nationalist movements." Defense Agency, ed., *Shittan, Meigō sakusen*, pp. 581–82.

[10] For the basis of the counterarguments of those who supported retaining the French regime in Indochina, see Shiraishi and Furuta, "Taiheiyō sensō ki," pp. 4ff.

[11] Policy proposal for French Indochina prepared by the Army General Staff, Second Department, and dated January 22, 1943. Army General Staff, War Plans Unit, "Daihon'ei kimitsu sensō nisshi" [Imperial Headquarters secret war diaries], War History Office, Defense Agency.

[12] Report on current activities of the embassy in French Indochina dated March 3, 1943. Ibid.

[13] Interview (May 26, 1979, in Tokyo) with Shōichi Kadomatsu, a staff officer in the Army General Staff Eighth Section from 1938 to the end of 1941; telephone interview (May 29, 1979) with Masaji Ozeki, a staff officer in the Army General Staff Eighth Section from the summer of 1940 to July 1945. See also Shiraishi, "Betonamu Fukkoku Dōmeikai," pp. 27, 34.

[14] Interviews (March 9, 21, 23, and 29, 1972, and June 15, 1976, in Tokyo) with Hidezumi Hayashi, a Kempeitai lieutenant colonel, later a colonel, first attached to the Operations Department of and then a staff officer of the garrison army in Indochina (January 1944–August 1945); interview (April 12, 1979, in Okayama) with Hiromasu Tabuchi, stationed in French Indochina from May 1940 to October 1941 and from July 1942 to August 1945, with ranks ranging from Kempeitai warrant officer to captain.

Shūmei Ōkawa,[15] and in Indochina there were Mitsuhiro Matsushita[16] of Dai Nan Kōsi, Dōichi Yamane[17] and Ōmi Komaki[18] of Indoshina Sangyō (a subsidiary of Taiwan Takushoku), and Kiyoshi Komatsu[19] of the Japanese Cultural Institute. However, these people did not act entirely on their own, as private citizens, but maintained links of some sort with people in the army and in the Foreign Ministry and its embassy in Indochina.[20]

A number of Vietnamese, for various reasons, were also in contact with Japanese individuals and organizations. The important role played by Cuong De in linking Vietnamese political groups, politicians, and intellectuals with Japanese cannot be ignored. Cuong De went to Japan for the first time in 1906 and participated in the Dong Du (Eastern Travel) movement, which encouraged Vietnamese youths to study in Japan. He left in 1909, after the movement's collapse, and wandered around China and Europe. He returned to Japan in 1915 and lived there for the most part from then on.[21] Being in the line of the crown prince of the founder of the Nguyen dynasty, and an activist since the time of the Dong Du movement, Coung De was a convenient political symbol for both Japanese and Vietnamese.

In February 1939, with the support of Colonel Takaji Wachi, head of the Ran Kikan (an intelligence organization in Hong Kong and Shanghai), and others, Cuong De assembled in Shanghai a number of Vietnamese living in exile in Guangdong, Thailand, and elsewhere, and organized the Viet Nam Phuc Quoc Dong Minh Hoi (League for the National Restoration of Vietnam), with headquarters in Tokyo. At around the same time, he began making contact with political groups and politicians in Vietnam.[22] These contacts were made through military channels, such as the

---

[15] Shiraishi, "Betonamu Fukkoku Dōmeikai," pp. 25, 31 (n. 9).

[16] Interviews (February 20 and March 8, 1975, in Saigon; June 30, 1976, in Tokyo) with Mitsuhiro Matsushita; interview (January 8, 1975, in Saigon) with his nephew Isooki Matsushita.

[17] Interview (March 31, 1981, in Kōchi) with Ōmi Uchikawa, who lived in French Indochina from 1937 to 1943 as an employee of Sawayama Shōji, Indoshina Sangyō, and Taiwan Takushoku.

[18] "Tanemakisuto 50 nen, Komaki Ōmi shi ni kiku" [Fifty years as a pioneer: A talk with Ōmi Komaki], part 5, *Mainichi Shimbun*, evening edition, March 5, 1971.

[19] Interview (April 13, 1976, in Tokyo) with Taeko Komatsu, Kiyoshi Komatsu's wife; interview with Tabuchi.

[20] An example is Mitsuhiro Matsushita, who originally had close ties to the navy and then in 1944 established close relations with the garrison army command in French Indochina. Komatsu also cooperated in sending Vietnamese who had been under the protection of the Kempeitai in Bac Ninh province to Taiwan and Japan. These facts cannot, however, be construed to mean that these men were undercover agents of Japan, though Philippe Devillers calls Matsushita the "chef de l'espionage civil dans le Sud de l'Indochine" in his *Histoire du Viêt-Nam de 1940 à 1952* (Paris: Éditions du Seul, 1952), p. 89. They should be seen as having acted not in a professional capacity but from a personal sense of mission. Nor were they seeking material gain; they invested their own funds, or at least paid their own way. Objective historical appraisals of their actions aside, their good intentions and personal sense of mission cannot be denied. This gives us a glimpse of the historical fact that the ideals of the Greater East Asia Co-Prosperity Sphere and Greater East Asian liberation, hollow though they were, had sufficient appeal to provide many Japanese with emotional support and justification of their war efforts and collaborative activities.

[21] For details, see Cuong De's dictated memoirs, *Cuoc Doi Cach Mang Cuong De* (Saigon: pub. by Cuong De's son Trang Liet, 1957).

[22] Shiraishi, "Betonamu Fukkoku Dōmeikai," pp. 24–30.

Eighth Section of the Army General Staff in Tokyo and the Saigon headquarters of the garrison army in Indochina; diplomatic channels, such as the embassy in Indochina; and individuals, such as Matsui, Matsushita, and Komatsu.

In 1943 the Viet Nam Ai Quoc Dang (Vietnamese Patriots' Party) in Hanoi sent Vu Dinh Dy to Cuong De in Japan, and Ngo Dinh Diem in Hue sent Pham Thuc Ngo.[23] In southern Vietnam, the Tay Ninh sect of the Cao Dai religion was in communication with Cuong De from 1939 onward.[24] And in 1942 Tran Van An established a branch of Cuong De's Phuc Quoc league in Saigon.[25]

The French authorities were extremely wary of these links between Vietnamese and Japanese.[26] Besides the above-mentioned contacts, in October 1942, with the help of the Kempeitai, the Japanese took the violent action of rescuing Huynh Phu So, founder of the Hoa Hao sect of Buddhism, who had been put under house arrest by the French authorities, and placing him under the protection of the Japanese army.[27] This further upset the French.

While the French authorities sometimes contented themselves with protesting verbally to the Japanese, they did not always refrain from taking more aggressive action. In the fall of 1943 many Vietnamese in Hanoi who were considered to be pro-Japanese were simultaneously rounded up. They included Tran Van Lai, Pham Loi, and Nguyen Trac.[28] To forestall further arrests,[29] the Japanese put Tran Trong Kim and Duong Ba Trac under protection in Hanoi and put Tran Van An and Nguyen

---

[23] Cuong De, *Cuoc Doi*, pp. 137–38. Also, for Dy, interviews with Hayashi, interview (January 25, 1975, in Saigon) with Yoshio Ebara, conscripted to work in French Indochina (1940–1945); for Ngo, interview (June 12, 1976, in Tokyo) with Masao Ishida, who worked at the consulate in Hue from May 1942 to August 1945.

[24] André Gaudel, *L'Indochine Française en face du Japan* (Romainville: J. Susse, 1947), pp. 45–47; Devillers, *Histoire du Viêt-Nam*, pp. 89ff; Jane Werner, "The Cao Dai: the Politics of a Vietnamese Syncretic Religious Movement" (Ph.D. diss., Cornell University, 1976), pp. 219ff.; Tran Quang Vinh, *Lich Su Dao Cao Dai trong Thoi Ky Phuc Quoc, 1941–1946* (Tay Ninh: Holy See of the Cao Dai Religion, 1946); interviews with Matsushita.

[25] Interview (Dec. 6, 1978, in Paris) with Tran Van An; [Sacks], *Political Alignments*, p. 55; Werner, "The Cao Dai," p. 235.

[26] See, for example, the memoirs of the governor general of French Indochina, Admiral Jean A. Decoux, *À la Barre de l'Indochine* (Paris: Plon, 1949), pp. 234ff.; report on the movements of French Indochina authorities prepared by the Southern Army General Headquarters and dated June 29, 1942, in Defense Agency, ed., *Shittan, Meigō sakusen*, p. 539.

[27] Devillers, *Histoire du Viêt-Nam*, p. 91; Hue-Tam Ho Tai, "The Evolution of Vietnamese Millenarianism" (Ph.D. diss., Harvard University, 1977), pp. 207ff.

[28] Tran Van Lai boarded trainees from the Japanese embassy in his home, and Pham Loi taught them Vietnamese. They and Nguyen Trac belonged to the pro-Japanese Dai Viet group. Interview (July 16, 1975, in Tokyo) with Keizō Kobayashi, first a trainee and then a staff member of the embassy in Indochina (1941–1945); interview (July 13, 1975, in Tokyo) with Kichisaburō Inoue, first a trainee and then a staff member of the embassy (1941–1945); interview (July 9, 1976, in Tokyo) with Kazunobu Terakawa, an embassy trainee later drafted into the garrison army (1942–1945). For more on the 1943 roundup of pro-Japanese Vietnamese, see Quang Huy, "Si Khi Ai Chau," *Sai Gon Moi*, nos. 82–92 (October 25–November 5, 1968); Tran Huy Lieu and Nguyen Khac Dam, eds., *Xa Hoi Viet Nam trong Thoi Phap Nhat* (Hanoi: N. X. B. Van Su-Dia, 1957), vol. 2, p. 14.

[29] The French authorities did not actually arrest anyone in Saigon, but they did ask the Japanese to turn over a number of Vietnamese. Devillers, *Histoire du Viêt-Nam*, p. 92.

Van Sam under protection in Saigon and sent them all into exile abroad (Singapore, Bangkok, and Taiwan).[30]

In July 1944 Ngo Dinh Diem, who felt himself to be in danger of arrest, sought protection from Masao Ishida of the consulate in Hue, with whom he had been in contact for some time. Ishida turned Diem over to the Kempeitai. The garrison army headquarters in Saigon decided to protect Diem, who was sent to Da Nang and flown from there to Saigon on a Japanese military plane.[31] In August, at Diem's request, the Japanese army also placed Cuong De's two sons in Hue under protection. Diem had asked that they be left with him, but the army did not want to harbor too many Vietnamese in Saigon because of what the French authorities would think and therefore sent them in a Japanese bomber to Bangkok, where they joined Tran Trong Kim in exile.[32] That Diem came under the direct protection of the garrison army headquarters through this series of events is significant, because the headquarters from this time on played a major role in drawing up the original plan for governing Vietnam after the overthrow of the French.

Meanwhile, Iwane Matsui's group in Tokyo sent Vu Dinh Dy to Saigon with a letter of introduction from Yatsuji Nagai, head of the Eighth Section of the Army General Staff, who was also Matsui's son-in-law. Dy's purpose in going to Vietnam was to contact pro-Japanese Vietnamese on behalf of Cuong De and send them to Japan.[33] The garrison army headquarters put Dy in touch with Ngo Dinh Diem. In September the two arranged a meeting with Hanoi members of Dy's organization, the Viet Nam Ai Quoc Dang, such as Nguyen Xuan Chu and Le Toan. In October they agreed to cooperate under Diem's leadership. They also asked the Japanese army to set up a new regime under Diem if opportunity permitted.[34] When Major General Saburō Kawamura, chief of staff of the garrison army, went to Tokyo in October, Le Toan and one other Vietnamese accompanied him.[35]

---

[30] Ibid., p. 193; Lieu and Dam, *Xa Hoi Viet Nam*, p. 14. For Tran Trong Kim, see his memoirs, *Mot Con Gio Bui* (Saigon: Vinh Son, 1969); interviews (November 19, 1979, in Chitose; November 20, 1979, in Sapporo) with Tomomi Yamaguchi, who worked first for the embassy and then for Dainan Kōsi (1941–1945). These interviews are included in Masaya Shiraishi, ed., "Intabyū kiroku C" [Collected Interviews C], in *Nihon no nampō kan'yo* [Japan's southern involvement], vol. 6, pub. Tokutei kenkyū "bunka masatsu" jimukyoku [Secretariat for the study of cultural friction] (Tokyo: University of Tokyo, 1981). Yamaguchi accompanied Kim as far as Bangkok. For Tran Van An, interview with An.

[31] Devillers mistakenly dates this incident several weeks after October 1943. Devillers, *Histoire du Viêt-Nam*, p. 93. All the Japanese parties concerned agree that it was lieutenant colonel Hayashi who gave the order to send Diem to Saigon from Hue for protection. Hayashi was assigned to Saigon in January 1944. Interviews with Hayashi; interview with Ishida; interview (June 26, 1976, in Tokyo) with Michio Kuga, a captain who headed the army's liaison office in Hue from February to June 1944 and worked in the liaison office in Saigon from June 1944 to August 1945; Toyofumi Tominaga, "Chinurareshi kūdetā" [A bloody coup d'état], in *Hiroku Dai Tōa senshi: Marē, Taiheiyō tōsho hen* [Secret records of the Greater East Asia War: Malaya and the Pacific islands], ed. Fuji Shoen (Tokyo: Fuji Shoen, 1953), pp. 157–59; Takeshi Tsukamoto, "Betonamu ni tsuite" [On Vietnam] (mimeo, n.p., 1965), p. 12.

[32] Interviews with Hayashi, Kuga, and Tabuchi. Tabuchi accompanied them to Bangkok. Kim mentions meeting Cuong De's sons in Bangkok. Kim, *Mot Con Gio Bui*, p. 34.

[33] Dy went to Vietnam in the ostensible capacity of an officer attached to the Japanese army. Interviews with Hayashi.

[34] Interviews with Hayashi; Tominaga, "Chinurareshi kūdetā," pp. 159–60.

[35] Interviews with Hayashi; Defense Agency, ed., *Shittan, Meigō sakusen*, p. 594.

These moves indicate that there was a consensus at this time among Matsui's group, the Eighth Section, and the garrison army command that the time for over-throwing the French was approaching. And indeed, the Supreme War Plans Council decided on "Measures Toward French Indochina to Deal with Changes in the Situation"[36] at a meeting convened on September 14, 1944, to deal with the situation evolving in Europe following the collapse of the Pétain regime in France on August 20 and the Allied liberation of Paris and the establishment of a provisional govern-ment under General Charles de Gaulle on August 29. The decision stipulated that force was to be used in Indochina only in the event of an "unavoidable situation." This reflected the cautious position of the army mainstream, which was opposed to an early military overthrow of the French regime in Indochina because it had to concentrate its forces for the time being on operations in the Philippines. The Japa-nese forces stationed in Indochina, however, interpreted this decision to mean that the time had come for an armed overthrow.[37] Upon his return to Saigon from Tokyo, Kawamura ordered the drafting of a proposal for governing Indochina after a mili-tary coup.[38]

According to Hidezumi Hayashi, at the time a Kempeitai lieutenant colonel and Kawamura's chief political aide, the draft plan drawn up by the garrison army was modeled on Japanese military rule in other parts of Southeast Asia.[39] But Hayashi opposed this plan for three reasons. First, by this time the war outlook was bleak; the Japanese army in Indochina needed to concentrate its forces in the Plaine de Jarres and therefore should not involve itself deeply in political matters. Second, Indochina did not possess the resources indispensable to military rule. Third, it was necessary to win the hearts of the "natives" to prevent them from going over to the Allies. To ensure their loyalty it was essential to recognize their deepest desire, liberation from French rule—in other words, independence. However, since it was not possible immediately to transfer the authority of the central administration (the French Indochina government general) to the three countries of Indochina (Vietnam, Laos, and Cambodia), the Japanese army should rule "temporarily," until conditions for the transfer of power obtained in the three countries.[40]

---

[36] "Jōsei no henka ni ōzuru tai Futsuin sochi ni kansuru ken." For the entire text see Army General Staff, *Haisen no kiroku* [Record of the defeat] (Tokyo: Hara Shobō, 1967), pp. 182–83; Defense Agency, ed., *Shittan, Meigō sakusen*, p. 584. The significance of this decision is dis-cussed in Shiraishi and Furuta, "Taiheiyō sensō ki," pp. 13ff.

[37] Ibid., pp. 15, 20.

[38] Interviews with Hayashi.

[39] Ibid. The garrison army began studying an armed overthrow of the French under the code name "Ma Measures" in 1943. The plan for post-French government of Indochina reported to army central headquarters on December 26, 1943, after consultations between Colonel Masao Kushida of the Southern Army General Headquarters and officers of the Thirty-eighth Army called for establishing military rule. At that point, as far as the army was concerned it was a foregone conclusion that military rule would follow the overthrow of the French. However, Kushida's report also noted that "if the bait of independence in some form is not dangled before the natives, it will be difficult to gain their allegiance." Defense Agency, ed., *Shittan, Meigō sakusen*, pp. 579–80. One can see here the idea of using the independence issue as "bait" to ensure the maintenance of order and to secure the cooperation of the "natives" in the war. Hayashi's own plan for post-French rule, discussed below, can be seen as reinforcing and expanding this aspect.

[40] Interviews with Hayashi.

Based on these considerations, Hayashi drew up a proposal that had as its main features rejection of a military government, the immediate granting of independence to the three countries of Indochina, and the formation of a "pro-Japanese" administration in Vietnam after independence. This plan presupposed a pro-Japanese government in which Cuong De would be head of state and Ngo Dinh Diem prime minister.[41]

Hayashi's plan was fairly well known even outside the garrison army. Takeshi Tsukamoto, a minister in Saigon at the time, relates in his memoirs: "Cuong De, relying on Iwane Matsui's Greater Asia Society [Dai Ajia Kyōkai] and with the support of the Army General Staff in Tokyo, planned to make contact with Ngo Dinh Diem and exclude Bao Dai. The army command in Indochina also planned to call Cuong De back to Indochina. A Kempeitai colonel was sent to Saigon for this purpose."[42] The Kempeitai colonel referred to was none other than Hidezumi Hayashi (then a lieutenant colonel, later a colonel, attached to the garrison army headquarters in Saigon). Tran Trong Kim also states in his memoirs that before the 1945 coup d'état Cuong De had entrusted Diem's group with the establishment of a new government and that this was supported by the Japanese.[43]

Hayashi's plan was approved by the chief of staff of the Thirty-eighth Army (as the Indochina garrison army was renamed in December 1944; see p. 122). Hayashi explained his plan at a study meeting at Thirty-eighth Army headquarters in Saigon in mid-December 1944. In addition to headquarters staff officers, some important officers of the Southern Army General Headquarters (then in Saigon) attended, including Lieutenant General Tadakazu Wakamatsu, the newly appointed assistant chief of staff. Many of those present expressed reservations or opposition to the plan. As will be seen in part two, they had assumed that military rule would follow the removal of the French.[44] Wakamatsu, however, who was familiar with Hayashi's skill in political affairs from Hayashi's days with the Shanghai Kempeitai, said, "Leave the government plan to Hayashi and you won't have to worry," and Hayashi's plan was approved.[45] On December 27 Hayashi presented his proposal in

---

[41] Ibid.

[42] Tsukamoto, "Betonamu ni tsuite," p. 11. Incidentally, Tsukamoto is identified variously in different documents—and in the present paper—as *kōshi* (minister), *sōryōji* (consul general), and *taishifu Saigon jimushochō* (head of the embassy's Saigon office).

[43] Kim, *Mot Con Gio Bui*, p. 45.

[44] Thirty-eighth Army Chief of Staff Kawamura expressed the opinion that independence be confined to Annam (central Vietnam), with military rule imposed in Tonkin (northern Vietnam) and Cochinchina (southern Vietnam), because there was a plan to make a present of Tonkin at the time of peace talks with Chungking and because it was considered desirable to place Cochinchina under direct Japanese jurisdiction in order to make it a naval base. A staff officer of the Southern Army General Headquarters stated his fear that, given the "low standard of living and cultural level" of the people of the three Indochinese countries, it would be unwise to grant them independence immediately and expressed uncertainty about the ability to maintain order and carry out labor conscription unless military rule were imposed. To this Hayashi replied that it would be easier to gain the cooperation of the "natives" in supplying labor and food for the Japanese army if independence were granted than if military rule were imposed and that, as far as maintaining order was concerned, with the exception of certain cities Vietnam had never had a police system. He expressed the opinion that the maintenance of order in rural areas could be left to the existing village councils of notables. Interviews with Hayashi.

[45] Ibid.

written form to Kawamura, Thirty-eighth Army Chief of Staff, and it was accepted at an army conference the following day.[46]

The above is based on Hayashi's own recollections as related to me, but documents in the Foreign Ministry Archives substantiate his account. A telegram dated February 25, 1945, from Shun'ichi Matsumoto, ambassador to French Indochina, to Mamoru Shigemitsu, foreign minister and Greater East Asia minister, makes it clear that Hayashi's plan for "Annamese independence" had been approved by Kawamura at the end of December 1944 and was merely awaiting the approval of Lieutenant General Yūichi Tsuchihashi, the new commander of the Thirty-eighth Army. The telegram reads in part: "Main points of discussions on February 23 and 24 with a Thirty-eighth Army staff officer (name withheld) follow. 1. In October last year [1944], drafting of a plan for the disposition of French Indochina was secretly ordered by Chief of Staff Kawamura. A plan in keeping with the [policy] line of Annamese independence was drawn up, was approved at the end of December by the chief of staff [Saburō Kawamura], and proceeded as far as point-by-point deliberation under the commander."[47] The staff officer mentioned must have been Hayashi himself.

The point to note here is the existence of a new commander, Tsuchihashi. As can be seen from the above, up to December 1944 Tsuchihashi had absolutely nothing to do with the process within the garrison army leading to the decision on the plan for governing Indochina after ousting the French. According to Tsuchihashi's postwar recollections, he arrived in Saigon on November 14, 1944, from his previous assignment on Timor and received his assignment in Saigon on December 14 from his predecessor, General Kazumoto Machijiri. He then left for Hanoi on December 18 to meet the French governor general, Admiral Jean Decoux.[48] Thus he would not have taken part in the conferences at Thirty-eighth Army headquarters in Saigon from mid-December onward. In other words, the Hayashi plan, which had been approved by Kawamura, had not received final approval from the new commander. Tsuchihashi was free to reject it at any time, should he be so inclined. And that is precisely what happened.

II. THE INDEPENDENCE ISSUE

As we have seen, because of operations in the Philippines the army headquarters in Japan wanted to avoid a military solution in Indochina. The Ministry of Foreign Affairs, however, particularly after the appointment of Mamoru Shigemitsu as foreign minister in April 1944,[49] was increasingly outspoken in calling for a military solution and the speedy granting of independence, in line with the spirit of the Greater East Asia Declaration [issued at the Greater East Asia Conference, held in Tokyo in November 1943]. At a Supreme War Plans Council meeting on October 28, 1944, Shigemitsu urged that "the Imperial Government issue a statement amplifying

---

[46] Ibid.

[47] Telegram dated February 25, 1945, from Matsumoto to Shigemitsu, in the file "Dai Tōa sensō kankei ikken: Jōsei no henka ni ōzuru Futsuin shori mondai" [Items on the Greater East Asia War: The problem of the disposition of French Indochina to deal with changes in the situation], Foreign Ministry Archives.

[48] "Tsuchihashi Yūichi chūjō no sengo no kaisō" [Postwar recollections of Lieutenant General Yūichi Tsuchihashi], War History Office, Defense Agency.

[49] Shiraishi and Furuta, "Taiheiyō sensō ki," n. 36.

the Greater East Asia Declaration, make clear our war objectives, and elucidate our future policy," then "proposed the urgency of resolving the French Indochina problem." General Yoshijirō Umezu, chief of the General Staff, replied that he agreed in principle, but that since military preparations were not complete, careful study was necessary. The exchange at this meeting illustrates clearly the fundamental difference in the positions of the Foreign Ministry and the army.[50] While the former called for forcibly removing the French in keeping with the spirit of the Greater East Asia Declaration, the latter rejected early action because of strategic concerns.

However, the failure of operations in the Philippines in December 1944 led to a change of policy within the army with respect to an early military solution in Indohina. The army's contention that it could ill afford to divert troops from the Philippines to Indochina no longer held. In fact, faced with the Allied occupation of the Philippines, Indochina's strategic significance shifted from that of a rear supply base to that of a battlefront. Accordingly, the Indochina garrison army was reorganized as a field army and renamed the Thirty-eighth Army. Troop reinforcements also began.[51]

At a meeting of the Supreme War Plans Council on December 30, 1944, the foreign minister stated: "In regard to undertaking the exercise of force in French Indochina, we will determine the timing around the middle of January on the basis of the information available at that time"—to which there were "no objections" by the other participants.[52] This consensus was probably made possible because the army, having concluded operations in the Philippines, expressed basic agreement with a military solution in Indochina.

From then on, conflict between the Foreign Ministry and the army revolved around the issues of the pretext for ejecting the French and the form of government that would follow. The Foreign Ministry had for some time been urging "resolving to restore independence to Annam" and bringing an end to French rule by military means, in accordance with "the spirit of the Greater East Asia Declaration."[53] Of course this does not mean that all ministry officials were in accord. Some were opposed to a military solution and the granting of independence, instead favoring maintenance of the status quo. For example, Tōru Hagiwara, director of the Second Political Affairs Division of the Foreign Ministry (in charge of all of Asia except China) from January to July 1945, told me the following in an interview: Shigemitsu believed that independence movements should be launched in all Japanese-occupied areas so that, even if Japan lost the war, the Americans and Europeans would be unable to return. However, Hagiwara and others were cool toward the idea of a military overthrow of the French regime in Indochina because of diplomatic considerations in regard to France. Vichy France was under the control of Japan's ally,

---

[50] Army General Staff, "Daihon'ei kimitsu," October 28, 1944. In response to Prime Minister Kuniaki Koiso's suggestion, at the December 7, 1944, meeting of the Supreme War Plans Council, that Japan "deal with French Indochina by a speedy exercise of force," the assistant chief of the General Staff declared, "The high command considers that we should decide independently, according to the degree of operational readiness." Ibid., December 7, 1944.

[51] For information on the reorganization of the garrison army and troop reinforcements, see Defense Agency, ed., *Shittan, Meigō sakusen*, p. 566ff.

[52] Army General Staff, "Daihon'ei kimitsu," December 30, 1944.

[53] "Futsuin mondai" [The French Indochina problem], Foreign Ministry document dated November 2, 1944. For the text see General Staff Headquarters, *Haisen no kiroku*, pp. 209–11. See also Shiraishi and Furuta, "Taiheiyō sensō ki," pp. 16–17.

Germany, and since the Vichy regime was neutral toward Japan, they did not want to create problems over the Indochina question. Nor did they want this to be a cause of friction with France after de Gaulle came to power.[54]

Tsukamoto, the head of the embassy's Saigon office from 1943 to 1945, said after the war that at the time he had advised Tokyo that the ideal was to "maintain the status quo" (in other words, he opposed a military solution). He added that he had stressed that, if that was not possible, when a military solution was imposed all three countries of Indochina should be granted independence, the Japanese embassy should be transformed into a government general, French laws should be retained, and the existing administrative apparatus should be used as far as possible.[55]

Conflicting (or at least differing) opinions among diplomatic officials were also reflected in a series of proposals for the administration of Indochina cabled to the Foreign Ministry from the embassy in the latter half of January 1945.[56] These proposals were basically consistent with the mainstream Foreign Ministry position advocated by Shigemitsu. A document dated January 16 maintained that compliance with "the spirit of the Greater East Asia Declaration" was the basic policy underlying a military solution and that after this was accomplished military rule should be eschewed; instead, "our immediate objective [should be] policy measures to promote the independence of Annam," to be followed by the independence of Cambodia and Laos and promotion of the formation of a "Federation of Vietnam" including all three countries. The document further stressed that diplomatic rather than military authorities should take the initiative with regard to "internal direction" and "guidance" of the federation and of the three Indochinese countries after independence; "advisory departments (consisting of two sections, political and military)" should be "attached" to the Japanese embassy (which was to be located in Saigon) and its subordinate offices, which were to be in Hue, Hanoi, Phnom Penh, and the capital of Laos.[57] However, the document also recommended that "the present [administrative] system in Annam not be changed in the least except in unavoidable circumstances" and that

---

[54] Interview (June 7, 1976, in Tokyo) with Tōru Hagiwara.

[55] Kokumin Gaikō Kai [Society for Citizen Diplomacy], ed., *Indoshina sangoku dokuritsu no hiwa* [The secret story of the independence of the three nations of Indochina] (Tokyo: Kokumin Gaikō Kai, 1955), pp. 56–57.

[56] This series of proposals, sent as telegrams from Tsukamoto to Shigemitsu, includes "Futsuryō Indoshina shori yōkōan" [Draft outline of the disposition of French Indochina], dated January 16; "Etsunan rempō kessei ni kansuru sangoku kyōdō sengen yōkōan" [Draft outline of the joint statement by three countries (Annam, Cambodia, and Laos) on the formation of a Federation of Vietnam], dated January 23; "Nichi-An dōmei jōyakuan" [Japan-Annam alliance draft treaty] and "Nichi-An dōmei jōyaku fuzoku giteisho yōryō" [Main points of the protocol attached to the Japan-Annam alliance treaty], dated January 24. "Dai Tōa sensō."

[57] "Futsuryō Indoshina shori yōkōan." Ibid. There is a slight discrepancy with respect to the handling of Cochinchina (southern Vietnam) in this document and in "Etsunan rempō kessei." While the former clearly states that "Tonkin (northern Vietnam) and Cochinchina are to revert to the jurisdiction of Annam" (on the condition that "consideration is to be given to the timing of implementation so as not to bring about results that would increase the burden of the Empire in the execution of the war"), the latter states that "Cochinchina and regions heretofore under the direct jurisdiction of the Republic of France should be under the direct jurisdiction of the Federation [of Vietnam] until, through the establishment of the federation, their final affiliation is determined."

"efforts [be] made to continue to use the present French personnel; if their cooperation cannot be obtained, they [are to be] replaced with Annamese."[58]

This document, while reflecting the basic mainstream position of the Foreign Ministry, that independence should be granted in line with "the spirit of the Greater East Asia Declaration," also reflected the position of those in the diplomatic corps concerned with maintaining the status quo as far as possible for the sake of relations with France. It can thus be regarded as the product of a compromise between two viewpoints within the diplomatic establishment.[59] The statement that "the independence of Annam [is to be realized by] carrying out a political coup d'état *under the present dynasty* [emphasis added] and setting up an independent government" was probably added to reflect the position of those favoring the status quo.[60] "The present dynasty" here meant the existing emperor, Bao Dai.

The embassy plan, though differing from the Hayashi plan in regard to retaining "the present dynasty," Bao Dai, after independence rather than replacing him with Cuong De, resembled it with respect to two points: not imposing military rule and speedily granting independence.

The mainstream at army central headquarters and in the Southern Army, meanwhile, intended to limit the pretext for overthrowing the French to one of strategic considerations (in this case, the need to strengthen defenses) and to impose the same kind of military rule in Indochina as in the other occupied regions. The problem of independence would be considered separately later, after the situation was under control.[61] This position was intrinsically incompatible with the Hayashi plan. Tsuchihashi, Machijiri's successor as commander of the garrison army (now the Thirty-eighth Army), supported the army mainstream view. Thus, at the level of the local army, Tsuchihashi continued to reflect the position of central headquarters, rejected Hayashi's plan, and ordered the drafting of an alternative proposal.

On January 11 and 12, 1945, an American task force conducted large-scale bombing raids in Indochina and the South China Sea, dealing Japanese naval forces in the area a mortal blow.[62] The Japanese army interpreted this as the prelude to an Allied landing in Indochina. In the event, no Allied landing took place, but the army's reading of the situation led it to conclude that military overthrow of the French regime in Indochina was unavoidable.[63] It also prompted Tsuchihashi to call for total rethinking of the Hayashi plan. Tsuchihashi contended that after forcibly ousting the French he would have to deal with the dangers of a US landing, Chinese attacks from the direction of Yunnan and Guangxi, and a French attempt to recover

---

[58] "Futsuryō Indoshina shori yōkōan." Ibid.

[59] It should be noted that the document was sent under the name of Tsukamoto, an advocate of maintaining the status quo, and thus can be assumed to reflect his own views.

[60] "Futsuryō Indoshina shori yōkōan." Ibid.

[61] See n. 44.

[62] For accounts of the damage caused, see Defense Agency, ed., *Shittan, Meigō sakusen*, pp. 597–98; Army General Staff, "Daihon'ei kimitsu," January 12 and January 16, 1945; "Isan ni den dai 138 gō" [Telegram 138 to Southern Army General Headquarters], dated January 12, 1945, in "Nampōgun (reika butai) kankei dempō tsuzuri" [File of telegrams concerning the Southern Army (subordinate troops)], War History Office, Defense Agency.

[63] Defense Agency, ed., *Shittan, Meigō sakusen*, p. 598; "Tsuchihashi Yūichi chūjō"; interviews with Hayashi.

Indochina. Therefore, he argued, Japan should be involved as little as possible in the administration of Indochina, instead retaining and utilizing the existing apparatus.[64]

The Hayashi plan was also based on the premise that the Japanese army would have its hands full on the military front and thus considered that the local administration in Indochina should be reorganized along "pro-Japanese lines" to encourage cooperation with Japan and facilitate procurement of goods and labor. Tsuchihashi disagreed on the grounds that this kind of reorganization would only create confusion and that in any case the Japanese did not have the time, personnel, or experience needed to reorganize successfully the local administrative organs.

Tsuchihashi ordered Hayashi to scrap his original proposal and come up with a new one.[65] The February 25, 1945, telegram from Ambassador Matsumoto to Shigemitsu stated: "[Hayashi's proposal for Annamese independence] proceeded as far as point-by-point deliberation under the commander, but one day the commander proposed his own plan (a plan to take over the French Indochinese government intact, without destroying the existing organs, because it would not be advisable to be preoccupied by the aftermath of independence); I imagine [the commander's plan] was influenced by the views of [Southern] Army General Headquarters."[66] This telegram portrayed Tsuchihashi's proposal as less his own idea than one influenced by the views of the Southern Army command, but actually Tsuchihashi held the same views as the army central headquarters mainstream and the Southern Army command.

In accordance with Tsuchihashi's order, in mid-January Hayashi drafted a new plan that was presented to the Southern Army General Headquarters as the proposal of the Thirty-eighth Army. On the basis of this, Colonel Sumikatsu Kojima, head of the Southern Army command's Political Affairs Unit, drafted a plan that was laid before the central army authorities when General Takezō Numata, Southern Army chief of staff, was in Tokyo.[67] According to the February 25 cable quoted above, Hayashi had explained developments to the embassy. "In the end, the independence plan was rejected, the Southern Army chief of staff presented the commander's [Tsuchihashi's] plan to army central headquarters, and a decision was made [the decision of February 1, which will be discussed below]. Having worked hard on the [independence] plan, [Hayashi] was very disappointed."[68]

A report from the embassy to the Foreign Ministry dated January 16, 1945, summarized the Thirty-eighth Army draft that was the basis for the Southern Army General Headquarters plan as follows: "To summarize the results of meetings of the ambassador [Matsumoto] and Consul General Tsukamoto with Commander Tsuchihashi and Chief of Staff Kawamura, the main points of the local army plan (it seems that the text has not yet been presented to the central authorities) are as follows: 1. Military rule will be established in the present French territories of Cochinchina [southern Vietnam], Hanoi, Haiphong, and Tourane [Da Nang]. (The commander scrupulously avoids using the term 'military rule' [gunsei], but since the commander himself will be the governor general of all of French Indochina and the

---

[64] "Tsuchihashi Yūichi chūjō"; interviews with Hayashi.

[65] Interviews with Hayashi.

[66] "Dai Tōa senso."

[67] Interviews with Hayashi. According to Hayashi, he personally helped Kojima draw up the plan.

[68] "Dai Tōa senso."

administration of these cities will be in the hands of military personnel, in fact these areas will be under military rule pure and simple.) 2. The form of independence will be assumed in the three countries of Annam [central Vietnam], Cambodia, and Laos, independence being recognized on the basis of agreements with the military commander. 3. The administration of several provinces of Laos will be entrusted to the Kingdom of Annam. 4. A viceroy will be sent from Annam to Tonkin [northern Vietnam]. 5. Advisory offices will be set up in Annam, Cambodia, Laos, and Tonkin and will provide guidance. Personnel will be sent to the advisory offices from the military administration inspectorate (governor general's office). (Ambassadors and other diplomatic delegations will not be sent. The commander says that stationing ambassadors in a war zone is out of the question, citing the de facto lack of authority of the ambassadors in Burma and the Philippines.) 6. As far as possible, the present lower-level Indochina government general personnel and Japanese embassy personnel will be utilized [under military control]."[69]

In other words, a "military administration inspectorate (governor general's office)" was to be set up under the local military commander in place of the old government general, and the existing administrative apparatus was to be retained and utilized as far as possible. Japanese diplomatic organs would be abolished and their personnel used in the military administration and "advisory offices." Military rule would be established in Tonkin and Cochinchina [and in Hanoi and other major cities], while Annam, Cambodia, and Laos would be made independent countries in form (protectorates in actuality). This was quite a different scenario from the one outlined in Hayashi's earlier plan.

The embassy interpreted this situation to mean that the army had decided to withdraw the original "Annamese independence" plan and establish "military rule pure and simple."[70]

Meanwhile, at army central headquarters in Tokyo, sentiment in favor of forcibly removing the French at an early date was hardening. Even before the American bombing raids of January 11 and 12, Major Akira Michitari had been sent to Saigon from Tokyo to act as local liaison with regard to "preparations for operations in connection with the disposition of French Indochina."[71] And in the "Comprehensive Plan of Future Operations" presented by Colonel Ichiji Sugita of the Second Section

---

[69] Ibid. Tsuchihashi's thinking is also referred to in a telegram from Tsukamoto to Shigemitsu dated February 11 and in a telegram from Matsumoto to Shigemitsu dated February 15. The Southern Army General Headquarters' intent is also seen in another February 11 telegram from Tsukamoto to Shigemitsu. See also Defense Agency, ed., *Shittan, Meigō sakusen*, p. 600.

[70] "Dai Tōa sensō." A telegram from Tsukamoto (in Saigon) to Shigemitsu dated January 16 reported that there did not yet seem to be a consensus on the establishment of military rule between the Thirty-eighth Army and the Southern Army General Headquarters. However, in a telegram to Shigemitsu dated January 26, Matsumoto reported from Hanoi that "the voices of those in the local army, navy, and other quarters who hitherto called for Annamese independence and so forth have become muted, while the views of those who anticipate that French Indochina will become a battleground and that to ensure our hold we must, like it or not, speedily settle [the] French Indochina [problem] have gained ground. Apparently this also being reflected at army central headquarters, which has been drawing up plans presupposing the imposition of military rule pure and simple and conveying them to the [Southern Army] General Headquarters and the local army." Ibid.

[71] Army General Staff, "Daihon'ei kimitsu," January 8, 1945.

of the Army General Staff on January 16, after the air raids, the "timely use of force" was spelled out as "policy toward Thailand and French Indochina."[72]

On January 17 an "Agreement Between the Army and Navy Central Headquarters on the Military Disposition and Subsequent Defense of French Indochina" was drawn up.[73] This document dealt mainly with operational measures, including the stipulation that "after the [military] disposition, military rule is to be speedily established." Apparently at this point the military central headquarters took for granted the imposition of military rule.

Major Shigetsugu Tsuneishi was ordered to Saigon. On January 26, after his return, he reported the views of the Thirty-eighth Army: "First, the purpose of the operation is to be solely to strengthen defenses; second, the handling of the issue of Annam's independence after the overthrow of the French regime is to be left to the local army."[74] On the same day the head of the War Plans Unit of the Army General Staff met with the foreign minister. According to the record of that meeting, they agreed on the following points: "1. The military disposition [of French Indochina] should take place as soon as possible, preferably before the three-leader summit meeting [the Yalta Conference]. 2. The pretext for the action will be to strengthen defenses. 3. The issue of Annam's independence will be left to the local leadership, and the Empire will recognize it at the appropriate time. 4. De facto military rule is to be implemented after the military disposition."[75] Doubt remains, however, as to whether the foreign minister really agreed with these conditions. This report was produced by Army General Staff personnel, and it is all too likely that they recorded the interpretation (or the impression they had received from the foreign minister) that suited them. In fact, a telegram dated January 30 from Tōru Hagiwara, director of the Second Political Affairs Section of the Foreign Ministry, to Gorō Morishima, a minister in the embassy in Indochina, reported that Shigemitsu staunchly maintained "a policy of Greater East Asian liberation and of national liberation" and that he was "at present engaged in discussions with military leaders on the basis of this intent."[76]

However, while there is doubt as to whether the foreign minister agreed with the stance of the military, the documents quoted above clearly show the position of the army at the time. First, army central headquarters had decided to bring an end to French rule in Indochina by the use of force in the near future. Second, along with conveying this intent to the local army, central headquarters was working out, with the local army, the details of a post-French system of rule. Third, the central headquarters plan called for limiting the pretext for disarming the French to "strengthening defenses" rather than referring to "the spirit of the Greater East Asia Declaration," imposing military rule "for the time being" after overthrowing the French, and leaving the independence issue to the judgment of the local army. Fourth, the army, having presented its views to the Foreign Ministry, was asking for the ministry's agreement.

---

[72] "Kongo no sōgō sakusen keikaku." Ibid., January 16, 1945.

[73] "Tai Futsuin buryoku shori oyobi shorigo no bōei ni kansuru rikukaigun chūō kyōtei." Defense Agency, ed., *Shittan, Meigō sakusen*, pp. 598–99.

[74] General Staff Headquarters, "Daihon'ei kimitsu," January 26, 1945.

[75] Ibid.

[76] "Dai Tōa senso."

The Supreme War Plans Council, meeting in Tokyo on February 1, arrived at a "Decision Regarding the Disposition of French Indochina to Deal with Changes in the Situation."[77] With this, the use of force to topple the French regime became official state policy. The language of the decision suggests that the position of the army had largely prevailed. First, it was stated clearly that the pretext for the forcible overthrow was to be "the absolute necessity of self-preservation and self-defense [*jison jiei*]." It was also stipulated that after the overthrow Indochina would "for the time being be placed under the administration of the army [*gun no kanri*]" and that "the local army" would take "appropriate" measures "to improve and support the independent status of Annam and the other countries [of Indochina] and to ensure [their] active cooperation with us." As far as the issue of independence was concerned, Japan would "recognize independence," "taking into consideration the general situation," but "the timing, means, and so on, [were] to be determined separately."

There was a considerable gap between the army's and the Foreign Ministry's interpretations of this decision. The army believed that its own position—that the pretext for the military termination of French rule should be based on "the absolute necessity of self-preservation and self-defense"—had been endorsed and that the Foreign Ministry's counterproposal supporting "national liberation" had been rejected.[78] According to Foreign Ministry documents, however, at the February 1 meeting the foreign minister had stressed that since most of the French Indochina army was composed of "native soldiers," it was necessary to "win the hearts of the people by fulfilling their national aspirations." Also, in view of the international situation and concern over the Soviet Union and other neutral countries, "a policy amounting to imposition of military rule carried out in the name simply of self-preservation and self-defense" was not advisable. In fact, the minister had called for "effecting without undue delay, even if not immediately, the independence of Annam and the other countries" of Indochina in accordance with "the spirit of the Greater East Asia Declaration" and considered that this had "been accepted."[79]

The army and the Foreign Ministry also had conflicting interpretations of the stipulation that post-French Indochina "be placed under the administration of the army [*gun no kanri*]." In a telegram dated February 7 to Ambassador Matsumoto explaining the February 1 decision, Shigemitsu noted that "although the initial draft contained the term 'military rule' [*gunsei*], this [term] was deliberately avoided and amended to 'placed under the administration of.'"[80] The Foreign Ministry tended to consider this revision a concession of sorts, an indication that the army had given up the idea of military rule in fact as well as in form. But the army regarded the choice of terminology as simply a rhetorical problem and maintained that what was actually meant was military rule. For example, Tsukamoto, the head of the embassy's Saigon office, reported in a February 9 telegram to Shigemitsu that Lieutenant Colonel Morio Tomura, then a senior staff officer at the Southern Army General Headquarters, had told the embassy that "the military [would] impose military rule in the areas under the direct jurisdiction of the French Indochina government general, but [would] not impose it in the protectorates, thus [would] use the term 'military administration'

---

[77] "Jōsei no henka ni ōzuru Futsuin shori ni kansuru ken." Army General Staff, *Haisen no kiroku*, pp. 227–28; Defense Agency, ed., *Shittan, Meigō sakusen*, pp. 586–87.

[78] Army General Staff, "Daihon'ei kimitsu," February 1, 1945.

[79] Telegram from Shigemitsu to Matsumoto dated February 7. "Dai Tōa sensō."

[80] Ibid.

[gun kanri] rather than 'military rule' *[gunsei]* although it actually signified the imposition of military rule." Also, "essentially the same thing was said" to Thirty-eighth Army Commander Kawamura.[81]

On the question of independence, the Foreign Ministry read a great deal into the phrase "improve and support the independent status." As has just been seen, the ministry believed that it had "been accepted" that Annam's independence was to be effected "without undue delay, even if not immediately." According to army documents, on the other hand, Major General Jōichirō Sanada, head of the War Ministry's Military Affairs Bureau, who was present at the February 1 meeting, responded to the foreign minister's doubts by recommending that "it would be best to leave the independence question to those on the scene." The document added that "the original draft prevailed."[82] In other words, the army understood that with the February 1 decision it had been agreed to entrust the problem of independence to the Thirty-eighth Army.

This conflict in views between the army and the diplomatic establishment carried over to, and was intensified in, Indochina itself. The embassy, in working out the details of the February 1 decision, decried the attitude of the army, and as discord with local army officials deepened, the embassy repeatedly requested the Foreign Ministry to obtain concessions from army central headquarters.[83]

As its reason for opposing the army's plan for military rule, the Foreign Ministry naturally cited the plan's inconsistency with "the spirit of the Greater East Asia Declaration and of national liberation." But there was the added concern that if military rule were imposed, the embassy would be abolished and its staff placed under military jurisdiction as military administrative staff. This fear was expressed most vividly in a February 10 telegram from Tsukamoto to the foreign minister: "Our intention to make the independence of Annam and the other countries the justification [for the coup] having been completely blocked, the disposition of French Indochina has become tantamount to the forcible overthrow of France. All that has been endured so far, all the efforts of the Empire to respect French sovereignty, have been for naught. . . . In particular, that we members of the embassy will bear the brunt by being made military administrative personnel is proof that the Empire's diplomacy is deceptive in both name and fact."[84]

---

[81] Telegram from Tsukamoto to Shigemitsu dated February 9. Ibid.

[82] Army General Staff, "Daihon'ei kimitsu," February 1, 1945. The document reads in part: "In response to the foreign minister's opinion that, in view of relations with the Soviet Union, national liberation would be a better pretext for disarming the French than self-preservation and self-defense, Sanada explained that the pretext of national liberation could easily degenerate into racial war *[jinshusen]* and that since at the moment there were no independence leaders in Annam, nor were any being trained, it was highly likely that independence would be empty of content; therefore, [he maintained,] it would be best to leave the independence question to those on the scene. The original draft prevailed."

[83] For developments during this period, see Shiraishi and Furuta, "Taiheiyō sensō ki," pp. 24ff.

[84] "Dai Tōa sensō." Embassy objections with regard to the problem of the treatment of its personnel are also found in the telegram from Tsukamoto to Shigemitsu dated February 11 and the telegram from Matsumoto to Shigemitsu dated February 14. This problem is also referred to in "Tsuchihashi Yūichi chūjō." Army and navy interference and overstepping of the bounds of their authority vis-à-vis the diplomatic establishment were a constant problem in Japanese diplomacy in the 1930s and 1940s. In fact, Kenkichi Yoshizawa, appointed the first ambassador to French Indochina when Japan established an embassy there in 1941, had been

In short, the conflict between the embassy and the army in Indochina, in addition to being a policy dispute—"the liberation of Greater East Asia" versus strategic needs—was also a conflict over which group would take the initiative in Indochina and over the two groups' positions and spheres of authority.[85]

In the latter half of February the Foreign Ministry sent Takezō Tōkō, director of the General Affairs Section, and the army sent Major Masatsugu Sakakibara, a staff officer in the Southern Affairs Unit of the War Ministry's Military Affairs Bureau, to Indochina to convey concrete instructions on the termination of French rule.[86] But they presented plans reflecting the views of the Foreign Ministry and army central headquarters, respectively, exacerbating confusion and conflict between the embassy and the Thirty-eighth Army.[87]

The embassy was particularly upset by the fact that the Southern Army General Headquarters and the Thirty-eighth Army were making preparations on the assumption that military rule would be established after the French had been ousted. In the February 10 telegram referred to above Tsukamoto wrote: "Since the local army is moving ahead rapidly, as I have reported in earlier telegrams, I urgently request that corrective measures of some kind be taken [in Tokyo]."[88] Around this time the embassy sent a barrage of telegrams to the ministry, requesting that the army head-quarters plan for imposing military rule and for closing the embassy and transferring its staff be checked and that a strong case be made for a plan for rule that reflected the position of the diplomatic establishment.[89] The embassy stressed that in its view, "the status of the embassy and independence [were] indivisible issues" and the "military administration" stipulated in the Supreme War Plans Council's February 1 decision did not signify "military rule."[90]

In other words, the embassy took the position that the policy rationale for granting independence (the argument that "the spirit of the Greater East Asia Declaration and of national liberation" ran counter to the army's plan for military rule and that

concerned about this even before assuming office. Kenkichi Yoshizawa, *Gaikō rokujū nen* [Sixty years of diplomacy] (Tokyo: Jiyū Ajiasha, 1958), pp. 239ff.

[85] On this point, see Shiraishi and Furuta, "Taiheiyō sensō ki," pp. 22ff.

[86] Interviews with Hayashi; telegram from Shigemitsu to Matsumoto dated February 19 and telegram from Matsumoto to Shigemitsu dated February 22, "Dai Tōa sensō."

[87] Thirty-eighth Army Chief of Staff Kawamura told Tōkō: "It is indeed regrettable that, having been sent from Tokyo, you are still unable to bring us a unified plan." Telegram from Matsumoto to Shigemitsu dated February 22. Ibid.

[88] Telegram from Tsukamoto to Shigemitsu dated February 10. Ibid.

[89] Telegram from Tsukamoto to Shigemitsu dated February 10, third telegram from Tsukamoto to Shigemitsu dated February 11, telegram from Matsumoto to Shigemitsu dated February 15, and the first two telegrams from Matsumoto to Shigemitsu dated February 23. Ibid. An early, and typical, telegram expressing the point of view of the embassy at this time is one sent on January 16 by Matsumoto. It stated that "it is our earnest hope that a plan will speedily be adopted that will not be bound by the narrow perspective of operational needs but will, in terms of basic Imperial policy and the overall direction of the war, serve both *justice and the benefit of* [post-French] *government*" (emphasis added) and urged that everything possible be done to see that the embassy proposals submitted in January (see n. 56) were adopted by the cabinet. This telegram expressed clearly the two levels on which the embassy opposed military rule: "justice" and "the benefit of [post-French] government."

[90] Telegram from Matsumoto to Shigemitsu dated February 23. Ibid. It was actually written by Tōkō, who was in Indochina on business, and was addressed to Yutaka Ishizawa, head of the Southern Affairs Bureau of the Greater East Asia Ministry, to explain the embassy's position.

independence should be granted to the three Indochinese nations) could not be separated from the practical issues of the continued existence of the embassy and the treatment of its staff. If the three countries of Indochina were granted independence, diplomatic channels would have to be maintained to promote relations with these independent countries; if diplomatic agencies were not placed in the three countries, this would mean that they were not considered truly independent countries.

The Foreign Ministry, however, considered the question of independence to be separate from that of the status of the embassy and the treatment of its staff. While the ministry had sought concessions from the army on the issue of independence, its policy in regard to the status of the embassy and its staff was to concede to the army. In February 18 and 19 telegrams to the embassy, the ministry expressed the opinion that since the main point was to implement the independence policy, the embassy staff should cooperate with the army if the army so wished, and indicated that if the army intended to carry out "a basic policy of independence," diplomatic officials should make concessions on the issue of the embassy, on the principle that "overall responsibility" should rest with the military.[91]

What happened was that a kind of bargaining took place in Tokyo between the Foreign Ministry and the army. On the issue of independence, the army made concessions to the Foreign Ministry, which insisted on immediate independence because of diplomatic concerns involving the Soviet Union. The Foreign Ministry, in turn, made concessions on the issue of the status of its embassy in Indochina, agreeing not to send full ambassadors to the three Indochinese countries after independence and to allow its diplomatic personnel to be utilized "in their present status" by the army.[92]

On February 26 the Supreme War Plans Council reached a decision on the question of independence, embodied in "Outline of the Political Disposition of Indochina."[93] This document stated that with the disarming of the French, "Annam and the other countries [of Indochina] are to be made to abrogate spontaneously their treaties of protection with France to clarify the fact that independence has been restored." However, "the actual restoration of independence is to take place in a context that does not jeopardize [military] operations." Moreover, "the timing, means, and so on, of recognition of the independence of Annam and the other countries are to be determined separately" in Tokyo—an indication that the way was being left open for further negotiations between the Foreign Ministry and the army. It was also stipulated that "the government institutions peculiar to these countries are to be respected, and, under our internal leadership, appropriate affairs are to be entrusted to them" and that "in improving and supporting the independent status of Annam and the other countries, we are to secure the active cooperation of the natives and make a special effort to raise national consciousness."

However, the administrative extent of "Annam and the other countries" was limited to the existing protectorates: "In the regions under the direct jurisdiction of

---

[91] Telegrams from Shigemitsu to Matsumoto dated February 18 and February 19. Ibid. In the February 19 telegram Shigemitsu emphasized that he was still trying to win over the military on the issue of independence.

[92] The circumstances leading up to the agreement in Tokyo between the diplomats and the army is conveyed in a telegram from Shigemitsu to Matsumoto dated February 24. Ibid. See also Shiraishi and Furuta, "Taiheiyō sensō ki," pp. 24–26.

[93] "Indoshina seimu shori yōkō." Army General Staff, *Haisen no kiroku*, pp. 232–34; Defense Agency, ed., *Shittan, Meigō sakusen*, pp. 589–90.

France, military rule [*gunsei*] will be imposed. But this should not be made public; ostensibly, administrative control [*gyōsei no kanri*] is being entrusted temporarily to the Japanese army. . . . Matters affecting the entire region of Indochina will be entrusted to us for the time being." In fact, all the authority of the French Indochina government general would for the time being be placed under the control of the Japanese army (de facto military rule). And although there would be personnel changes in the top echelons of the government general, "its administrative machinery is to be utilized," which meant that the systems of the government general would remain basically intact.

Except for the stipulation that the three Indochinese countries were to be granted independence "speedily," the February 26 decision differed little from the plan drawn up by the Southern Army General headquarters on the basis of the Thirty-eighth Army's draft and presented to army central headquarters.[94] At least, that was the understanding of the local army command. As far as the army was concerned, it had given up the form but retained the substance. The Foreign Ministry, meanwhile, had the satisfaction of obtaining a concession from the army on the point of "speedily" granting independence, if nothing else. But it had had to concede to the army on such substantive issues as the actual implementation of independence and the handling of the embassy. Given the relative strengths of the Foreign Ministry and the army at the time, however, the diplomats were probably lucky to gain even that much.

On March 1 the directors general of the Foreign Ministry's Political Affairs Bureau, the Greater East Asia Ministry's General Affairs Bureau, and the War Ministry's Military Affairs Bureau reached an understanding on the handling of embassy staff. It was decided that except for consular staff, all embassy personnel would be "utilized by the army in their present status as civilian employees."[95] The stipulation that embassy personnel would retain their current status was a concession of sorts to the Foreign Ministry. Here was another case of bargaining in which the Foreign Ministry was left with only the form while the army got the substance.

The March 1 agreement stipulated a number of other matters. Consulates were to perform tasks for the army in addition to their normal functions. Documents and telegrams between the Foreign Ministry and the ambassador or consul general, except those dealing with accounting and personnel matters, were to be censored and approved by the army. And the ambassador, in his capacity as a civilian employee of the army, was to advise the military commander on administrative matters.[96] (However, Ambassador Matsumoto announced his resignation before the French were overthrown and returned to Japan after the March 9 coup.)

How did the embassy feel about the concessions that the Foreign Ministry was making to the army? The ministry repeatedly advised and instructed the embassy to do what it could in the circumstances to give substance to the independence of the three Indochinese countries.[97] Perhaps, having given in to the army on the status of the embassy and its staff, the ministry wanted to ensure that on the issue of independence, at least, it would gain something tangible in line with its own position. In any

---

[94] See pp. 125–26, n. 69.

[95] Second telegram from Shigemitsu to Matsumoto dated March 1. "Dai Tōa sensō."

[96] Three telegrams from Shigemitsu to Matsumoto dated March 1. Ibid.

[97] Telegrams from Shigemitsu to Matsumoto dated February 18 and February 19. Ibid.

case, the ministry considered the issue of independence to be distinct from—and certainly more important than—that of the embassy staff.

The embassy's attitude was just the opposite. Despite repeated admonishment from the ministry, it made only halfhearted efforts to work for meaningful independence. Most of its energy went into the struggle over conditions pertaining to the treatment of embassy personnel. For example, it made the extravagant proposal that Commander Tsuchihashi concurrently assume ambassadorial office, in the hope that a diplomatic presence could survive under the protection of a commander-cum-ambassador. If the embassy had to be closed down, at least a minister should be retained; if not a minister, then at least a consul. It also held that if diplomatic personnel had to be diverted to military administration, they should be limited to an advisory role; it was not diplomatically advisable for embassy personnel to fill posts corresponding to bureau head or regional governor in the defunct government general.[98] When it looked as though the fight for favorable conditions was going to fail, embassy officials individually announced their intention of resigning.[99]

Finally, there were embassy proposals that the coup itself be called off or at least postponed. After receiving a telegram from the Foreign Ministry on February 24 relating that the ministry and army central headquarters were near agreement,[100] the embassy cabled the ministry on February 26 requesting that military action against the French be postponed.[101] In other words, if the embassy could not get what it wanted, it would be better not to carry out the coup at all and to maintain the status quo. It is clear that the embassy considered treatment of its personnel to be a critical, nonnegotiable issue. At around the same time, Lieutenant Colonel Hayashi also took the position that the coup should be called off, telling the embassy that if his plan for the independence of Annam were not to be used, it would be better to maintain the status quo.[102]

III. Establishment of the Bao Dai-Tran Trong Kim Government

As we have seen, the Thirty-eighth Army and the Southern Army General Headquarters interpreted the February 1 decision to mean that their plan for disarming the French had been accepted by the central authorities in Tokyo, and they began concrete preparations on the assumption of a military administration, the de facto dismantling of the embassy and the utilization of its staff by the army, and deferral of the question of independence, which was to be considered as a separate issue.[103]

---

[98] Telegrams from Matsumoto to Shigemitsu dated February 15 (first telegram), February 23, and February 28. Ibid.

[99] Telegrams from Matsumoto to Shigemitsu dated February 14, February 15 (first and second telegrams), and February 28. Ibid.

[100] Telegram from Shigemitsu to Matsumoto dated February 24. Ibid.

[101] Telegram from Matsumoto to Shigemitsu dated February 26. Ibid. The ostensible reason was that the danger of a US landing had receded.

[102] Telegram from Matsumoto to Shigemitsu dated February 25, ibid.; interviews with Hayashi. The grounds for Hayashi's argument that it was not necessary to disarm the French were also that the danger of a US landing had lessened.

[103] The opinion of Lieutenant Colonel Morio Tomura, a senior staff officer in the Operations Section of the Southern Army General Headquarters, was reported in telegrams from Tsukamoto to Shigemitsu dated February 9, 10, and 11, while the opinion of Thirty-eighth Army Commander Tsuchihashi was conveyed in a telegram from Matsumoto to Shigemitsu dated February 15. Ibid.

Thirty-eighth Army Commander Tsuchihashi told Ambassador Matsumoto on February 13 that he had "no intention of abolishing the present status of Annam, Cambodia, and the other countries" of Indochina and "absolutely no intention of preparing them for future complete independence." He also stated that there was "no prospect whatsoever of independence for Annam until there is an improvement in the war situation."[104] The embassy observed that for the Southern Army command, as well, "the issue of independence for Annam and the other countries is only something included [in the February 1 decision]; there is no intention of implementing it. It will be deferred on the grounds that the time is not right."[105] Indeed, the Thirty-eighth Army and the Southern Army command gave priority to the restoration of order and the establishment of a defense system, and considered the time for independence to be "several months away."[106]

Army central headquarters took the same position. In a telegram sent to the chiefs of staff of the Southern Army and the Thirty-eighth Army on February 23, the assistant chief of the General Staff and the Army vice-minister added the following explanation of the February 1 decision's call for "appropriate [measures] in the local army to improve and support the independent status of Annam and the other countries": "Central headquarters will respond to the local army's implementation [of the February 1 decision] by utilizing [these measures] to make clear to foreign countries, particularly the Soviet Union, the nonaggressive nature of this exercise of force (we will declare that, having thrown off the yoke of French Indochina, the treaties of protection concluded between French Indochina and Annam and the other countries have died a natural death, and therefore we do not intend to force through specific independence measures in any particular hurry)."[107] What is important here is the fact that this instruction from army central headquarters was issued shortly before formal approval of "Outline of the Political Disposition of Indochina," whose content would already have been hammered out by the authorities concerned.[108]

The Southern Army command and the Thirty-eighth Army, having received the February 26 summary, were prepared to abide by the policy of granting independence to the three Indochinese countries immediately after disarming the French, but only because they understood that "the central authorities want the independence of Annam and the other countries declared simultaneously with the forcible removal [of the French] out of consideration for relations with the Soviet Union and foreign relations in general."[109] In other words, independence was thought of as a pretext, a mere expedient necessitated by relations with the Soviet Union.

---

[104] Telegram from Matsumoto to Shigemitsu dated February 15. Ibid.

[105] Telegram from Tsukamoto to Shigemitsu dated February 10. Ibid.

[106] Statement of Major Masatsugu Sakakibara to Tōkō (both visiting Indochina from Tokyo), reported in a telegram from Matsumoto to Shigemitsu dated February 22. Ibid.

[107] This telegram is included in "Dai Tōa sensō," though how the Foreign Ministry obtained this army communication is unknown. The Foreign Ministry notified Matsumoto of its content in a telegram dated February 27.

[108] Shigemitsu reported to Matsumoto in a telegram dated February 24 that "while there [might] be some changes in the wording of the 'Political Guidance Summary' [sic] as a result of discussion by the officials responsible," the document was ready to be confirmed at the Supreme War Plans Council meeting on February 26. "Dai Tōa sensō."

[109] Report in a telegram from Matsumoto to Shigemitsu dated March 3 on a liaison meeting between central and local representative at the Southern Army General Headquarters. Ibid.

This policy left no room for working out the kind of "pro-Japanese reorganization of the Annam government" outlined in the Hayashi plan. And involving Cuong De, who was in Japan, was out of the question. Major General Sanada, who attended the February 1 meeting of the Supreme War Plans Council, said at the time that "at the moment there were no independence leaders in Annam, nor were any being trained"[110]—a statement indicative of the attitude of army central headquarters. And on February 20 Thirty-eighth Army Commander Tsuchihashi stated to Consul General Tsukamoto: "For the time being, entry [to Vietnam] will not be granted to native politicians in exile in Japan."[111]

Naturally, this does not mean that no one in Tokyo thought of using Cuong De in Vietnam after the French were overthrown. According to Tsuchihashi's postwar recollections, a staff officer was sent from Tokyo about January 1945 to request that Cuong De be admitted in anticipation of the post-French period. Asked by Thirty-eighth Army Chief of Staff Kawamura for his opinion, Tsuchihashi replied, "It would be best to refuse." An envoy from Tokyo visited again at the end of February and reported to Tsuchihashi that Cuong De would be sent to Saigon. Tsuchihashi responded, "Send him, but understand that as soon as he arrives at Saigon airport I'll pack him off to Poulo Condore prison."[112] Tsuchihashi recalls that he gave that "crazy answer" because he felt that "Tokyo and the local [Southern Army] general headquarters and [Thirty-eighth Army] headquarters were in cahoots and plotting to make Conde [*sic*] emperor in place of Bao Dai," adding that "it was my policy not to interfere in any way in the internal affairs of a country that was even nominally independent as long as it cooperated actively with the army's operational preparations."[113] These remarks, written long after the fact, tend to be self-serving. Of course, Tsuchihashi may well have believed the above, but the main reason for rejecting Cuong De lay in the resolve of army central headquarters, the Southern Army General Headquarters, and Tsuchihashi himself to keep the independence of Annam a pretext and to avoid any systematic reorganization of the government.

Meanwhile, on March 9 the Foreign Ministry advised Ambassador Matsumoto that "in the event of the military disposition of French Indochina, utilization of the Annamese independence activists in Tokyo is not being considered by the local army at the moment, but since they have high hopes of undertaking activities, guidance is necessary; after you have consulted with the army, I would like you to reply by cable as soon as possible with your views on how those in Tokyo (especially Conde [*sic*]) should be handled."[114] Thus it can be seen that some people within the Foreign Ministry were also sympathetic to Cuong De. No doubt there were people in the local army and the embassy who supported him, as well. And private individuals, such as Mitsuhiro Matsushita and Kiyoshi Komatsu, did all they could to build him up. But

---

[110] See n. 82 for the context of this statement.

[111] Telegram from Tsukamoto to Shigemitsu dated February 11. Ibid.

[112] "Tsuchihashi Yūichi chūjō."

[113] Ibid.

[114] "Dai Tōa sensō."

in the end the diplomatic and military mainstream in both Tokyo and Indochina opted to retain Bao Dai.[115]

The Japanese army carried out a coup d'état on the night of March 9 in 1945 and disarmed the French Indochina army. After enjoying two days of hunting at Quang Tri, Bao Dai had returned by automobile to Hue with the empress, Nam Phuong. They were taken into custody by security personnel of the Japanese army unit sent to the Hue district (the 890th Battalion of the Independent Infantry) and their persons entrusted to Captain Noboru Kaneko of the Yasu Corps.[116] The Yasu Corps, composed mainly of graduates of Nakano Gakkō, a school for intelligence officers, had been organized to serve as an intelligence and propaganda unit directly under the Southern Army General Headquarters especially for the purpose of the military disposition of French Indochina.[117]

The next morning Minister Masayuki Yokoyama, who had been sent to Hue as supreme adviser to the Kingdom of Annam, went to the palace with Consul General Akira Konagaya and Consul Taizō Watanabe, who had also been specially sent to Hue, and met with Bao Dai.[118] Bao Dai knew that Japan supported Cuong De and naturally thought that he himself was to be deposed. He was unable to hide his surprise when he heard what Yokoyama had to say.[119]

Bao Dai accepted the Japanese offer. On March 11 he announced the abrogation of the 1884 treaty of protection with France and declared Vietnam's independence.[120] On March 17, in addition to announcing that *dan vi quy* (the most precious thing is the people) was to be the new national policy, he issued a decree calling for men of talent to cooperate with Japan in building Greater East Asia and laying the

---

[115] Interviews (September 8, 1975, and May 24, 1976, in Tokyo) with Akira Konagaya, consul general in Hanoi from 1942 to 1945; interview (June 11, 1976, in Tokyo) with Fujio Minoda, consul general in Saigon and Hanoi from June 1940 to August 1945; interview (February 13, 1980) with Jirō Takase, who was on the staff of the Foreign Ministry's Research Division 1940–1941. Shiraishi, ed., "Intabyū kiroku C." In addition, interviews with Kadomatsu and Hayashi; interviews (December 3 and 27, 1975, in Tokyo) with Toyofumi Tominaga, who worked as a foreign correspondent in Hanoi (September 1940 and May–July 1941) and in Saigon (November 1941–March 1945), then worked for Masayuki Yokoyama, supreme adviser to the Kingdom of Amman, in the Propaganda Bureau in Hue (March–August 1945).

[116] Interview (June 29, 1976, in Tokyo) with Noboru Kaneko, commander of the Yasu Corps in Hue; Defense Agency, ed., *Shittan, Meigō sakusen*, pp. 635–36; Maruyama, *Ushinawaretaru kiroku*, pp. 306–8; Tominaga, "Chinurareshi kūdetā," pp. 155–56; Bao Dai, *Le Dragon d'Annam* (Paris: Plon, 1980), pp. 99–101. Bao Dai has this taking place on the night of March 10, but it should be the night of March 9 or the morning of March 10. He seems to be one day off in his account of events at this time.

[117] Interview with Kaneko; interview (July 1976 in Tsurumi) with Shigemi Shinohara, a major and commander of the Yasu Corps in Hanoi; interviews with a number of Japanese conscripted into the Yasu Corps locally whose names cannot be divulged; Defense Agency, ed., *Shittan, Meigō sakusen*, p. 620.

[118] Interviews with Konagaya; interview (November 29, 1979, in Tokyo) with Seiji Urabe, a consul in Hue.

[119] Bao Dai, *Le Dragon*, pp. 101–3; Tominaga, "Chinurareshi kūdetā," p. 156.

[120] English translation of a monitored radio broadcast of the declaration of independence. US Office of Strategic Services, *Programs of Japan in Indochina* (Honolulu: Office of Strategic Services, 1945), p. 79; Defense Agency, ed., *Shittan, Meigō sakusen*, p. 645; Bao Dai, *Le Dragon*, p. 104. Bao Dai puts this on March 12.

foundations of the newly independent state.[121] People like Tran Van Chuong,[122] who had been pro-Japanese all along, and a group of young intellectuals including Hoang Xuan Han, Phan Anh, and Vu Van Hien received invitations from the emperor[123] and went to Hue.[124]

The problem was how to handle Ngo Dinh Diem. Bao Dai knew that Diem was then in Saigon and had long been close to the Japanese authorities. He considered Diem indispensable to smooth relations between the Vietnamese government and the Japanese occupiers.[125] Through Yokoyama, he asked the military authorities in Saigon to contact Diem,[126] but the authorities deliberately failed to relay the message. The army considered the disarming of the French to be solely an operational matter, so although the authorities recognized the need to satisfy to some extent "the national sentiment of the Annamese," they feared that recognition of "complete" independence would hinder military operations. Thus they allowed Bao Dai to stay on as emperor and felt "the need to limit [Annam] to a puppet regime" so that it would not go too far along "the road of independence and self-reliance." They rejected Diem as prime minister because they felt that, being a "nationalist," he would probably form an "independent government."[127]

Bao Dai awaited Diem's reply in vain. Bao Dai knew that the Japanese army, through its intelligence network, must know Diem's whereabouts, and thus judged that Diem must be out of favor with the military authorities.[128] Bao Dai then turned to Tran Trong Kim.[129] As we have already seen, Kim had been taken into protective custody by the Japanese army in the fall of 1943 and sent first to Singapore, then to Bangkok. Born in 1883, he was already over sixty years of age. The Japanese army agreed with this choice, no doubt in the belief that it would be easy to manipulate Kim.[130]

---

[121] Nguyen Ky Nam, *Hoi Ky, 1925–1964* (Saigon: Giap Thin, 1964), p. 169.

[122] It was Konagaya who delivered Bao Dai's invitation to Chuong in Hanoi. Interviews with Konagaya.

[123] Quang Huy, "Si Khi Ai Chau"; interview (November 26, 1976, in Paris) with Hoang Xuan Han. He said that he arrived in Hue on April 1.

[124] Apparently Bao Dai sent invitations to twenty or so people and asked Yokoyama to deliver them. All except Diem were assembled in Hue by the army. Defense Agency, ed., *Shittan, Meigō sakusen*, p. 646.

[125] Bao Dai, *Le Dragon*, p. 106.

[126] Ibid.; interviews with Hayashi and Tominaga.

[127] Tominaga, who visited Saigon in July 1945, says that Hayashi told him this (interviews with Tominaga). Hayashi's own explanation lacks consistency and concreteness (interviews with Hayashi). In view of the extremely clear and specific nature of his testimony on other points, his vagueness on this point is probably due to his wish to avoid criticizing his superiors and colleagues. According to Kim's memoirs, when the Japanese army took him to Saigon on March 30, Thirty-eighth Army Commander Kawamura showed him a list of the people Bao Dai had invited to form a cabinet. Kim, who had arrived in Vietnam only that day, was on the list, as well as Hoang Xuan Han and others, but Diem's name was missing. Kim, *Mot Con Gio Bui*, pp. 42–43. Since it is certain that Bao Dai did extend an invitation to Diem, Japanese army officials must have deliberately removed his name.

[128] Bao Dai, *Le Dragon*, p. 106.

[129] Ibid.

[130] Interviews with Tominaga.

Captain Michio Kuga of the army's Saigon liaison office flew to Bangkok to bring back Kim, who touched down at Saigon airport on March 30. Kim met with Lieutenant Colonel Hayashi and Major General Kawamura and, after spending three days at the home of Mitsuhiro Matsushita, headed for Hue.[131] During the three days he spent in Saigon, Kim also met with Diem at Matsushita's home. It was the first time the two had met. As Kim later recalled, Diem did not know at the time that Bao Dai was in the process of inviting people to form a cabinet.[132]

Kim arrived in Hue on April 5 and had an audience with Bao Dai two days later. This was their first meeting. Kim firmly refused to form a cabinet, citing his age and his lack of any party organization or political experience (precisely the reasons he was acceptable to the Japanese military) and suggested that Diem be called upon instead.[133] After all, Kim had been brought back from Bangkok without knowing why, and had only learned what was happening from the military authorities in Saigon; in addition, he was reluctant to serve under Bao Dai.[134]

Bao Dai learned from Kim that Diem did not know the emperor had summoned him and once again asked the Japanese to contact Diem.[135] The Japanese authorities in Saigon ordered Hayashi to contact Diem, who was staying in Vinh Long, where his older brother was bishop. Hayashi took advantage of a visit by Diem to Saigon to relay Bao Dai's message, but Diem told Hayashi that he did not intend to accept the emperor's invitation.[136] It would be one thing if Cuong De returned to Vietnam and took over from Bao Dai, but Diem too had no intention of leading a government under Bao Dai. Diem thoroughly disliked Bao Dai and reportedly had spread the rumor among the Japanese that he was not really the son of Emperor Khai Dinh.[137]

The cool attitude of the Japanese military authorities can also be considered a factor that made Diem less than enthusiastic. He was particularly angered that Hayashi, with whom he had established close personal ties when in the custody of the Japanese army in Saigon, had not notified him in advance of the coup.[138] The fact that at the most crucial time, just before and after the coup, Hayashi, who was supposed to have been in charge of political affairs, was not in Saigon but was traveling in central and northern Vietnam on an irrelevant assignment struck Diem as strange.[139] Shortly after Hayashi returned to Saigon, around March 27, Diem visited him. Hayashi strongly advised Diem not to become involved in politics under the present circumstances.[140]

Hayashi's attitude carried considerable weight with Diem, for Hayashi was the central figure who had promoted the concept of a Cuong De-Ngo Dinh Diem govern-

---

[131] Interviews with Kuga and Hayashi; Kim, *Mot Con Gio Bui*, pp. 41–46.

[132] Kim, *Mot Con Gio Bui*, pp. 44–45.

[133] Ibid., pp. 48–52.

[134] Interviews with Hayashi.

[135] Kim, *Mot Con Gio Bui*, pp. 48–52.

[136] Interviews with Hayashi.

[137] Ibid.; interviews with Tominaga. Some said that Diem was in love with Empress Nam Phuong and therefore hated Bao Dai. But the major reason probably had to do with events in the 1930s, when Diem was appointed home minister under Bao Dai but then was forced to relinquish power.

[138] Interviews with Hayashi.

[139] Ibid.

[140] Ibid.

ment. That Hayashi, who had acted as a bridge between the Japanese military authorities and Diem, had been out of Saigon on the day of the coup bespoke a change in Hayashi's role in the military. Diem apparently inferred a change in the Japanese military authorities' intent from Hayashi's attitude toward him around the time of the coup. Another reason for declining Bao Dai's invitation was Diem's judgment that, with the war situation rapidly worsening for the Japanese, it would not be wise to be in charge of a government under Japanese occupation.

Diem responded to Hayashi's request by writing a long, abstruse letter of explanation to the emperor in French. Hayashi understood the letter to have said that the situation in Vietnam was not favorable to Diem; if he formed a cabinet, the Japanese would believe that it would accept all their demands, while the Vietnamese would think that it would accept all their demands to the Japanese, and both sides would be unhappy. On the grounds that such an explanation would lead to "misunderstanding," Diem was made to write another letter stating simply that he was declining the emperor's invitation for reasons of health.[141] Yokoyama also conveyed to Kim the message that Diem could not return to Hue because of illness.[142] Kim accepted Bao Dai's second request to form a cabinet. The Kim government came into being on April 17, one month and eight days after the coup d'état executed by the Japanese army.[143]

CONCLUSION

Some Vietnamese political parties, religious groups, politicians, and intellectuals forged links with the Japanese using the political symbol of Cuong De. But Ngo Dinh Diem, who in 1944 was placed under the protection of the Japanese military authorities in Saigon (particularly Hayashi, who was in charge of political affairs) occupied a special place. Diem, in collaboration with Nguyen Xuan Chu, Vu Dinh Dy, and other members of the Viet Nam Ai Quoc Dang in Hanoi, promoted Cuong De and even had hopes of establishing a government that would be approved by the local Japanese military authorities. But their plans were doomed by opposition in the army mainstream in early 1945, when the military coup against the French finally approached execution. Hayashi's plan, which had formed the heart of the concept of a government led by Diem and his allies, rejected military rule and called for granting immediate independence to the three countries of Indochina and for reorganizing the new governments, particularly that of Vietnam, along pro-Japanese lines. This, in fact, is why the plan failed in the end to win the support of the army mainstream.

The diplomatic establishment also rejected military rule, taking a position close to that of the Hayashi plan with respect to support for independence. But some diplomatic officials differed; whereas one school of thought supported the independence movement insofar as this accorded with the tenets of the Greater East Asia Declaration, another favored maintaining the status quo in French Indochina out of concern for relations with France. While some support for Cuong De and Diem persisted, the diplomatic establishment as a whole, as seen in the series of proposals issued by the embassy at the beginning of 1945, had to settle for retention of "the present dynasty," that is, Bao Dai.

---

[141] Ibid.

[142] Kim, *Mot Con Gio Bui*, p. 50.

[143] Ibid., pp. 51–53; Bao Dai, *Le Dragon*, p. 107.

Furthermore, there were two aspects to the diplomats' support for independence. One had to do with maintaining a semblance of consistency in national policy; the other had to do with bureaucratic sectionalism and involved concrete issues of status and scope of authority. In terms of the latter aspect, the diplomats' support for independence was support by default: they were opposed to military rule because it was in conflict with their position on the issue of survival of the embassy and treatment of its staff. This gave rise to a tendency to be willing to compromise in other areas if they were thereby able to protect their diplomatic territory. (One example was the argument for retaining Bao Dai and the government general under the diplomatic authorities' "internal direction"—a plan that presupposed an ambassador and embassy. Another was the inverted logic that if the alternative were imposing military rule and abolishing the embassy, it would be better to maintain the status quo, in other words, not overthrow the French.)

Conversely, when the embassy realized that, as a result of bargaining in Tokyo, it would be subordinated to the military in exchange for military concessions on the issue of granting immediate, if nominal, independence, it lost its taste for the fight to make independence as meaningful as possible under the circumstances (something the Foreign Ministry repeatedly advised). Instead it put all its energy into the struggle over the issue of the treatment of embassy personnel. And when it looked as if that struggle would fail, individuals began announcing their resignations. As we have seen, the embassy finally proposed postponing or even canceling the coup. Under a wartime setup, in which the word of the military had absolute priority, resistance to the military, particularly on the part of the officials in Indochina who were pushed to the wall on the issue of abolishing the embassy, was no longer a matter of lofty ideological debate or of policy debate on the meaning of independence for the three Indochinese countries. The embassy's last bastion fell when the embassy completely lost its autonomy and was placed under the jurisdiction of the military.

Thus the Hayashi plan faced the rejection of central army headquarters, the Southern Army General Headquarters, and the commander of the local army. The diplomats, meanwhile, particularly those attached to the embassy, who had originally wanted to retain Bao Dai, were now in no position to engage in leisurely discussion of the meaning of independence since their own position had been undermined. From the perspective of Japan's civilian and military bureaucracies as they were at the time, Hayashi's plan for governing Indochina bordered on the heretical.[144]

Ngo Dinh Diem and others, unfortunately, came to be linked with this plan. Or perhaps just the opposite could be said: they became significant players on Vietnam's political stage for the first time, in the final stage of the Pacific War, precisely because they were linked to the Hayashi plan. In any case, their potential for political activity shared the same fate as that plan.

Of course, anyone observing all this from the outside, unaware of the conflicts among Japanese officials, would have found the rise and fall of certain Vietnamese political figures enigmatic. Arriving in Saigon from exile in Bangkok, Tran Trong Kim thought it strange that there was no sign that Ngo Dinh Diem and Nguyen Xuan

---

[144] However, as pointed out in n. 39, in Hayashi's plan independence was first and foremost an expedient to enable the Japanese army to conduct operations more smoothly. At base, his thinking was the same as that of the army mainstream at the time.

Chu were going to have any role in the post-French political scene in Vietnam. They had planned to form a government under Cuong De, and this had had the support of at least some Japanese. They also had their own party organizations. Why then, now that their hour had arrived, were they making no move? Kim writes in his memoirs that Diem withdrew to Vinh Long and Chu hastily returned to Hanoi from Saigon.[145]

Tran Trong Kim was a second card, picked after the first had been discarded. His background made him acceptable to both Bao Dai and the Japanese military authorities. He was a "sincere patriot" but had no history of activity in party politics. A pro-Japanese intellectual, he had been protected by the Japanese army. He also had a reputation as a scholar of Vietnamese history and culture and had a quiet, dignified bearing. In short, he possessed the right qualities for both a puppet and a "nationalist."

Given the circumstances that led to its birth, the Kim cabinet could not have been made up of pro-Japanese politicians. The establishment of such a cabinet had been rejected by the army mainstream and was of no interest to the diplomats (at least not in their official capacity). Thus, the cabinet formed on the 17th of April 1945 was composed of technocrats and intellectuals and, with only one exception, included no pro-Japanese politicians.[146]

This paper was originally published under the title "Chan Chon Kimu naikaku setsuritsu (1945 nen 4 gatsu) no haikei: Nihon tōkyoku no tai Betonamu tōchi kōsō o chūshin to shite" [The background to the formation of the Tran Trong Kim cabinet (April 1945): The Japanese authorities' plans for governing Vietnam], in Kenji Tsuchiya and Takashi Shiraishi, eds., *Tōnan Ajia no seiji bunka* [Politics and culture in Southeast Asia] (Tokyo: Tokyo Daigaku Shuppankai, 1984), pp. 33-69.

---

[145] Kim, *Mot Con Gio Bui,* pp. 42–46.

[146] The exception was Tran Van Chuong, who became foreign minister. Interview with Han.

5

THE INDOCHINA COMMUNIST PARTY'S DIVISION INTO THREE PARTIES: VIETNAMESE COMMUNIST POLICY TOWARD CAMBODIA AND LAOS, 1948–1951

Motoo Furuta

INTRODUCTION

The recent strife in Indochina has heightened global interest in Vietnamese communist policy toward Cambodia and Laos, but very little study has been made of the two decades of the Indochina Communist Party's existence (1930–1951), a period that needs to be explored for an adequate historical analysis. Only recently have studies of this period been published in the West,[1] and many points have yet to be clarified. Recent studies, including an earlier paper of mine,[2] summarize the development of Vietnamese communist policy toward Cambodia and Laos more or less as follows.

The Vietnamese Communist Party, formed in February 1930, changed its name to the Indochina Communist Party in October of the same year. This name change was made at the behest of the Comintern rather than on the initiative of the Vietnamese communists themselves.[3] In the 1930s, in line with a policy emphasizing class struggle, the ICP proclaimed its intention of forming an Indochinese Soviet Union, but though the organization encompassed Cambodia and Laos, the Vietnamese communists were not very successful in attracting Cambodians and Laotians to their cause, their influence being limited to people of Vietnamese descent.

The situation changed when the ICP shifted its emphasis to a nationalistic perspective. By 1941 the party had laid the groundwork for a "revolution for national

---

[1] Such studies include Pierre Rousset, *Communisme et Nationalisme Vietnamien* (Paris: Édition Galilée, 1978); Gareth Porter, "Vietnamese Policy and the Indochinese Crisis," in *The Third Indochina Conflict*, ed. David W. P. Elliott (Boulder, Col.: Westview Press, 1981), and "Vietnamese Communism and Cambodia" (unpublished MS, 1981); Ben Kiernan, "Origins of Khmer Communism," in *Southeast Asian Affairs 1981*, ed. Institute of Southeast Asian Studies (Singapore: Institute of Southeast Asian Studies, 1982).

[2] Motoo Furuta, "Indoshina kyōsantō ni okeru chiiki saihensei no kokoromi" [Regional restructuring within the Indochina Communist Party], *Ajia kenkyū* [Asian studies] 26, no. 4 (January 1980).

[3] This does not mean that we can ignore the Vietnamese people's endeavor, in the 1910s and 1920s, to arrive at a new interpretation of the concept of Indochina. This issue is discussed in Furuta, "Indoshina kyōsantō."

liberation" and developed the concept of a Democratic Republic of Vietnam as a steppingstone to the eventual formation of an Indochinese Soviet Union. The idea of a Democratic Republic of Vietnam presupposed similar frameworks for national liberation in Cambodia and Laos and made it possible for the Vietnamese communists to rationalize their interest in these neighboring countries.

In 1945, toward the end of World War II and immediately after, the Vietnamese communists finally began to see the fruits of their efforts to promote national awareness among Cambodians and Laotians in the formation of the Khmer Issarak and Lao Issara movements, respectively. Fighting a resurgent France in cooperation with these two movements, the ICP exerted a strong influence over them.

At the ICP's Second Party Congress, in February 1951, it was decided to divide the party into three parties, Vietnamese, Cambodian, and Laotian. For the Vietnamese communists this was a means of strengthening solidarity in Indochina, not an indication of a diminishing sense of the importance of Cambodia and Laos.

Here I will examine the context in which this decision was made. In my earlier paper, I concluded that the division into three parties was the logical outcome of the ICP policy, formulated in the early 1940s, of a revolution for national liberation, which required that Vietnam, Cambodia, and Laos be liberated as separate nations; that the Vietnamese, Cambodian, and Laotian peoples form a united front against colonial domination of Indochina; and that Vietnam help Cambodia and Laos, where the liberation movement was less well developed, to form their own popular political entities.

While my basic premise has not changed, I now feel that this view does not adequately explain the decision to divide into three parties.[4] First, it does not clarify

---

[4] I did not have access to sufficient data at the time I wrote my 1980 paper, "Indoshina kyōsantō." Subsequently I visited Vietnam, where I was able to copy relevant sections of the documents listed below. Hereafter, the letters TLGC followed by a number indicate references to or quotations from these documents. Thus, "TLGC 8" refers to document 8 in the list. In the list I have also noted the location of the documents in parentheses, using the letters S (Social Sciences Library), SS (library of the Institute for Southeast Asian Studies, Committee for Social Sciences), and P (archives of the Commission for the Study of the History of the Party).

1. Nghi quyet Hoi nghi Trung uong mo rong 15, 16, 17-1-1948 (S)
2. Nghi quyet Hoi nghi can bo Trung uong lan thu IV (mien Bac Dong Duong 20-5-1948) (S)
3. Phat dong phong trao thi dua ai quoc (chi thi cua Trung uong ngay 27-3-1948) (S)
4. Nghi quyet Hoi nghi can bo Trung uong lan thu V (tu 8 den 16-8-1948) (S)
5. Nghi quyet cua Hoi nghi can bo Trung upong lan thu V ve cong tac dan van va cong tac mat tran dan toc thong nhat (tu ngay 8–16-8-1948) (S)
6. Nghi quyet cua Hoi nghi can bo Trung uong lan thu V (tu 8–16-8-1948) [chung ta chien dau cho doc lap va dan chu] (bao cao doc o hoi nghi) (S)
7. Kiem thao mua he va chuan bi Thu Dong nam 1948 (bao cao cua dong chi Vo-nguyen-Giap tai Hoi nghi can bo Trung uong lan thu V) (S)
8. Cong tac dan van va cong tac Mat tran dan toc thong nhat (bao cao cua dong chi Hoang-quoc-Viet, uy vien Thuong vu Trung uong tai Hoi nghi can bo Trung uong lan thu V) (S)
9. Tinh hinh va nhiem vu moi cua Dang (bao cao cua dong chi Le-duc-Tho, uy vien Thuong vu Trung uong tai Hoi nghi can bo Trung uong lan thu V) (S)
10. Nghi quyet Hoi nghi can bo Trung uong lan thu VI (tu 14 den 18-1-1949) (S)
11. Tich cuc cam cu va chuan bi tong phan cong (bao cao o Hoi nghi can bo lan thu VI ngay 14 den 18-1-1949) (S)
12. Chuyen manh sang tong phan cong, Nghi quyet cua Hoi nghi toan quoc lan thu III (tu 21-1 den 13-2-1950) (S)
13. Hoan thanh nhiem vu chuan bi chuyen manh sang tong phan cong (bao cao cua dong chi Truong-Chinh tai Hoi nghi toan quoc lan thu III 21-1 den 3-2-1950) (S)

exactly when and why the ICP decided it was necessary for Cambodia and Laos to have their own independent party organizations. There was, after all, no indication of such a policy in the first half of the 1940s. Second, my earlier theory implies that the ICP waited until the conditions were right in Cambodia and Laos to implement a policy formulated at the beginning of the 1940s. This scenario is incomplete. Certainly the Vietnamese communists were beginning to meet with some success in their efforts to organize Cambodian and Laotian resistance to French colonial rule, but very few Cambodian and Laotian party members attended the Second Party Congress in 1951. Altogether, there were only 150 to 300 Cambodian and 31 to 140 Laotian party members.[5] Not even the Vietnamese believed that the time was ripe to form separate parties in Cambodia and Laos.[6] Why, then, did they divide the ICP as early as 1951? This is not adequately explained in my earlier paper.

In the present paper, therefore, I will focus on the period of resistance to French colonial rule, specifically the years between 1948 and 1951; the factors that led to the ICP's decision to establish separate parties in Cambodia and Laos; and finally, the reason that this decision was implemented in 1951.

---

14. Cong tac mat tran va dan van trong nam chuyen sang tong phan cong (bao cao cua dong chi Hoang-quoc Viet tai Hoi nghi toan quoc lan thu III 21-1 den 3-2-1950) (S)
15. Thuyet trinh ve Chinh quyen va Nha nuoc dan chu nhan dan Viet-nam (truoc Hoi nghi toan quoc lan thu III 21-1 den 3-2-1950) (S)
16. Dien van khai mac cua dong chi Ton-duc-Thang (ngay 11-2-1951) (S)
17. Ho Chu tich noi chuyen voi dai hoi (trong buoi khai mac ngay 11-2-1951) (S)
18. Ban ve cach mang Viet-nam, bao cao cua dong chi Truong-Chinh (S)
19. Dong chi Truong-Chinh giai dap cac y kien ve van de doi ten Dang (ngay 14-2-1951) (S)
20. Cung co khoi doan ket de chien thang, bao cao cua dong chi Hoang-quoc-Viet (ngay 14-2-1951) (S)
21. Ve to chuc va dieu le Dang Lao dong Viet-nam, bao cao cua dong chi Le-van-Luong (ngay 14-2-1951) (S)
22. May van de cot yeu cua chinh quyen dan chu nhan dan Viet-nam, bao cao cua dong chi Pham-van-Dong (ngay 15-2-1951) (S)
23. Xay dung quan doi nhan dan, hoan thanh chien tranh giai phong, bao cao cua dong chi Vo-nguyen-Giap (S)
24. Nghi quyet ve bao cao chinh tri cua dong chi Ho-chi-Minh (ngay 17-2-1951) (S)
25. Nghi quyet ve cach mang Mien Lao (ngay 17-2-1951) (S)
26. Dieu le cua Dang Lao dong Viet nam (S)
27. Du thao duong loi cach mang Mien Lao va de nghi ve van de Dang o Mien Lao trinh Dai hoi Dang lan thu II (1951) (P)
28. Nguyen Xuan Hoang, "Qua trinh van dong xay dung dang Marx-Lenin o Cam-pu-chia," 9-1979 (SS)
29. Bao cao tong hop cua thoi ky 1946–1954 (SS)
30. De hoan thanh nhiem vu va day manh cong tac truoc mat, bao cao cua dong chi Truong-Chinh truoc Hoi nghi Trung uong lan thu VI mo rong (15 den 18-7-1954) (S)

[5] TLGC 27 gives the number of Cambodians as 150, while Thanh Dam refers to 300 in "Nhan dan Campuchia chong de quoc phap," in Uy ban Khoa hoc xa hoi Viet Nam, *Tim Hieu Dat Nuoc Campuchia Anh Hung* (Hanoi: Nha xuat ban Khoa hoc xa hoi, 1979). TLGC 27 cites 31 Laotians, while TLGC 29 cites 140.

[6] These are not especially low or insufficient numbers compared with the number of members in other countries' communist parties during the formative period. For example, the Vietnamese Communist Party had around 300 members when it was formally organized in February 1930. When I say that the time was not yet ripe for the establishment of parties in Cambodia and Laos, I mean that their organizations were not yet strong enough to take political and military command of the resistance movement against France. The Vietnamese communists did not feel that this condition had been met either in 1951 or later, in July 1954 (TLGC 30).

I. THE RESISTANCE MOVEMENTS IN CAMBODIA AND LAOS AND THE ICP

After World War II the French resumed their hold over Cambodia in October 1945 and over Laos in March 1946. The resistance movements in these countries at that time were led by the Khmer Issarak and the Lao Issara, respectively. Below I will discuss these movements and their relationship to the ICP.

THE EARLY STAGE OF THE RESISTANCE

I will begin by reviewing the characteristics of the two movements in the early stage of their resistance to the French, between 1945 and 1947.[7] First, the two movements were only loosely organized and represented a variety of political trends. They had neither well-defined structures nor any goals other than opposition to French rule. Second, both movements had the support of the Free Thai regime. It is well known that when the French resumed control of Laos, the Lao Issara government exiled itself to Bangkok. What is not so well remembered is that in the autumn of 1946 the Khmer Issarak launched its first military attacks against the French in Battambang and Siem Reap, two western Cambodian provinces that had been ceded to Thailand during the war and in which Thai influence remained strong.

Third, both movements were also receiving support from the ICP and the Viet Minh. Immediately after its successful revolution in August 1945, the Vietnamese government dispatched emissaries to Cambodia and Laos to proclaim its support for the resistance movements in those countries. By early 1946 a cooperative system had been established that enabled the Viet Minh mission in Bangkok, headed by Tran Van Giau, to play a major role in the resistance.

Prior to this, ICP organizations within the Vietnamese populations in Thailand, Cambodia, and Laos had been cooperating with the Cambodian and Laotian resistance movements and supplying them with Vietnamese fighting men. With the help of the Free Thai government, the Viet Minh mission in Bangkok directed the resistance movements in Cambodia and Laos, organizing squads of ethnic Vietnamese fighters, such as the Cuu Long I, II, and III, the Tran Phu, and the Quang Trung, and building cooperative relations with various resistance groups in northwestern Cambodia and with the militant faction of the Lao Issara.[8] Thus in the early years of the resistance joint Cambodian-Vietnamese and Laotian-Vietnamese forces were at the core of the Khmer Issarak and the Lao Issara, respectively. Nevertheless, the ICP was not yet in a position to take full command of the Khmer Issarak and Lao Issara movements. Between December 1946, when Vietnam initiated nationwide resistance, and the end of 1947, the ICP had its hands full with the resistance movement in Vietnam and had no leeway for active involvement in the affairs of Cambodia and Laos.[9]

---

[7] See Furuta, "Indoshina kyōsantō" for more on the Lao Issara movement. My major sources for the Khmer Issarak are Roger M. Smith, *Cambodia's Foreign Policy* (Ithaca, N.Y.: Cornell University Press, 1965); Malcom Caldwell and Lek Tan, *Cambodia in the Southeast Asian War* (New York and London: Monthly Review Press, 1973); Pham Viet Trung, Do Van Nhung, and Chiem Te Chu Bien, *Dat Nuoc Cam-pu-chia Lich Su va Van Minh* (Hanoi: Truong dai hoc Tong hop Ha-noi xuat ban, 1977); Thanh Dam, "Nhan dan Campuchia"; Kiernan, "Origins."

[8] Author's interview with Professor Tran Van Giau, Ho Chi Minh City, July 9, 1982.

[9] ICP central committee resolutions from the autumn of 1945 to the end of 1947 are recorded in Ban nghien cuu lich su Dang truc thuoc Ban chap hanh Trung uong Dang Lao dong Viet Nam, *Van Kien Dang tu 25-11-1945 den 31-12-1947* (Hanoi: Nha xuat ban Su that, 1969).

EQUILIBRIUM AND ITS EFFECTS

Changes triggered by events in late 1947 and early 1948 enabled the ICP to focus much of its attention on Cambodia and Laos once again. First, there was a shift in the battle situation in Vietnam.[10] In October 1947 the French initiated an all-out assault on the Viet Minh base at Viet Bac, near Vietnam's border with China, with the intent of destroying the nucleus of the resistance movement. The assault failed, however, and it became apparent that the Indochina War was going to be a protracted struggle. Judging that the war had advanced from the defensive stage to equilibrium, the ICP began to intensify its resistance activities.[11] At its fourth central executive conference (Hoi nghi can bo trung uong), in April 1948, the ICP decided to extend its operations into enemy-held territory, which included Cambodia and Laos.[12]

There was also a change in Thailand's situation. In November 1947 the Free Thai government was toppled in a coup d'état that returned Phibun Songkhram to power. The new government was anticommunist, and not only refused to support the Indochinese national liberation movement but also regarded the Viet Minh as its enemy.[13] This deprived the Khmer Issarak and the Lao Issara of a powerful ally but gave new weight to support from Vietnam.

The above factors combined to renew ICP interest in Cambodia and Laos. Cambodia and Laos were first discussed as major topics at the fifth central executive conference, held in August 1948, at the peak of the Vietnamese struggle against the French. The primary focus of interest was military. "If the Rhine was the first line of defense for Britain, the Mekong River was Vietnam's first line of defense,"[14] and Cambodia and Laos represented crucial second lines of defense. In 1948 and 1949, guerrilla activity directed by the ICP did increase in Cambodia and Laos. At the end of 1947 an external affairs committee headed by Nguyen Thanh Son was set up within the southern Vietnam regional committee specifically to direct support for Cambodia. The seventh, eighth, and ninth southern military zones were given responsibility for northeastern, southeastern, and southwestern Cambodia, respectively, and instructed to expand the resistance in these regions.[15]

Vietnamese and Khmer Krom (Khmer residents of Vietnam) units accompanied by Cambodian cadres were sent into Cambodia, and the Khmer Issarak movement spread quickly into northeastern, southeastern, and southwestern Cambodia. In each region the ICP had Cambodian leaders under its control: Son Sichan in the northeast, Keo Moni and Tou Samouth in the southeast, and Son Ngoc Minh in the southwest. But though the Khmer Issarak movement was rapidly spreading nationwide, no control center was ever created; instead, the resistance movement in northwestern

---

[10] My description of the military development of the Indochina War is based on André Teulires, *La Guerre du Vietnam 1945–1975* (Paris: Éditions Lavauzelle, 1978); Ban nghien cuu lich su quan doi thuoc Tong cuc chinh tri, *Lich Su Quan Doi Nhan Dan Viet Nam* (Hanoi: Nha xuat ban Quan doi Nhan dan, 1974). The latter work is referred to hereafter as LSQDNDVN.

[11] This view of the war's progress was first stated at the ICP's enlarged central committee meeting in January 1948 (TLGC 1).

[12] TLGC 2.

[13] Peter A. Poole, "Thai-Vietnamese Relations: Implications for United States Policy" (Ph.D. diss., American University, 1968), pp. 51–52.

[14] TLGC 7.

[15] Author's interview with Nguyen Thanh Son, Ho Chi Minh City, July 10, 1982.

Cambodia was directed by the ICP organization in Thailand, and the movement in other regions was directed by the military zones in southern Vietnam.[16]

New developments were also seen in guerrilla activities in Laos in late 1948 and early 1949. As part of its program of infiltrating enemy territory, the ICP strengthened its Viet Minh armed propaganda units in northwestern Vietnam, bordering Laos. These units made their way into upper Laos, where they organized local resistance groups and intensified guerrilla warfare against the French,[17] eventually forming a guerrilla unit led by Laotian ICP cadre Kaysone Phoumvihan.[18]

In conjunction with these events, toward the end of 1948 the ICP reorganized its chain of command, adding military zones in Sam Neua (upper Laos) and lower Laos to its original three western zones and one eastern zone.[19] Vietnamese military support thus played a major role in the expansion of the struggle in Cambodia and Laos. Nevertheless, at the time of the fifth central executive conference in August 1948 the Vietnamese communists did not assume simplistically that Cambodia and Laos could be liberated by sending in Vietnamese troops. They had long since concluded that their efforts should be directed toward getting the Cambodians and Laotians to form their own independent organizations.

The political report delivered at the fifth central executive conference observed that the Cambodian and Laotian revolutions should be carried out by the Cambodian and Laotian masses and reminded the party that the Cambodian and Laotian revolutions represented an essential part of the "new democratic revolution" of all Indochina. The Vietnamese communists were admonished for their tendency to take advantage of the Cambodian and Laotian revolutions to secure recruits for their own revolution, while the Cambodian and Laotian revolutionaries were reassured that there was no basis to their fear that cooperation with the Vietnamese would lead to absorption into Vietnam.[20] In short, the purpose of mobilizing the Cambodians and Laotians was to form popular political entities to liberate the Cambodian and Laotian peoples, a policy that was a natural extension of the line adopted at the beginning of the 1940s.

The ICP saw the Khmer Issarak and the Lao Issara as the foundations of popular governments in Cambodia and Laos. The fifth central executive conference political report criticized the two movements for pitting workers, farmers, and petty-bourgeois intellectuals against anti-French royalty and patriotic Buddhist priests. The Laos party organization's attempt to displace Prince Phetsarath as the leader of the Lao Issara government-in-exile because of his group's "national feudalism" and to establish a "national liberation committee" of intellectuals instead was cited as an

---

[16] This information is based on my interview with Nguyen Thanh Son and on Thanh Dam, "Nhan dan Campuchia"; Kiernan, "Origins"; Nguyen Hao Hung, "Lien minh chien dau Viet Nam-Campuchia mot nhan to bao dam thang loi cua cach mang Campuchia trong thoi ky chong Phap 1945–1954," in Uy ban Khoa hoc xa hoi Viet Nam, *Hoi Nghi Khoa Hoc vc Quan He Viet Nam Cam-pu-chia trong Lich Su* (Ho Chi Minh City: Vien Khoa hoc xa hoi va Ban Dong Nam A, 1980).

[17] LSQDNDVN, pp. 350–51; TLGC 11.

[18] Phan Gia Ben et al., *Luoc Su Nuoc Lao* (Hanoi: Nha xuat ban Khoa hoc xa hoi, 1978), p. 183. The day this unit was formed, January 10, 1949, is commemorated today as Laotian Army Foundation Day.

[19] TLGC 29.

[20] TLGC 6.

example of misguided thinking. The report added that constitutional monarchies were viable choices for Cambodia and Laos in the postcolonial era.[21]

From the above it can be concluded that the Vietnamese communists thought it more important at this point to help the Cambodian and Laotian upper classes establish popular political entities than to push for organization of the masses.[22] This view was probably based on the pragmatic need to enlist the support and cooperation of the Cambodian and Laotian royal families and Buddhist clergy in the fight against France.

This does not mean that the Vietnamese communists were indifferent to the need to recruit Cambodian and Laotian members of the party. The report on party affairs delivered at the fifth central executive conference pointed out that though the war for liberation was escalating in Cambodia and Laos, the party had almost no base in these countries, and suggested that in addition to recruiting Vietnamese living in Cambodia and Laos, party membership requirements should be eased for native Cambodians and Laotians in order to encourage them to join.[23]

The assumption that Vietnamese would form the core of the Cambodian and Laotian party organizations indicates that at this point the ICP had no intention of establishing independent party organization in these two countries. While the Vietnamese were encouraging Cambodians and Laotians to join the party, this was not yet perceived as an important step toward the creation of popular political entities in Cambodia and Laos.

The sixth central executive conference, held in January 1949, stressed the need to continue the military buildup initiated the previous year and to expand operations in Cambodia and Laos in order to disperse the French forces. Specifically, it was suggested that the Khmer Issarak military zones in Cambodia be combined and that a base of operations be established in Laos.[24]

PREPARATIONS FOR UNIFIED RESISTANCE

New developments in the Indochina War in 1949 and 1950 caused further changes in ICP policies toward Cambodia and Laos. As is well known, the emergence of the People's Republic of China in October 1949 served to place the Indochina War in the context of East-West confrontation. From the perspective of the ICP, the establishment of a communist China raised the specter of US intervention in the Indochina War,[25] but

---

[21] Ibid.

[22] For further discussion of this issue, see Motoo Furuta, "Indoshina no minzoku to kakumei no seiji" [The peoples of Indochina and the politics of revolution], in *Betonamu kara mita Chūgoku* [China as seen from Vietnam], ed. Motoo Furuta (Tokyo: Nitchū Shuppan, 1979).

[23] TLGC 9.

[24] TLGC 11.

[25] By January 1949 it had become clear that the communists would triumph in China. While noting that the victory of the People's Liberation Army was certain to have a beneficial effect upon the revolution in Vietnam, the report of the ICP's sixth central executive conference warned that "at the same time, the Vietnamese people may face new difficulties as a result of the victory of the People's Liberation Army. . . . We must not forget that the United States has not abandoned its support for the anti-Chinese forces. There is a very real possibility, for example, that the United States will intervene directly in the Vietnamese-French war to prevent the People's Liberation Army's advance into southern China or provide aid to the French to ensure that they will in turn help Chiang Kai-shek rally his forces against the People's Liberation Army and thereby obstruct the Chinese revolution" (ibid.).

it also brought the war to the world's attention and ensured stable support for the communist struggle, and this was welcomed by the ICP.[26]

It had already been pointed out at the sixth central executive conference that a communist victory in China would generate conditions enabling a rapid escalation of the Indochinese resistance from equilibrium to a "general counteroffensive" against the French.[27] At the beginning of 1950 the ICP decided to begin preparing in earnest to escalate the struggle.[28] The fronts in Cambodia and Laos took on added significance as the party declared its intention to persist until all Vietnamese, Cambodian, and Laotian territories had been recovered.

Another important development was the signing in 1949 of agreements between France on the one hand and the Bao Dai government in Vietnam and the monarchies in Cambodia and Laos on the other, granting each of these countries independence within the French Union. These agreements triggered discord within the Khmer Issarak and the Lao Issara. In September 1949 the Dap Chhuon, based in Siem Reap, the northwestern province, surrendered to the Cambodian monarchy. This was followed by the defection of several other resistance groups.[29] Meanwhile, the Lao Issara's government-in-exile in Bangkok was dissolved with the signing of the Laos-France accord, and Souvanna Phouma and other moderates returned to the royal government in Vientiane.[30]

The aim of the 1949 agreements was to isolate the Vietnamese resistance by promoting Cambodian and Laotian nationalism,[31] and they did cause the Vietnamese to lose some of their support among Cambodians and Laotians. In the circumstances, the ICP saw no way to achieve peace except by striking a decisive military blow against the French forces. Since 1947 the party had envisioned the conclusion of a peace between the Viet Minh and France.[32] Though the likelihood of this diminished with the passage of time, the party continued to cling to the possibility until 1949. The original scenario had Vietnam concluding an independent peace with France so that the Viet Minh government could later intercede between the Cambodian and

---

[26] The keynote report of the third national conference, early in 1950, stated that "the People's Republic of China has been established and has initiated diplomatic relations with Vietnam. We are no longer encircled; a pathway to the world has been opened for Vietnam. We now have a large and powerful ally at our side" (TLGC 13).

[27] The slogan of the day was "Prepare for a general counteroffensive by direct confrontation" (TLGC 11).

[28] TLGC 12.

[29] Kiernan, "Origins"; TLGC 28. The keynote report of the third national conference described the Dap Chhuon as "opportunists" (TLGC 13).

[30] The Lao Issara's government-in-exile in Bangkok was disbanded on October 24, 1949. See Phan Gia Ben et al., *Luoc Su Nuoc Lao*, p. 182.

[31] The first French high commissioner for Indochina after World War II, Admiral Thierry d'Argenlieu, stated that "the Laotians, Cambodians, and other minority groups continue to exist because of us. It is thanks to us that these groups have not been absorbed by Annamese imperialism." Quoted in Ellen Hammer, *Indoshina gendaishi* [The struggle for Indochina], trans. Noboru Kawai (Tokyo: Misuzu Shobō, 1970), p. 156.

[32] For example, at the sixth central executive conference, in January 1949, the possibility was raised that the French might be willing to negotiate a peace through the Bao Dai government. In such an eventuality, Vietnam's condition for peace was that "the French must withdraw their military forces in Vietnam to France, not simply to Cambodia and Laos. They cannot be allowed to attack Vietnam from behind the shield of puppet governments in Cambodia and Laos" (TLGC 11).

Laotian resistance movements and France.[33] But at the beginning of 1950 the ICP abandoned all hope of concluding such a peace[34] and decided to organize a unified resistance to fight for the independence of all Indochina. The first step was to reorganize the resistance movements in Cambodia and Laos so as to bring them under the ICP's direct control.

At the ICP's third national conference, held in late January and early February 1950, the urgency of preparing for a general counteroffensive was stressed. Notable is the fact that at this point all Indochina was viewed as a single battlefield, as the keynote report to the conference made clear: "In this war of resistance all Indochina is a single battlefield. Unified resistance requires the participation of Vietnam, Laos, and Cambodia. The goal of the resistance is not only to expel the enemy from Vietnam but to free Laos and Cambodia as well. This is because Vietnam, Laos, and Cambodia are extremely close both geographically and politically. Without freeing Laos and Cambodia, Vietnam cannot be free; and without victory in Vietnam, Laos and Cambodia cannot achieve independence. . . . In this unified resistance, we cannot wait to achieve our goal in Vietnam and then rest a while before we fight for the independence of the rest of Indochina. Even though fighting has not ceased in Vietnam, we must follow a unified plan of resistance for all Indochina and fight at the same time to liberate at least part of Laos and Cambodia."[35]

The perception of Indochina as a single battlefield grew out of the idea that Indochina was an organic whole in which the strategic front could move anywhere in Vietnam, Cambodia, and Laos, depending on the circumstances. This reasoning not only rationalized Vietnamese participation in the fighting in Cambodia and Laos[36] but also emphasized the importance of linking the Vietnamese, Cambodian, and Laotian revolutions.

Another major change in the ICP's attitude toward the Cambodian and Laotian fronts was expressed in the keynote report, which observed that "at present national united fronts have not yet taken clear form in Laos and Cambodia" because of insufficient mass participation and because of the party's inherent weakness in these regions.[37] The ICP was well aware that, unlike the party-controlled Viet Minh, the various anti-French factions within the Khmer Issarak and the Lao Issara were too loosely organized, and therefore too weak, to constitute true national united fronts with broad popular bases. The ICP's 1948 target of an alliance with the upper classes had changed to a drive for grass-roots organization of the masses.[38]

---

[33] See TLGC 11 for the party's position in January 1948. The idea of an independent peace was considered as early as March 1946, when a preliminary agreement with France was concluded. See Hoa de tien: chi thi cua Ban thuong vu Trung uong, 9-3-1946, Vu bien soan Ban tuyen huan trung uong, *Lich Su Dang Cong San Viet Nam*, vol. 2 (Hanoi: Nha xuat ban Sach giao khoa Mac Le-nin, 1978), p. 34. This work is referred to hereafter as LSDCSVN 2.

[34] There is no reference to peace negotiations with France in the documentation of the ICP's third national conference, in 1950. See TLGC 12, 13.

[35] TLGC 13.

[36] This rationalization became a reality after the upper Laos action in the spring of 1953. See LSQDNDVN, pp. 504–7.

[37] TLGC 13.

[38] This trend was also evident in Vietnamese domestic policy toward minority groups. The report on the united front delivered at the ICP's third national conference stated, in regard to minority groups, that "emphasis will be placed on organizing the masses from the bottom up. Through government intervention and the lessening of oppression and exploitation, the people

At the conference a new policy was worked out to strengthen the organizations of the Khmer Issarak and the Lao Issara, with the aim of creating national united fronts in Cambodia and Laos that would eventually grow into a united front of all Indochinese peoples.[39] The aim was to help the Khmer Issarak and the Lao Issara develop strong, well-organized structures like that of the Viet Minh. An important element of this policy was the creation of "national, democratic" independent parties capable of becoming "the primary support of national united fronts in Cambodia and Laos."[40] As far as I know, this was the first time the formation of independent parties for Cambodia and Laos was proposed.[41]

To strengthen ties among the three Indochinese revolutionary movements in order to achieve a unified resistance, the Vietnamese communists attempted to tighten the loosely knit organizations of the Khmer Issarak and the Lao Issara. In the process, it became clear that it would be necessary first to establish independent parties in Cambodia and Laos. The party line adopted at the beginning of the 1940s, to assist in the formation of popular political entities in Cambodia and Laos, had thus reached its logical conclusion. This is my answer to the question of why and how the ICP decided that it was necessary to divide into three separate parties.

At the conference it was proposed that to establish party organizations in Cambodia and Laos it would be necessary to (1) recruit more Cambodians and Laotians into the party, (2) encourage workers, farmers, and progressive intellectuals to join forces in order to create a solid foundation for the party among the masses, (3) train Cambodian and Laotian party cadres and place them in leadership positions at various levels, and (4) plan revolutionary schemes tailored to the special conditions within Cambodia and Laos.[42]

The third national conference, unlike the fifth central executive conference in August 1948, gave priority to recruiting more Cambodian and Laotian party members. This did not mean that the ICP intended to create purely Cambodian and Laotian parties immediately. It was assumed that Vietnamese cadres would remain in leadership positions until Cambodian and Laotian cadres could be trained to take their place.

At the conference it was also decided to create centralized resistance governments to direct and coordinate the resistance against French domination, by establishing a "national liberation committee" to function as a provisional government in

---

must be made to realize the need to fight for the distribution of land to the poor. A resolute attitude toward reactionary comrades is necessary" (TLGC 14).

[39] TLGC 12.

[40] The keynote report stated that independent parties would be established in "Cambodia and, if necessary, Laos" (TLGC 13). As this indicates, the movement was considered to be more developed in Cambodia than in Laos at that time. TLGC 27 provides more detailed information on this point.

[41] In November 1949 a central-level conference was held to discuss the issue of Cambodia and Laos. See TLGC 28, 29; Nguyen Hao Hung, "Lien minh chien dau Viet Nam-Campuchia." I have not seen the report of this conference, but on the basis of the sources cited above it can be surmised that the party's policy toward Cambodia and Laos outlined at the third national conference was probably worked out at the November 1949 conference. It is therefore equally possible that the idea of forming independent parties in Cambodia and Laos was also first presented at that time.

[42] TLGC 13.

Cambodia and by reorganizing the resistance government in Laos.[43] In 1950 events in keeping with these policies took place in both Cambodia and Laos. In March the First All-Cambodia Cadre Conference was held, at which it was decided to unify the separate regional lines of command by establishing the Cadre Committee of All-Cambodia. At the outset this committee included eight Vietnamese cadres and two Cambodian cadres (Son Ngoc Minh and Tou Samouth) and was headed by Nguyen Thanh Son. At a conference held at the end of June 1951, after the ICP's Second Party Congress, this committee was reorganized into the Canvassing Committee for the Creation of a Khmer People's Revolutionary Party, headed by Son Ngoc Minh, and the Vietnamese cadres were made advisers.[44]

Meanwhile, on the government and resistance level, at a national conference of the Khmer Issarak convened April 17–19, 1950, shortly after the party's First All-Cambodia Cadre Conference, it was voted to establish the National Central Executive Committee of the Unified Issarak Front, chaired by Tou Samouth, and the People's Liberation Central Committee, chaired by Son Ngoc Minh, the latter to function as a provisional resistance government.[45]

In Laos, a national conference of party cadres was convened in June 1950 and a blueprint for the Laotian revolution was discussed. No central party leadership organ was created; instead the country was divided into military zones according to the Vietnamese military inter-zones from which they received their main support. Thus, by the end of 1950 three military zones had been established, for upper Laos, central Laos, and lower Laos, corresponding to the Viet Bac, fourth, and fifth Vietnamese inter-zones. Each zone had its own command network and individually organized group of Laotian party members and candidates for party membership and functioned in the same way as the Cambodian Canvassing Committee for the Creation of a Khmer People's Revolutionary Party.[46] At the Lao Issara national congress held on August 13, 1950, Prince Souphanouvong was elected chairman of a resistance government and the name Lao Issara was changed to Neo Lao Issara.[47]

In this way, in 1950 the groundwork was laid for the Khmer Issarak and Lao Issara movements to be transformed into the Issarak and Issara fronts. While the new organizations retained their original motivation, they were now coordinated into a well-knit united front under party leadership and followed a clear-cut master plan. The stage had been set for the establishment of independent parties in Cambodia and Laos.

II. THE PEOPLE'S DEMOCRATIC REVOLUTION AND THE 1951 PARTY DIVISION

The ICP's decision to divide into three separate parties in 1951 is connected to trends evident in the international communist movement at the time and to the Vietnamese communists' switch to new policies.

---

[43] Ibid.

[44] TLGC 28; interview with Nguyen Thanh Son.

[45] Thanh Dam, "Nhan dan Campuchia."

[46] TLGC 29.

[47] Phan Gia Ben et al., *Luoc Su Nuoc Lao*, pp. 184–85.

THE FRAMEWORK OF THE IDEA OF A REVOLUTION FOR NATIONAL LIBERATION

At the eighth Central Committee Plenum of the ICP, in May 1941, the imminent Indochinese revolution was characterized as a revolution for national liberation. This characterization remained intact after World War II, as can be seen in the Central Standing Committee's "Directive on the Resistance and Nation Building," issued on November 25, 1945, which hailed the end of the war as ushering in "an era of development of peace and democracy"[48] and described the revolution in Indochina as "a revolution for national liberation."[49] The ICP adhered to this line through 1947.

In practical terms, this line meant first that the focus of all revolutionary activity was to be national liberation, in other words, independence, and that priority was to be placed on unifying all classes of people. Feudalism was to be combated only insofar as doing so did not threaten unity.[50] Thus the Viet Minh government restricted the land-reform program introduced immediately after the founding of the Democratic Republic of Vietnam to tax and interest-rate reductions, just as the Chinese Communist Party had done during its struggle against the Japanese, and refrained from demanding that land be confiscated from owners and given to cultivators.[51]

Second, while the importance of the working class, specifically, communist-party leadership, was acknowledged, it was believed that in the postwar era of peace and democracy the government should be a coalition reflecting the union of all classes and that the party's existence should not be overly emphasized. During its formative stage the Viet Minh government is believed to have patterned itself on the Chinese Communist Party's pre-civil war concept of a coalition government.[52] The ICP's declaration of its own dissolution, however insincere, in November 1945[53] must be considered in the light of this background and the Viet Minh government's international isolation.

Third, no disparity was seen in the basic nature of the Vietnamese, Cambodian, and Laotian revolutions, all three being regarded as revolutions for national liberation. By the mid-1930s the Vietnamese communists had come to recognize that there were qualitative differences in the societies of Vietnam, Cambodia, and Laos. Compared with Vietnam, Cambodia and Laos had had minimal exposure to colonialism,

---

[48] LSDCSVN 2, p. 5.

[49] Ibid., p. 11.

[50] The idea that antifeudalism was subordinate to national liberation was presented at the Sixth Central Committee Plenum, in November 1939. See Ban nghien cuu lich su Dang Trung uong, *50 Nam Hoat Dong cua Dang Cong San Viet Nam* (Hanoi: Nha xuat ban Su that, 1979), p. 60. This work is referred to hereafter as *50 Nam.*

[51] The land-reform policies of the ICP, and later of the Vietnamese Workers' Party, are discussed in Tsutomu Murano, "Kita Betonamu no tochi kaikaku" [Land reform in northern Vietnam], in *Ajia tochi seisakuron josetsu* [An introduction to land reform policies in Asia], ed. Hitoshi Saitō (Tokyo: Institute of Developing Economies, 1976).

[52] Kazuo Arahata, "Taisenki Betonamu o meguru shokuminchi shihai saihensei to jinmin no teikokushugi ninshiki" [The reorganization of colonial rule in wartime Vietnam and the Vietnamese people's perception of imperialism], *Ajia, Afurika kenkyū* [Journal of Asian and African studies] 14, no. 10 (October 1974).

[53] Japanese debate over the dissolution of the ICP is summarized in Shigehiko Tanikawa, "Betonamu sensōshi kenkyū josetsu" [An introduction to the study of the history of the Vietnam War], *Hōsei kenkyū* [Journal of law and politics] 47, no. 1 (October 1980). The impact of the party's dissolution on the history of the Vietnamese communist movement is discussed in Huynh Kim Khanh, *Vietnamese Communism 1925–1945* (Ithaca, N.Y.: Cornell University Press, 1982), pp. 328–33.

and hence capitalism, and their societies retained feudalistic characteristics. As a consequence, little progress had been made in breaking down class distinctions.[54] Thus, in terms of a class-struggle orientation, the Vietnamese revolution would be quite different in character from that of Cambodia or Laos. But in terms of a nationalist revolution there was little need to be concerned with this difference. That is why, from the beginning of the 1940s—when the Indochinese revolution was perceived as three separate revolutions taking place in Vietnam, Cambodia, and Laos—through 1947, no difference was recognized in the nature of these three revolutions; all three were perceived to be based on the same nationalist principles.

PAVING THE WAY FOR A PEOPLE'S DEMOCRATIC REVOLUTION

The first indication of a change in perception appeared in 1948. At its enlarged central committee meeting in January 1948, the ICP referred to the formation of the Cominform in September of the preceding year and endorsed the Cominform's view of an international community divided into the two opposing power blocs of East and West.[55] At the fifth central executive conference, in August 1948, the basic character of the Indochinese revolution was redefined as a "new democratic revolution." Through 1947 the ICP had accepted the definition used by Mao Zedong when he introduced the concept in 1940. As redefined, however, "new democratic revolution" meant a "people's democratic revolution" possessing the potential to evolve into socialism under communist-party direction.[56]

From this we can conclude that it was around this time that the idea of a "people's democratic revolution" to be carried out by the ICP took root. The use of the term "new democratic revolution" at the fifth central executive conference was very much an attempt to keep in step with the international communist movement. The ICP was highly sensitive to such events as the formation of the Cominform and Yugoslavia's expulsion from the organization.[57] This is clearly indicated by the proposal of an "Asian Cominform," made by the Committee for Liaison with Friendly Parties of East Asia (East Asia included Southeast Asia) at the fifth central executive

---

[54] This perception is reflected in the resolution on activities within minority groups passed at the ICP's first party congress, in March 1935. See Motoo Furuta, "Shoki Indoshina kyōsantō no chiiki haaku ni kansuru sōkō" [Notes on early Indochina Communist Party regional control], *Tōkyō Daigaku kyōyōgakubu kyōyōgakka kiyō* [Journal of the Department of Liberal Arts, College of Arts and Sciences, University of Tokyo], no. 11 (March 1979).

[55] TLGC 1.

[56] The political report delivered at the fifth central executive conference declared that "the new democratic system has the character of a people's democracy. . . . The new democratic system has the potential to evolve into a socialist system without going through a further revolution" (TLGC 6). For the concepts of people's democratic revolution and new democratic revolution, see Hiroshi Momose, "Soren, Tō-Ō ken no keisei to jinmin minshushugiron no hensen" [The formation of the Soviet and East European bloc and changes in the theory of people's democracy], *Rekishigaku kenkyū* [Journal of historical studies], no. 465 (February 1979); Robert M. Rodes, "Soviet Attitudes toward the Independence Movements in South and Southeast Asia 1945–1952" (Ph.D. diss., Columbia University, 1966), pp. 196–211. For changes in the interpretation of the concept of new democracy in China, see Seiji Imahori, *Mō Takutō kenkyū josetsu* [An introduction to the study of Mao Zedong] (Tokyo: Keisō Shobō, 1966); Isao Nakanishi, *Chūgoku kakumei to Mō Takutō shisō* [The Chinese Revolution and the ideology of Mao Zedong] (Tokyo: Aoki Shoten, 1969).

[57] The formation of the Cominform is mentioned in the report of the January 1948 enlarged central committee meeting (TLGC 1). The Yugoslavia problem is mentioned in the report of the fifth central executive conference in August (TLGC 6).

conference: "The communist parties of Europe are more mature [than those of Asia], but despite its proximity to Russia the Yugoslavian communist party has made an irrevocable mistake because of insufficient mutual liaison and mutual support. The communist parties of Asia are still in their infancy. Without a system of mutual liaison and mutual support, how can they possibly avoid making the same mistake?"[58]

At this point, in 1948, the ICP saw the resistance movement in Indochina as belonging to the democratic camp in the East-West confrontation[59] and was fully willing to become part of the new communist world order presaged by the formation of the Cominform. Acceptance of the idea of a "new democratic revolution" was just one facet of this worldview. But though Indochina's armed resistance against the French was applauded at the February 1948 Calcutta Youth Conference as indicating a new phase in the communist struggle in Asia,[60] this did not alter the fact of the Indochinese resistance movement's international isolation, and the ICP was still hesitant to implement the new definition.

Indicative was the way in which the party handled the issue of land reform. The idea of a "new democratic revolution" implied that even within the context of a revolution primarily directed at national liberation it was possible to pursue simultaneously antifeudalistic goals, such as land reform.[61] This was a significant change, in view of the fact that land reform had not been a major goal back when the revolution had been defined as a revolution for national liberation. Still, in 1948 the ICP did not yet perceive land reform as a policy that needed to be implemented immediately. The party still sought to attract "enlightened" and "patriotic" landowners to its cause, claiming them as allies of the revolution, and land-reform policy remained limited to advocacy of lower taxes and interest rates.[62]

The same attitude was seen in regard to the issue of communist-party leadership. In a "new democratic revolution" the communist party would theoretically play a major leadership role in both the revolution and the government to follow, laying the foundation for socialism; but in actuality it was still considered premature to bring the ICP out into the open. The report on party affairs delivered at the fifth central executive conference gave two reasons for this view: according to the party, official

---

[58] TLGC 9. It is not clear what effect this proposal had, but, as Bernard Fall notes, at that time the Vietnamese communists sought to link all the communist movements in Southeast Asia. See Bernard B. Fall, *The Viet-Minh Regime* (New York: Institute of Pacific Relations, 1956), pp. 58–59.

[59] TLGC 6.

[60] J. H. Brimmell states that the main report delivered at the Calcutta Youth Conference was that of the Vietnamese delegation and that it was the Vietnamese model that was being urged on all of Southeast Asia. See J. H. Brimmell, *Communism in South East Asia* (London and New York: Oxford University Press, 1959), p. 258. An analysis of the Calcutta conference is found in Tatsumi Okabe, "Chūgoku no Tōnan Ajia seisaku" [China's Southeast Asia policy], chap. in *Gendai Chūgoku no taigai seisaku* [Contemporary China's foreign policy] (Tokyo: Tōkyō Daigaku Shuppankai, 1971), pp. 244–49.

[61] At the fifth central executive conference it was declared that, because of two factors—the establishment of a people's government with the August Revolution of 1945 and the rise of new democratic forces in the postwar world—"while it is urgent that we fight imperialism, it is necessary at the same time to carry out a land-reform program that will gradually eliminate feudalistic exploitation" (TLGC 6).

[62] Ibid.

status would expose it to assault from international anticommunist reactionary forces and would stir up domestic unrest among participants in the united front.[63]

The ICP's adoption of the concept of a "new democratic revolution" was thus, at least in 1948, mainly a ploy to keep in step with the international communist movement and had very little impact upon the actual situation in Indochina. Still, it did have an important effect on the ICP's policy toward Cambodia and Laos in that the party acknowledged differences in the character of the Vietnamese, Cambodian, and Laotian revolutions. The political report delivered at the fifth central executive conference stated that "there are differences of degree among Vietnam, Cambodia, and Laos, and Vietnam is, in every aspect, economically, politically, culturally, and socially more developed than Cambodia and Laos. Because of this the party's new democratic revolution must be implemented differently in each of these countries. . . . The present Vietnamese revolution is a struggle against imperialism and feudalism, but in Cambodia and Laos the primary aim of the revolution must be to liberate the people and achieve their independence."[64]

The reasoning was that the Vietnamese revolution was a "new democratic revolution" of antiimperialism and antifeudalism, while the Cambodian and Laotian revolutions were "revolutions for national liberation" directed at the liberation of their peoples from imperialism. Acceptance of the concept of a "people's democratic revolution" had compelled the Vietnamese communists to acknowledge the necessity of redefining the Vietnamese revolution and differentiating it from the Cambodian and Laotian revolutions. In other words, the concept of a "people's democratic revolution" was employed to emphasize the nature of the Vietnamese revolution within the context of the Indochinese revolution.

This does not mean that the Vietnamese communists did not change their perception of the Cambodian and Laotian revolutions. In fact, by emphasizing their own revolution, the Vietnamese communists put themselves in the position of having to recognize the characteristics of the Cambodian and Laotian revolutions that set them apart from the revolution in Vietnam. That is why the fifth central executive conference could envision the possibility of constitutional monarchies in Cambodia and Laos following their revolutions.

THE PEOPLE'S DEMOCRATIC REVOLUTION: FROM THEORY TO ACTUALITY

Application of the concept of a people's democratic revolution to the Vietnamese revolution was a gradual process that did not affect the reality of the situation in Vietnam until 1950, shortly after the establishment of the People's Republic of China. The need to clarify that the Viet Minh government was a people's democratic government was stressed at the ICP's third national conference, early in 1950. Even within the ICP, it was noted, this important concept was only vaguely understood, partly because the party had not formally declared its existence and partly because the Indochinese resistance movements had had no overseas allies and thus had been internationally isolated.

The Viet Minh government needed to be perceived as a people's democratic government for three reasons: to enable a "people's dictatorship" under the leadership of

---

[63] TLGC 9. In the autumn of 1948, when the Vietnamese communists were taking a cautious stance, a paper was published in the Soviet Union on the working class in Vietnam and its struggle under communist-party leadership. See Rodes, "Soviet Attitudes," p. 227.

[64] TLGC 6.

the working class to be established; to enable a people's democracy to be realized and progress to be made toward socialism; and, on the international level, to enable Vietnam to align itself with the democratic front led by the Soviet Union.[65]

With the People's Republic of China as its ally, the Vietnamese resistance movement was no longer internationally isolated and the Vietnamese communists saw no reason to hide any longer the fact that the Viet Minh government was under communist leadership. They also saw the founding of the People's Republic of China as an opportunity to bring the Vietnamese resistance movement into conformance with the Chinese model, which had become the paradigm for all communist movements in Southeast Asia. At the World Trade Union Conference, held in Beijing in November 1949, Liu Xiao Ji presented four points characterizing the Chinese revolution that, he argued, made China's experience an appropriate model for revolutions in areas under colonial or semicolonial control. His four points were a broad-based national united front, communist-party leadership of the united front, communist-party stability, and an armed struggle and a base of operations.[66] In the case of Vietnam, where the Viet Minh formed the core of the resistance against the French, there was no problem with the first and fourth points, but the second and third points were problematic. The ICP had grown from a mere 5,000 members in 1945 to 760,000 in the 1950s,[67] and the party's leadership position in both the united front and the Viet Minh government was secure. But the Vietnamese communists could not see themselves as conforming to the Chinese model unless the party declared itself openly.

It was in these circumstances that the Vietnamese communists held their Second Party Congress—the first in sixteen years—February 11–17, 1951. The central themes of the congress were application of the Chinese model and of the concept of a people's democratic revolution to the Vietnamese revolution and public declaration of the existence of a communist party in Vietnam.[68]

Party Secretary General Truong Chinh explained why it was felt necessary to apply the concept of a people's democratic revolution to the Vietnamese revolution and why the Vietnamese revolution had to be differentiated from the Cambodian and Laotian revolutions: "Vietnam is more developed than Cambodia and Laos in every aspect, economically, politically, socially, and culturally. With the August Revolution we saw the birth of the Democratic Republic of Vietnam and the establishment of a people's democracy in Vietnam. Events since then have further distinguished the Vietnamese revolution from the Cambodian and Laotian revolutions. . . .

---

[65] TLGC 15.

[66] A Japanese translation of Liu Xiao Ji's speech is published in Nihon Kokusai Mondai Kenkyūsho [Japan Institute of International Affairs], ed., *Shin Chūgoku shiryō shūsei* [Documents from the new China], vol. 3 (Tokyo: Nihon Kokusai Mondai Kenkyūsho [Japan Institute of International Affairs], 1969), pp. 9–15. For a discussion of the speech, see Okabe, "Chūgoku no Tōnan Ajia seisaku," pp. 241–43.

[67] *50 Nam*, p. 113.

[68] In the opening speech, Ton Duc Thang identified three tasks to be carried out at this congress: analyze domestic and international conditions and define the party's general plan and strategy for a people's democratic revolution; discuss and draft a resolution on the public declaration of the party's existence and the formation of a strong new party; and elect a new central committee (TLGC 16).

The time has come when we must recognize that the Vietnamese revolution confronts different issues from the revolutions in Cambodia and Laos."[69]

At this congress the Vietnamese communists officially declared their intention of following the Chinese model in their own revolution. The Vietnamese Workers' Party rules adopted at the congress stipulated that the party's ideological basis and action policies derived from Mao as well as Marx, Engels, Lenin, and Stalin.[70] The rules stated that "the situation of the colonies and semicolonies of Asia closely resembles that of China. [Mao Zedong's ideology] provides a guide for revolution in these countries. Vietnam's experience, especially, testifies to the validity of applying Mao Zedong's ideology."[71]

Another notable event at the Second Party Congress was the labeling of the Vietnamese revolution a "national people's democratic revolution." The Vietnamese revolution, a people's democratic revolution that had as its primary goal national liberation, had three missions: to achieve national liberation, to sweep away all feudalistic exploitation, and to build a foundation for socialism.[72] The report on the government explained that there were two kinds of people's democracies: one was the dictatorship of the proletariat seen in Eastern Europe; the other was the people's democratic dictatorship practiced in China and Vietnam. The report added that insofar as it still had not achieved national liberation, the Vietnamese people's democratic dictatorship was inferior to that of China.[73]

The initial effect of this redefinition of the Vietnamese revolution was to pave the way for the communists to emerge into the open as the Vietnamese Workers' Party. A representative of the party spoke at a joint meeting of the Viet Minh and Lien Viet united fronts on March 3, 1951. This was the first overt activity of the communist party since its announcement of its dissolution in November 1946.[74]

In contrast to these events, in the interest of maintaining national unity the party remained cautious in its implementation of a land-reform program.[75] This was also why the party chose to call itself a "workers' party" rather than assume the controversial label "communist."[76]

---

[69] Truong Chinh, *Ban ve Cach Mang Viet Nam*, vol. 1 (Ban chap hanh Trung uong xuat ban, 1952), p. 7. The handwritten transcript differs slightly from this version. The transcript does not include the opening sentence, "Vietnam is more developed than Cambodia and Laos in every aspect, economically, politically, socially, and culturally." And the transcript of the sentence beginning "Events since then" does not include the word "further."

[70] TLGC 26.

[71] TLGC 21.

[72] "Chinh cuong Dang Lao dong Viet Nam," LSDCSVN 2, p. 205.

[73] TLGC 22.

[74] Ban nghien cuu lich su Dang Trung uong, *Nhung Su Kien Lich Su Dang*, vol. 2 (Hanoi: Nha xuat ban Su that, 1979), p. 258.

[75] The report on the Vietnamese revolution delivered at the Second Party Congress stated: "It is our task to fight feudalism even as we fight imperialism. To enable the resistance to swiftly annihilate the imperialist invaders and liberate the people, we must act systematically and gradually, enhancing the revolutionary power of the people and maintaining the unity of all the people" (TLGC 18). The Vietnamese Workers' Party did not address the issue of land reform until its fourth Central Committee Plenum, in January 1953. See Murano, "Kita Betonamu no tochi kaikaku"; Motoo Furuta, "Betonamu ni okeru jishu rosen no mosaku" [Vietnam's search for an independent line], *Rekishigaku kenkyū* [Journal of historical studies], no. 478 (March 1980).

[76] Fall, *The Viet-Minh Regime*, p. 40; TLGC 19.

Having put the Vietnamese revolution on a new track, how did the party congress of 1951 perceive the Cambodian and Laotian revolutions? The idea that the Cambodian and Laotian revolutions differed in character from the Vietnamese revolution was reasserted more explicitly. Truong Chinh observed: "Although Cambodia and Laos have no unified working class, because of the Indochina Communist Party's creation of party organizations in Cambodia and Laos the revolutions in these countries are being directed by the working class. However, these countries have no capitalists, and their industries remain undeveloped. These differences in social structure make the Cambodian and Laotian revolutions different in character and aims from the Vietnamese revolution."[77]

A resolution was adopted declaring the Cambodian and Laotian revolutions to be revolutions for national liberation aimed at attaining national independence and *limiting* feudalistic exploitation. That these revolutions were not directed at *eliminating* feudalistic exploitation or at building a foundation for socialism was interpreted as differentiating the struggles in Cambodia and Laos from the national people's democratic revolution of Vietnam.[78]

Truong Chinh also spoke of the party's leadership of the government and the united front in Cambodia and Laos as well as the party's decision to come out into the open: "One feature that distinguishes Cambodia and Laos [from Vietnam] is that communists do not control [the leadership]. Officially, certain members of the royal families in these countries run the government, but unofficially the foundation of government is actually controlled by communists. . . . While we have decided to bring the communist party out into the open in Vietnam, there is no need to do so yet in Cambodia and Laos."[79]

This view of the situation contributed to the decision to divide the ICP into three independent parties. In 1951, legitimizing the communist party by accepting China as a role model and adopting the theory of a people's democratic revolution were the most urgent issues on the party agenda. Since no corresponding need for legitimacy was seen in the case of Cambodia and Laos, the granting of official status only to the communist party in Vietnam necessitated a complete reorganization of the ICP. Adoption of the policy of setting up independent parties in Cambodia and Laos and of the view that the revolutions in Cambodia and Laos differed in character from the revolution in Vietnam led to the decision at the Second Party Congress to divide the ICP into three separate parties, one of which was the Vietnamese Workers' Party.[80]

If we accept the fact that in 1951 the Vietnamese communists were primarily concerned with organizing the Vietnamese Workers' Party and legitimizing its existence, we can understand why the ICP was divided even though the Cambodians and Laotians were not yet ready to maintain their own party organizations. It is important to bear in mind that the Vietnamese communists did not decide to divide the ICP because Cambodia and Laos had become less important to their cause or because they wanted to reduce their involvement in the revolutions underway in those two coun-

---

[77] TLGC 19.

[78] TLGC 25.

[79] TLGC 19.

[80] The resolution regarding this stated: "In keeping with the new conditions evident in Indochina and the world, the Vietnamese Workers' Party will be established with a program and rules tailored to the situation in Vietnam. Revolutionary groups conforming to conditions in Cambodia and Laos will also probably be formed in these two countries" (TLGC 24).

tries. On the contrary, the decision to divide the ICP was made at the same time that the Vietnamese communists were declaring all Indochina to be a united front. Cambodia and Laos were, after all, essential to a successful unified resistance.[81]

The Vietnamese were well aware of the weakness of the newly independent Cambodian and Laotian communists and made supporting them a prime obligation of the newly formed Vietnamese Workers' Party. The resolution stated that "the Vietnamese Workers' Party has an obligation to support its Cambodian and Laotian comrades in their endeavors to gain national independence and to establish people's revolutionary parties that conform to democratic principles."[82]

CONCLUSION

This paper has focused on the factors behind the ICP's policy of establishing independent communist parties in Cambodia and Laos and the reasons behind the ICP's 1951 decision to divide into three parties. I would like to conclude with a broader analysis of the division of the ICP.

Vietnamese communist policies toward Cambodia and Laos during the period in question were tailored to the needs of the Vietnamese resistance movement and revolution and to the security concerns of the newly founded Democratic Republic of Vietnam. This is evinced by the emphasis on the military importance of the Cambodian and Laotian fronts and the division of the ICP into three separate parties primarily as a means of furthering the Vietnamese revolution.

Certainly it was in Vietnam's interest to ensure that the resistance movement spread throughout Indochina. The French controlled the deltas and part of the central coastal plain, and Cambodia and Laos provided sorely needed communication and supply routes linking Viet Minh bases in the north and the south.[83] Expanding the front to encompass Cambodia and Laos also served to disperse the already small French force and lessen the pressure on Vietnam.[84]

Vietnamese support was just as vital to the Cambodian and Laotian resistance movements. After the fall of the Free Thai government, they had nowhere else to turn for armed support. For Cambodia and Laos to distance themselves from Vietnam would be tantamount to giving up their armed resistance against the French. The Vietnamese communists' concept of a united Indochinese front was an acknowledgment of this symbiotic relationship.

The most effective political means of consolidating a unified resistance against the French, in the view of the Vietnamese communists, was solidarity among Vietnamese, Cambodians, and Laotians, all fighting for their own national liberation. This view had many points in common with the concept of Vietnam, Cambodia, and Laos

---

[81] For example, 500–700 political and military agents were sent from Vietnam to Laos at the end of 1946 and the beginning of 1947. The number had grown to 5,000–7,000 at the end of 1950 and the beginning of 1951, and to 17,000 in 1953 (TLGC 29).

[82] TLGC 24.

[83] For example, when the French army attempted to seize the coastal plain around Hue, in central Vietnam, and thereby cut off the Viet Minh fifth military inter-zone from the other resistance zones, the party's central committee commanded the southern regional committee to open up a supply route from southern Vietnam through Cambodia and Laos to northern Vietnam. See Nguyen Hao Hung, "Lien minh chien dau Viet Nam-Campuchia."

[84] When a nationwide resistance movement was launched in Vietnam, in December 1946, the French had only 7,000–8,000 soldiers in Cambodia (ibid.).

as separate nation-states but departed from that concept in positing a reorganization of relations among the peoples of Indochina as a whole.

That the Cambodian and Laotian communist parties were conceived as being made up solely of Cambodian and Laotian members, respectively, illustrates this most clearly. However, if the three-way division of the ICP had been simply a cosmetic change designed to make party organization reflect the existence of three separate nation-states (the French were thinking along these lines at the time), it should have sufficed to transfer the affiliation of the Vietnamese who made up the vast majority of ICP members in Cambodia and Laos to the new parties formed in those countries.[85] This would have been in keeping with the organizational principle of the Comintern, which dictated that communists join the party of the country in which they resided.

Instead, the Vietnamese ICP members in Cambodia and Laos were made members of the new Vietnamese Workers' Party, some of whom acted as "advisers" to the organizations promoting the establishment of Cambodian and Laotian communist parties.[86] The Vietnamese communists took great pains to ensure that the parties in Cambodia and Laos would be made up purely of Cambodians and Laotians, respectively. They envisioned a framework of national liberation for those countries in which the Cambodians (Laotians) fighting for liberation and the formation of an independent government would be supported by a communist party of fellow Cambodians (Laotians). The Cambodian and Laotian nation-states envisioned by the Vietnamese communists did not include Vietnamese residents of those countries. This was because the Vietnamese saw themselves as having their own battle of national liberation to fight within the broader framework of Indochinese independence.

The Vietnamese envisioned an Indochina divided along national lines, arguing that this was the most advantageous way of organizing the unified resistance movement in Indochina. It did not occur to them that creating separate Cambodian and Laotian communist parties was in any way a threat to Indochinese solidarity. Thus, in 1951, the Vietnamese saw it as their duty to support their comrades in Cambodia and Laos by sending Vietnamese advisers to guide them in the organization of their own party structures.

The result was the creation of three independent parties—Vietnamese, Cambodian, and Laotian—that were linked in solidarity with regard to Indochina as a whole while fighting individually for national liberation, and with the Vietnamese party aiding its weaker counterparts in Cambodia and Laos. In my view, this situation was generated by circumstances peculiar to Indochina and by the history of the communist movement in that region and would later contribute to the special relationship among the three countries.

We must also realize, however, that in 1951 the Vietnamese communists saw their support of Cambodia and Laos as being part of a greater "proletarian internationalism," as well. This was evident in Truong Chinh's characterization, at the ICP's

---

[85] According to a report delivered at the Second Party Congress, at the time of the congress the ICP had 1,784 members in Cambodia. Of this number 150 were Cambodians, the remainder Vietnamese. In Laos the party had 2,091 members, only 31 of whom were Laotians, while the remainder were all Vietnamese (TLGC 27).

[86] The report cited in note 85 declared that in reforming the ICP "the Vietnamese communists active in Cambodia and Laos will be regarded as members of the Vietnamese Workers' Party. Cambodian and Laotian communist party members cannot join the Vietnamese Workers' Party" (ibid.).

Second Party Congress, of the Cambodian and Laotian revolutions as "people's revolutions," which he explained as a concept used in the Comintern's analysis of "backward countries."[87] He was referring to the Sixth Comintern Congress of 1928, at which revolutions had been categorized by the degree to which capitalism had developed. In his view, Cambodia and Laos were not as advanced as other countries under colonial or semicolonial domination,[88] and therefore their revolutions necessarily differed in character. At the root of this concept was a theory of noncapitalistic development according to which it was possible to "achieve socialism without ever passing through a capitalistic stage if backward countries can be ensured of strong aid from countries already under proletarian dictatorship."[89] As he saw it, "the development of society in Cambodia and Laos is at a low level, but with help from the Soviet Union and other democratic counties they should be able to skip the capitalistic stage of development."[90]

In thus justifying aid to a "national uprising," the Vietnamese were interpreting the Comintern view broadly, but no doubt they felt it was necessary to define their aid to Cambodia and Laos in terms that would accord with the idea of a greater "proletarian internationalism."

The division of the ICP in 1951 enabled Cambodian and Laotian communists to assume positions of greater importance within their own governments, but at the same time paved the way for new problems in the relationship among the three parties, a subject that is beyond the scope of this paper.

This paper was originally published under the title "Indoshina kyōsantō kara mittsu no tō e: 1948–51 nen no, Betonamu kyōsanshugisha no tai Kambojia, Raos seisaku" [From the Indochina Communist Party to three parties: The Vietnamese communists' policies toward Cambodia and Laos, 1948–1951], in *Ajia kenkyū* [Asian studies] 29, no. 4 (January 1983): 42–78. It is based on a paper delivered at the 1981 national convention of the Japan Association for Asian Political and Economic Studies. I am indebted to the many people at the convention who made valuable comments on that paper.

---

[87] TLGC 19.

[88] See Yōichi Murata, ed. and trans., *Kominterun shiryōshū* [Collected Comintern documents], vol. 4 (Tokyo: Ōtsuki Shoten, 1981), p. 352.

[89] Ibid.

[90] TLGC 19.

6

CHANGES IN THE LITERARY POLICY OF THE VIETNAMESE WORKERS' PARTY, 1956–1958

Hirohide Kurihara

INTRODUCTION

Nikita Khrushchev's denunciation of Joseph Stalin at the Twentieth Congress of the Communist Party of the Soviet Union (CPSU), held in February 1956, had significant effects on the Party itself and on the international communist movement as a whole. It not only precipitated the collapse of Stalin's once-invincible prestige but also signaled a sweeping reappraisal of the Stalinist political system and worldview.

This reappraisal represented a serious problem, especially for the communist parties in power in socialist countries, since it directly affected their own political hegemony. To be sure, different parties dealt with the problem differently. Some parties, like those of Poland and Hungary, went so far as to change the Party leadership, while others, notably the Chinese Communist Party (CCP), skirted the issue by asserting that the problems raised by the denunciation of Stalin were peculiar to Stalin.[1] Despite such differences, however, every communist party in the socialist camp was obliged to refer to the role of Stalin in one way or another and to reconstruct the legitimacy of its own policies and strategy.

The Vietnamese Workers' Party (VWP) was no exception. In the wake of the denunciation of Stalin, the Party undertook to reexamine itself using denial of the cult of personality and expansion of intraparty democracy as the two criteria of self-evaluation. However, this effort, coupled with the influence of China's "Let a hundred flowers bloom, let a hundred schools of thought contend" campaign, stirred up a whirlwind of criticism of the Party by writers, intellectuals, and students in the autumn of 1956. The criticisms voiced by these writers and intellectuals, many of whom had fought in the Resistance War against France (the First Indochinese War; 1946–1954) along with the Party, and some of whom were party members, were a matter of grave concern to the VWP.

Some of the dissident writers and intellectuals, echoing the CCP's "hundred flowers" policy and the Soviet denunciation of Stalin in the pages of the newspaper *Nhan van* and the journal *Giai pham* (referred to hereafter as the NV and the GP,

---

[1] Nakajima 1971, pp. 97–102.

respectively),[2] openly attacked the policies of the VWP and the Government of the Democratic Republic of Vietnam (DRV), including their literary policy. Though the direct impact of the publication of such criticisms was limited mainly to the capital, Hanoi, from the standpoint of the Party it still constituted pressure to reconsider its strategy toward the literary sphere. Moreover, given the fact that these writers and intellectuals bolstered their criticisms by citing the policies of the CCP and other communist parties, the VWP had to bring its own policy into balance with the policies of the other parties.

At first the VWP took the stance of tolerating the publication of the NV and the GP and engaging them in open debate. In December 1956, however, the Party changed its stance and banned the two publications. Thereafter, it further stiffened its attitude, finally expelling from literary organizations the dissident writers and intellectuals who had been affiliated with the two publications. Thus, the Party's attitude toward literary circles changed significantly within the short span of less than two years.

The Party itself has always regarded NV and the GP as vehicles of an antirevolutionary force that took advantage of the Party's weakness at a time when it was trying to deal with various difficulties.[3] Most Western studies of these events interpret them as merely a manifestation of the failure of the VWP's effort to introduce Chinese policies, especially the "hundred flowers" policy.[4] Such interpretations, however, are problematic on many counts. For one thing, neither interpretation offers a convincing explanation of the fact that the VWP's leadership criticized itself during the same period for having tried to carry out land reform uncritically modeled on the Chinese experience.

The overall picture of the changes in the VWP's literary policy in the 1956–1958 period has been seriously blurred because the problem has been interpreted simply as a rift between the group of writers and intellectuals that contributed articles to the NV and the GP on the one hand and the Party leadership on the other. The purpose of this paper is to view this process of policy change in a much wider perspective and reexamine its significance both in relation to international political developments in the socialist camp following the denunciation of Stalin, which had a significant bearing on the views and activities of writers and intellectuals in the DRV, and in relation to the internal process of socialization.

It is important to take into account the problems involved in socialization because the 1956–1958 period coincided with what the VWP officially labeled the period of transition from "economic recovery" to "socialist transformation." Thus, these two years saw the VWP play an increasingly strong leadership role in society. In the literary sphere, this took the form of the mobilization of writers and intellectuals in the service of a "cultural revolution."

---

[2] *Nhan van* means "humanism," and *Giai pham* means "masterpieces." Both periodicals were privately published in Hanoi. Their first issues appeared between the end of August and mid-September 1956: August 29 for the GP and September 20 for the NV. Each periodical published five issues before being banned in December. (The GP had also published an issue in January 1956; withdrawn from circulation on the order of the VWP, it was reprinted in the autumn of that year and thus is included in the five issues published in the autumn of 1956.)

[3] See, for example, To Huu 1973, pp. 132–219.

[4] See, for example, Hoang Van Chi 1964; Honey 1957, 1963; Nhu Phong 1962. See also the analysis of the political process of the 1957–1958 period in Furuta 1980, which, unlike other studies, characterizes this period as one in which the VWP was searching for an independent line.

I. The Emergence of the Problem: The Denunciation of Stalin and the "Hundred Flowers" Policy

In August 1956 the Vietnamese Literary Association (Hoi Van Nghe Viet Nam) held an eighteen-day literary theory study meeting to analyze Mikhail Sholokhov's speech at the Twentieth Congress of the CPSU and Lu Dingyi's May 1956 speech expounding the "hundred flowers" policy. Many of the participating writers strongly demanded that the VWP launch a policy similar to the CCP's "hundred flowers" policy in Vietnam, as well. They also voiced many complaints about the VWP, criticizing it for its failure to devise concrete literary policies, for its narrow-minded guidelines on creative writing, for its formalistic application of the principle that "literature should serve politics," and for its unjust practice of denouncing writers by stigmatization.[5]

Even though the difference in aesthetic views between writers and the Party leadership had surfaced as early as the period of the Resistance War,[6] it was only after the conclusion of the Geneva agreements in July 1954 that writers began to voice collective demands to the Party.

Immediately after the conclusion of the Geneva agreements the VWP had to undertake the task of rebuilding the economy, exhausted by a nine-year war, and of providing relief for the people. In the urban districts that had been under French control during the war, the most urgent task was to resolve the serious problems of unemployment and food shortages and to resume factory production. The devastated villages that had been turned into battlefields also had to be rehabilitated.

The VWP accorded the highest priority to economic problems during the years from 1954 to 1956, even though what the Party called the "period of economic recovery" extended through 1957. This does not mean that the VWP paid no attention to cultural affairs during these years.[7] Yet given the Party leadership's strong belief that only economic recovery and development could lay the groundwork for cultural development,[8] there is no denying that culture was treated as secondary to economics. Moreover, in keeping with the basic policy of "consolidating the North under any circumstances" for the achievement of national unification, soon after the signing of the Geneva agreements the Party leadership set forth a long-term plan to build socialism in the North step by step[9] and described concretely how the plan was to be implemented. The plan was concerned primarily with economics. One major feature was the call for socialist transformation of the national economy by such means as gradual fostering of the state-run and cooperative economic sectors, gradual transformation of the private-capital sector into a state-capital sector, and socialist transformation of commerce and industry. Another was emphasis on the importance of organizing production activities in a well-planned manner.[10]

---

[5] Nguyen Chuong 1956a.

[6] GPMT II, pp. 5–7. Since 1948 controversies had occurred over popular criticism of the arts, Picasso's works, and the banning of a play by Chu Ngoc.

[7] The Ministry of Culture was established in 1955 to raise the cultural and ideological standards of the people. Also, when Prime Minister Pham Van Dong met with university students in Hanoi in 1955, he emphasized the importance of promoting science, literature, and the arts (*Tap san Dai hoc su pham*, pp. 4–10).

[8] *Tai lieu hoc tap ve khoi phuc kinh te*, p. 2.

[9] Vien Mac–Le-nin 1982, pp. 29–31.

[10] Ibid., pp. 40–41.

The VWP had made no changes or additions to its literary policy since Truong Chinh's 1948 speech, delivered during the First Indochinese War, on the theme "Marxism and Vietnamese Culture." On the one hand, this speech pronounced "nationalism, promotion of science, and popularization" to be the new direction for Vietnamese culture and laid down a code of conduct to be followed by cultural organizers, which demanded that they "remain absolutely loyal to the Fatherland and the Resistance War," that they "base their activities on Marxist doctrine," and that they "serve the people." At the same time, because of the urgent need to incorporate a wide spectrum of writers and intellectuals into a united cultural front for the purpose of winning the Resistance War against France, Truong Chinh specified the minimum qualifications necessary for membership in the front: support of the causes of national independence and of freedom and democracy.[11] This means that when, upon the conclusion of the Resistance War, the VWP leadership began to regard construction of a socialist state as the national goal, it should have started to work out a new literary policy adapted to the new phase.

One noteworthy feature of the VWP's literary policy in the 1954–1956 period was tolerance of a variety of views. For instance, a collection of poems titled *Viet Bac* by To Huu, a member of the VWP's central committee, was widely discussed among the masses, and even views critical of his work were published in VWP organs. The Party also allowed writers to engage in creative activities without censorship. On the other hand, this period saw friction arise between a group of writers and the VWP cadres in charge of the literary sphere. Broadly speaking, the friction was brought about by the decisive change in the status of the VWP from a resistance force at war with France to the Party controlling all of the North. After the signing of the Geneva agreements the VWP began to assert increasingly strong dominance over both the population and organizations, including not only the former inhabitants of the districts controlled by the French during the war who had chosen to remain in the North after the war but also the Party followers who had fought in the Resistance War.

Most of the writers in this period had taken part in the Resistance War and had returned from base camps to Hanoi after the conclusion of the Geneva agreements. For instance, in 1955 a group of writers within the military, including such party members as Tran Dan, Hoang Cam, and Tu Phac, drafted a "Proposal for the Establishment of Literary Organizations Within the Military" that demanded a number of organizational reforms: return of the right to supervise literary activities to writers themselves, abolition of the commissar system of the Army Literary Corps, abolition of the existing military system governing literary activities within the army, and establishment within the army of a literary branch affiliated with the Vietnamese Literary Association directly, not through the Propaganda Bureau or the Commissariat.[12] Thus, some of the issues that were to come to the fore later, such as the relationship between politics and literature and the return of the right to supervise creative writing to writers, were raised as early as 1955.

The spring 1956 issue of the GP, published in January of that year by the Minh Duc publishing house, carried Tran Dan's poem "We Shall Win" (Nhat dinh thang), some passages of which could be interpreted as advocating national unification by means of military advance into the South.[13] Even though this may have been no more

---

[11] Truong Chinh 1975, pp. 145–235.

[12] To Huu 1973, p. 142.

[13] THDN, pp. 103–12; Elliott 1976, pp. 200–201. A party document also attests to the fact that

than an honest expression of the author's feelings after having fought against France, it was at odds with the policy of peaceful unification that the VWP was officially proclaiming at the time. It should also be pointed out that the VWP regarded the poem as defaming the DRV, and the spring 1956 issue of the GP was ordered withdrawn from circulation.

The evidence referred to above shows that by early 1956 at least some writers had started to voice objections to the actual conditions of literary organizations and to the Party's policy toward literature. To be sure, the above-mentioned two incidents did not develop into a movement involving all literary circles but remained isolated and local in impact. Nonetheless, judging from the atmosphere prevailing at the August 1956 literary theory study meeting, it suffices to say that discontent with the official literary policy was by no means a phenomenon peculiar to the participants in the two incidents. Thus the VWP was criticized for its lack of a new literary policy just when it was busy tackling the urgent task of economic recovery. But the Party did not respond to the writers immediately.

This was the state of affairs in Vietnamese literary circles when the Twentieth Congress of the CPSU was convened. The VWP's response to the issues raised by that congress, including the denunciation of Stalin, was made public at the Party's Ninth Plenum, in April 1956. The VWP's basic attitude toward the denunciation of Stalin was similar to the CCP's in that the VWP interpreted the implications of the denunciation narrowly, as ascribable primarily to the evils of the cult of personality and to Stalin's individual faults.[14] Nor did the various propositions put forward at the Twentieth CPSU Congress, such as those concerning peaceful coexistence, the possibility of preventing another world war, and the potential for a peaceful transition to socialism, induce the VWP to readjust its own policies; the Party responded to these propositions cautiously, emphasizing the necessity of maintaining "vigilance" against imperialists and of taking into account shifts in the "balance of power" that could easily change the international situation.[15]

This is not to say that the VWP reacted totally negatively to the propositions made at the Twentieth CPSU Congress. At the Ninth Plenum the VWP leadership admitted that the cult of personality, which was practiced "to some extent" both inside and outside the Party and at both the central and the local levels, was an obstacle to "collective leadership and intraparty democracy" and to "the creativity and initiative of ordinary party members and the people at large." The party emphasized the need to overcome these evils by reinforcing collective leadership, encouraging intraparty democracy and criticism from below, strengthening the Party's relationship with the masses, and struggling against bureaucratism.[16] Pursued properly, these proposed countermeasures could have prompted reexamination of the VWP's policies and encouraged the democratization of society.

It was under these conditions that the literary theory study meeting was held. Despite its stated purpose of helping writers and intellectuals improve their theoretical understanding of creative writing, in fact it provided the participants with a chance to join forces and express their discontent. The main tenet of Lu Dingyi's "hundred flowers" speech, one of the subjects of study at the meeting, was its call for

---

there was opposition to peaceful unification (HT 1956a, p. 9).

[14] HT 1956b, pp. 34–36.

[15] Ibid., pp. 19–27.

[16] Ibid., pp. 37–38.

"breaking through the stagnancy of intellectual activities" in China.[17] The speech urged that intellectuals be allowed to enjoy various freedoms—"freedom of independent thought in literary, artistic, and scientific research activities; freedom of expression; freedom to engage in creative work and to criticize the work of others; freedom to express opinions; and freedom to withhold opinions"—although these freedoms were based on the concept "among the people." The speech also objected to the sectarianism practiced by some members of the CCP.[18]

These messages, coupled with the positive image conveyed by the slogan "Let a hundred flowers bloom, let a hundred schools of thought contend," seem to have evoked strong sympathy among DRV writers and intellectuals dissatisfied with their situation.[19] Indeed, the literary theory study meeting marked the starting point of the controversy between writers and the VWP leadership.

II. The Development and Outcome of Criticism of the VWP by Writers and Intellectuals

The NV and the GP began publication between the end of August and mid-September, shortly after the literary theory study meeting, and both reflected the atmosphere of that meeting. The first issue of both publications addressed a wide array of topics, including the Party's guidance of literary activities, that is, the proper relationship between politics and literature; the need to improve the living conditions of writers; criticism of policies not directly related to literature, such as land-reform and economic policies; and criticism of the bureaucratic trend of society.[20] It was the question of guidance of literary activities that ignited the most heated criticism of the VWP.

Phan Khoi, an influential figure in literary circles, who had begun his writing career in the second decade of the century, contributed an article titled "Criticism of the Leadership in Art and Literature" to the autumn 1956 issue of the GP, published on August 29. Viewing the two-year period since the signing of the Geneva agreements as a time of conflict between the leaders in art and literature and "the masses of writers and artists," he attributed the conflict to the VWP's erroneous literary guidance, especially excessive interference with literary activities by party cadres in charge of literature. Believing that politics could never supervise literature, Phan Khoi emphasized that the special nature of literature, the individuality of writers, and their creative methods should be respected, because this was the only way of ensuring "mutual benefits" to both politics and literature.[21] He further elaborated his argument by criticizing various errors of the VWP, such as the practice of forcing writers to change wording that was deemed unacceptable, the imposition of complicated

---

[17] Nakajima 1971, p. 105. In the DRV, too, a mood of inactivity seems to have prevailed among intellectuals after the signing of the Geneva agreements. The writer To Hoai later lamented that writers showed less enthusiasm for creative writing after the Geneva agreements than during the Resistance War against France (To Hoai 1957, p. 74).

[18] The limitations and arbitrary nature of the lecture are discussed in some detail in Nakajima 1971, pp. 142–44.

[19] Although Sholokhov's speech received less attention than the CCP's "hundred flowers" policy, the passages in which he urged the Soviet Writers' Union to act to improve the living conditions of writers and to support their research activities aroused sympathy among Vietnamese writers (GPMT II, pp. 69–70).

[20] The above is based on GPMT II; THDN; Hoang Van Chi 1958.

[21] THDN, pp. 60–72.

conditions on authors, the banning of the spring 1956 issue of the GP, the launching of an ad hominem attack on Tran Dan that had nothing to do with literary criticism, and the arbitrary way in which the winners of literary awards were selected.[22]

Truong Tuu, a scholar of Vietnamese literature, echoed Phan Khoi's argument, asserting that "at no time has the act of telling the truth, telling it straightforwardly and thoroughly, been so important a yardstick of the loyalty of intellectuals to the people's democracy." Citing concrete instances of conflict between writers and the Party leadership dating back to the Resistance War against France, he concluded that the stagnancy prevailing in literary circles had been generated by the Party cadres in charge of literature, who, because of their idolization of party leaders, had tried to direct literary activities in a highly bureaucratic manner.[23] Truong Tuu described the situation of the literary circles of the time as follows: "These men—who despise the masses and destroy their unity, act arbitrarily on their own authority, fawn to their superiors, and exclude their subordinates—have been guiding literature for years, have been complimented by their superiors for their supposedly superb performance, and have even won official commendation. It need hardly be said how suffocating the atmosphere of literary circles is.

"Add to this method of guidance their shallow and biased understanding of literature, their mechanical application of the principle that writers should serve [politics] without hesitation, their formalistic imposition of policies and plans on artistic works, the monopolistic and sectarian control they exercise at the time of publication of works, their administrative and militaristic oppression of writers who dare to tell the truth straightforwardly and thoroughly. . . . All these are features of the suffocating situation from which literary circles have been suffering for the last five or six years."[24]

Many other contributors to the NV and the GP referred to the problems caused by interference in literary matters by party cadres in charge of literature. There was the story of an artist who was forced to revise a painting many times on insistent instructions from above, and the story of a writer who was severely overburdened with clerical work, which left him virtually no time for creative writing.[25] The historian Dao Duy Anh wrote an exposé of party cadres' meddling in the study of periodization and the formation of the Vietnamese nation. He questioned the behavior of party cadres who, because of their stubborn adherence to the writings of Marx and the opinions of their superiors, tried to suppress "individuals whose opinions overstep traditional theories and conventional frameworks of thinking" and labeled them "reformists." He ascribed this problem to dogmatism and the cult of personality.[26]

On the basis of their critical perception of the situation, the contributors to the NV and the GP began to articulate demands to the Party: that the cult of personality be abolished, that a policy similar to the Chinese "hundred flowers" policy be intro-

---

[22] Ibid. It should be pointed out that in October the Association of Writers accepted Phan Khoi's critique in part, admitting that the way in which it had criticized Tran Dan and the method of selecting winners of literary awards were improper (ND 1956a).

[23] GPMT II, pp. 3–11.

[24] Ibid., p. 12.

[25] THDN, pp. 258–60.

[26] Ibid., pp. 284–87. The expression "cult of personality" was used here not to indicate the object of a cult but to connote the ubiquitous phenomenon of uncritical subservience to superiors. Other contributors used the word in more or less the same sense.

duced, that policies concerning literary activities and intellectuals be established, and that "the right to guide literary affairs be returned to writers themselves" and "matters concerning a profession be left to those practicing that profession."[27] We should bear in mind that at that time top VWP officials met with representatives of the writers to exchange views on the "hundred flowers" policy.[28] It should also be remembered that discontent was rife among intellectuals, who felt that they were being deprived of opportunities to put their expertise to good use and that they were being constantly and closely watched and restrained. In fact, the Party organ *Nhan Dan* took a serious view of the problem and published an article about it.[29]

All this suggests that the demands articulated in the NV and the GP were by no means peculiar to their contributors but reflected opinions shared by the wider community of writers and intellectuals. Indeed, this explains, at least in part, why the VWP refrained from taking a hard line, as it had earlier in withdrawing the spring 1956 issue of the GP, and chose instead to allow continued publication of the NV and the GP and to indicate willingness to debate the issue publicly.[30]

It should also be pointed out that the VWP itself was beginning to reexamine its policies. Indicative of this is the decision by the Tenth Plenum, in September 1956, to correct the "errors" committed in the course of implementing land reform, to expand democracy, and to guarantee the people's freedom and democratic rights.[31] This decision was intended to take the plan adopted at the Ninth Plenum a step further by having it reflect the voice of the masses.

With these points in mind, let us look at how the VWP's reactions to the NV and the GP changed, focusing primarily on the opinions expressed in the *Nhan Dan* and the Party's theoretical journal, the *Hoc Tap*. In September, a statement representing the Party's official position admitted that the criticisms raised by Phan Khoi were "partly in accord with reality," thus acknowledging faults in the VWP's guidance of literary activities.[32] With regard to the wide range of demands concerning the "hundred flowers" policy, the Party declared that, though this policy was "correct in principle," the situations in Vietnam and China were different and Vietnam should not hastily imitate the Chinese policy but should, rather, continue to study it carefully for the time being.[33]

The latter statement was natural, in the light of the following two facts. On the one hand, the VWP leadership at the time was openly acknowledging that uncritical importation of a Chinese-style land-reform program was one of the primary reasons

---

[27] This demand was made not only by Phan Khoi and Dao Duy Anh but also by Truong Tuu (GPMT II, pp. 3–14), Hoang Hue (ibid., pp. 67–70), and Sy Ngoc (THDN, pp. 258–60).

[28] Truong Chinh 1957, TCVN 2, pp. 12–16.

[29] Dao Anh Kha 1956. It can be inferred from the *Nhan Dan* article that there was discord between intellectuals who had taken part in the Resistance War against France and those who had not, and that among the former, party cadres in charge of political affairs were receiving preferential treatment.

[30] There were only nine contributors to the spring 1956 issue of the GP, but I have been able to identify thirty-seven contributors to the NV and the GP in the autumn of that year.

[31] HT 1956c, pp. 6–12. The major "errors" committed in implementing land reform included misconstruing of the demarcations between different classes, excessive rectification of rural party cells, and excessive implementation of measures to suppress subversive activities. For details, see Murano 1976, pp. 97–108.

[32] Nguyen Chuong 1956a.

[33] Nguyen Chuong 1956b.

the land-reform policy was not progressing smoothly in Vietnam and, on the basis of this self-criticism, was emphasizing the need to take the realities of Vietnam into fuller consideration.[34] On the other hand, there was still no knowing at the time, even in China, how the "hundred flowers" policy was likely to develop.

In contrast, the question of whether the VWP should accede to the writers' demand for restoration of the right to guide literary activities for themselves was an extremely delicate one. Compliance with that demand might oblige the VWP to accept a pluralistic political system—specifically, a multiparty system—which would represent a total denial of the principle of one-party rule by the VWP. Insofar as one-party rule was regarded as the indispensable prerequisite to membership in the socialist camp at the time,[35] to allow this possibility to become a reality would seriously affect the DRV's status within the camp.

The viewpoints expressed in September and October by the VWP on the question of the right to guide literary activities can be summarized in the following two points. First, to return the right of supervision over literary activities to literary circles is to separate literature from politics and deny the Party's leadership in the literary sphere, and is therefore unacceptable. In a class society, where literature is one of the major weapons of class struggle, literature is inseparable from politics and should be subordinate to certain political objectives. In the context of Vietnam, this means that literature should be subordinate to the interests of the working class and to the Party representing these interests.[36] Second, what is at issue is not the question of returning the right to guide literary activities but the question of how to qualitatively improve guidance. The VWP will continue to guide literary circles ideologically and organizationally, in line with its own policy objectives, and it will do so basically by means of persuasion rather than coercive interference or peremptory orders. The Party pledges to respect the special nature of literature and writers' individuality and creative initiative.[37]

The VWP view of literature summarized above was much the same as the one Mao Zedong had expressed in "Lecture at a Discussion on Literature in Yenan."[38] The Party's guidance of literature, insofar as it was premised on the inseparability of literature and politics, obliged writers to follow the Party's policies when engaging in creative activities. In choosing the theme of a work, for instance, a writer was required to choose one that was directly relevant to issues of urgent importance, such as the struggle for national unification or economic recovery.[39] This stance was justified by applying to all writers, both party members and nonmembers, Lenin's theory of "party orientation [*partiinost'*] in literature," expounded in his 1905 article "Party Organizations and Party Literature."[40]

---

[34] Truong Chinh 1956, p. 17.

[35] As exemplified by the Hungarian Revolt, even Khrushchev, who had denounced Stalin, found attempts to undermine the one-party system unacceptable (McCauley 1987, p. 170).

[36] Nguyen Chuong 1956a; Xuan Truong 1956a; Hong Chuong 1956, pp. 35–36.

[37] Hong Chuong 1956, pp. 42, 45.

[38] Mao Zedong 1968, pp. 822–24.

[39] Hong Chuong 1956, p. 40.

[40] Ibid., pp. 35–36. Lenin used the term "party-oriented" (*partiinaia*) in relation to internal problems of the Russian Social-Democratic Workers' Party before it assumed power. For a detailed discussion of how the term came to be used in a wider sense, see Fujii 1976, pp. 203–34. This issue is also referred to in the NV (THDN, pp. 136–40).

Evidently, the VWP made little effort to propound new theories concerning literary guidance. The opinions expressed by the Party in response to critics writing in the NV can be summed up more or less as above. Nonetheless, it is worth noting that the VWP, in responding to the conflict that had emerged between writers and party cadres in charge of literary affairs, indicated its intention of introducing a degree of flexibility to the implementation of guidance. This seems to show that the situation was such that the VWP felt obliged to take some steps to soothe the discontented writers.

The VWP changed its attitude abruptly in early November, when it began to criticize the NV and the GP in a tone of harsh accusation and condemnation. In conjunction with this, administrative pressure was brought to bear on the NV editors with regard to publication procedures. Finally the paper was banned in December. The reversal in the Party's attitude was apparently prompted by at least two factors. One was that, to the VWP's displeasure, the NV was expanding its criticism of the VWP from the sphere of literature to that of politics and was beginning to gain increasing social influence. The other was an international factor, that is, the Hungarian Revolt in October and November, which prompted the Party to act decisively to prevent a similar occurrence in the DRV.

In October both the NV and the GP began to direct their criticisms not only to the literary sphere but to the political sphere, as well. One such criticism was raised by the philosopher Tran Duc Thao, who argued that the removal of Stalinist evils, such as narrow-minded and authoritarian methods of supervision and the cult of personality, was the prerequisite for the expansion and reinforcement of communism on a global scale. Extolling the significance of the popular struggle being waged in the DRV "under the leadership of the Party and the Government" against "bureaucratism, sectarianism, and the cult of personality," he proposed that the method of criticism, which is open to the public and which ensures "all people the freedom to criticize the leadership," be adopted as a means of promoting this struggle.[41]

What is noteworthy here is that his view serves as a clear example of the impact the denunciation of Stalin had on Vietnamese intellectuals. The popular struggle, Tran Duc Thao maintained, was part of the "movement for freedom and democracy that is growing among the people" of Vietnam, and which in turn formed part of a larger international movement that "was initiated by the Twentieth Congress of the CPSU and has spread worldwide."[42] He also maintained that striving to let "individual freedom" grow in order to create a communist society in which individuals, together with their individuality, are liberated is the ultimate "task of the proletarian dictatorship."[43]

At that time, the contentions of the NV and the GP were finding an expanding audience not only within the literary sphere but in the wider intellectual community, as well. A group of students began publishing a journal, *Dat Moi*, whose criticisms of the Party echoed those in the NV and the GP. Moreover, the positions of the NV and the GP were supported not simply by the party members who were regular contributors but also, if not too openly, by other party members. It is reported that some of

---

[41] *So phan tri thuc mien Bac*, pp. 11–14.

[42] Ibid., p. 11.

[43] Ibid., p. 16.

the latter went so far as to express their opinion that all political groups and organizations be granted freedom of association and activity.[44]

The social climate of the DRV was by no means calm and stable, either. It is true that following the Tenth Plenum measures to correct the "errors" in land reform were undertaken, but the administrative machinery in some rural districts was in a state of total paralysis.[45] On top of this, peasants' disturbances erupted in Quynh Luu district, Nghe An province, in November. Hanoi and other cities, where inflation was rampant, were shaken by clashes between citizens and administrative authorities over surveillance and taxation.[46]

Relations between the North and the South were disturbed, as well. The Ngo Dinh Diem regime in the South began to cite the NV's criticisms of the VWP in its anticommunist propaganda. The Party saw this as evidence that the NV was leaking information on the North to the South and backing the Diem regime's attempt to damage the prestige of the North.[47]

It was at this very moment that the Hungarian Revolt broke out. Interpreting it as an antirevolutionary revolt instigated by imperialist forces outside Hungary and antirevolutionary elements within Hungary that had exploited a legitimate movement of the Hungarian people,[48] the VWP supported the Soviet military intervention in Hungary. It is true that there was almost no possibility that the Hungarian Revolt would directly affect the political affairs of the DRV, because the situation in the DRV was far different from that in Hungary in many respects, including the processes of the seizure of power by the communists and the domestic and international environments of the two nations. Moreover, the Vietnamese intellectuals affiliated with the NV and the GP were no match for their Hungarian counterparts in the Petöfi Circle in terms of either the scale or the intensity of their activities.[49] Despite the many differences between Vietnam and Hungary, however, by its nature the Hungarian Revolt raised serious questions for the VWP and all other socialist regimes, because it undermined the cold-war belief in the "indestructibility of communist systems from within,"[50] which had long been shared by the political and military leaders of the West.

The grave implications of the Hungarian Revolt led the VWP to take a wary look at the activities of the opposition groups within the country and their growing influence, and to take steps to prevent a similar crisis from erupting in the DRV. This point of view was reflected clearly in the editorial published in the *Nhan Dan* on November 9, shortly after the second Soviet Army intervention in Hungary. Titled "Democracy and Dictatorship," the editorial affirmed the importance of upholding the policy of expanding democracy but emphasized that in the circumstances certain limits should be set on the expansion of democracy and that the "proletarian dictatorship" should play a key role.

---

[44] Dao Duy Tung 1957, pp. 25–27.

[45] HT 1956d, p. 2.

[46] Nguyen Duy Trinh 1956, p. 28.

[47] Xuan Truong 1956b.

[48] ND 1956b.

[49] The NV and the GP did not organize popular forums, as did the Petöfi Circle. For information on the Petöfi Circle, see Vali 1961, pp. 225, 228, 254.

[50] Fehér 1983, p. 3.

"When our nation is divided into two," it argued, "when imperialists are hatching malicious plots against our people, and when the independence and unity of our Fatherland is jeopardized, it is a grave mistake to speak only of the expansion of democracy and make no mention of the [proletarian] dictatorship." The editorial continued: "We will never tolerate anybody who takes advantage of freedom and democracy, and of freedom of expression, to conspire or actually attempt to set the people at variance with the Party and the Government, attack our regime, spread confusion among the people, and disseminate reactionary, corrupt, and decadent ideas."[51] Though their names were not actually mentioned, it is clear that the NV and the GP were the major targets of this warning directed at forces critical of the VWP.

After the publication of this editorial the NV came under harsher attack, and the opinions expressed by those speaking for the Party began to place greater emphasis on the need to limit "democracy" and "freedom," the importance of the "proletarian dictatorship," and the need to "differentiate between friends and enemies." Moreover, all these arguments took for granted that judgment of the kinds of limitation and differentiation appropriate, as well as their actual implementation, should be left to the VWP. This indicates that there was no chance that the writers' demands, including the demand for the return of the right to guide literary activities, would receive any consideration from the VWP.

Take, for instance, the VWP's reaction to the demand for expanded "individual freedom." The VWP countered this demand with the argument that "absolute freedom" is impossible, because the extent of "freedom" is determined by the objective conditions existing at any given time, such as "the balance of power between us and our enemies," the relationships and interactions between the two parties in a struggle, the relationships among the antisocialist forces, the relationships among the socialist forces, "the party's ability to lead the people," and "the level of our people's accomplishments in economic, political, cultural, and ideological construction."[52] No effort was made to debate the questions raised by Tran Duc Thao, which could have had extremely important implications both theoretically and practically, that is, his questions on the proper relationship between communism and individuals and the proper method of democratizing society.

Received with equal disfavor was an article in the NV that emphasized the importance of encouraging a "hundred flowers" to bloom even if these flowers "inevitably include poisonous flowers and foul-smelling flowers as well as pleasant-smelling flowers" and insisted that the people should be free to decide which flowers they liked best. Focusing exclusively on the phrases "poisonous flowers" and "foul-smelling flowers," the VWP leadership denounced this argument as an attempt to "blur the line between friends and enemies."[53] Underlying this denunciation was the perception that enemies of the proleratian dictatorship should not be allowed to enjoy "freedom" in the sphere of creative activities, and certainly should not be allowed to make use of literature to enable "poisonous flowers" and "foul-smelling flowers" to bloom in the DRV.[54]

---

[51] ND 1956c.

[52] Tran Cong Tuong and Huu Trong 1956, p. 34.

[53] Quang Dam 1956.

[54] Ibid.

During the period immediately after the Hungarian Revolt through early December, the *Nhan Dan* not only hurled criticisms at the NV and the GP from the standpoint of the VWP leadership but also published Hanoi citizens' letters to the editor denouncing the NV. These steps were followed by the imposition of a ban on the NV on December 15 by the Hanoi Administrative Council on the grounds that "many of the articles in the paper distort truth, are slanderous, sow discord, spread confusion, and arouse suspicion of the people's democratic regime, and have actually harmed the order and public peace of the city."[55] The other publications critical of the VWP were also banned, ending their short lives of a little over three months. Concurrently, the Law on the Press System was promulgated, in effect making it illegal to publish periodicals similar to the NV and the GP.[56]

III. Presentation of a Literary Policy and Developments in Literary Circles in 1957

It was not until the Second National Congress on Art and Literature, held in Hanoi in late February 1957, that the VWP announced its official view of the criticisms and demands raised in the autumn of 1956 by literary circles, including the NV and the GP. The Party executive addressed a letter to the congress elucidating the Party's literary policy, and Truong Chinh, a member of the Politburo, delivered a speech at the congress.

In its letter the VWP executive acknowledged that the criticisms raised by writers about the shortcomings of the Party's literary guidance were justified and declared that the Party was determined to rectify these shortcomings. At the same time, however, the letter outlined a new literary policy strongly oriented toward control over writers' creative activities. Specifically, it listed several criteria of creative writing: it should be socialist in substance and nationalist in form; it should serve workers, peasants and soldiers; it should assimilate both the national literary heritage and the world's most advanced literary art; and it should follow socialist realism, the best method of creative writing.

The letter also stipulated the obligations and behavior of writers, demanding that they contribute to the realization of a cultural revolution in the North, that they develop their ideological and artistic abilities by studying Marxism-Leninism and the programs and policies of the Party and the Government, and that they familiarize themselves with the life of workers, peasants, soldiers, and "brain workers."[57] In his speech Truong Chinh demanded that writers take the "position" of "love of the Fatherland, service to the people, defense of the people's democratic regime, promotion of socialism, and defense of world peace."[58]

It will be useful to examine briefly how the cultural revolution mentioned above was perceived. According to the VWP letter, it was an undertaking to be carried out parallel with economic transformation, in order to "extricate our people's cultural life from its low state; overcome backward ideologies, decadent customs, and remnants

---

[55] ND 1956c.

[56] ND 1956d. While ensuring freedom of expression and prohibiting prepublication censorship, this law obligated publishers to apply for permission to publish and to "serve the interests of the Fatherland and the people, defend the people's democracy, and support the Democratic Republic of Vietnam."

[57] HT 1957b, pp. 7–11.

[58] Truong Chinh 1957, TCVN 1, p. 21.

of the old society; gradually raise our country's cultural and technological standards; and build a new type of person deeply educated in patriotism and socialist ideals."[59]

This cultural revolution had the character of a cultural and ideological reform movement imposed from above, as can be inferred from Truong Chinh's remark that it was to be carried out under the leadership of the Party and the Government.[60] At the same time, the VWP's official mention of a cultural revolution was significant as an indication that the Party, heretofore preoccupied with economic recovery, was now beginning to address cultural and ideological issues and as the first clear statement of its view on the place these issues should occupy in the overall process of socialization.

But why did cultural and ideological problems begin to be perceived as so important at that particular time, and why was a cultural revolution imposed from above conceived as a means of dealing with these problems? One plausible explanation is that the Party, having witnessed the Hungarian Revolt and the state of affairs in DRV literary circles during the autumn of 1956, must have been convinced of the need to control culture and ideology. Another explanation is that the launching of the cultural revolution was closely related to the decision made shortly thereafter, at the Twelfth Plenum, in March 1957, to bring economic recovery to completion during fiscal 1957 by restoring the 1939 standard of living and to create "favorable conditions for the period of planned construction."[61]

In other words, the Party's ability to carry out the socialization of the North depended upon the successful implementation of the 1957 State Plan.[62] Indeed, bringing the economic recovery program to completion in 1957 was of crucial importance to the Party, which had had to postpone the original completion date of 1956 by one year owing to "many mistakes in economic and financial operations."[63] The Twelfth Plenum identified the resolution of ideological problems as the single most important prerequisite for successful completion of the 1957 State Plan: "Solving ideological problems is tantamount to solving half of all the problems." On the basis of this understanding, the Plenum proposed a policy centered on educating the people in "a new labor viewpoint" and intensifying work discipline.[64]

The same line of thinking found its way into the 1957 policy on cultural affairs that was adopted after the Second National Congress on Art and Literature. This policy proposed to promote further, on the basis of the cultural revolution, enhancement of cultural life, improvement of the people's general knowledge, education of the people in patriotism and socialist ideals, and construction and development of a new culture. The success of these efforts, it was emphasized, would play a significant role

---

[59] HT 1957b, p. 8.

[60] Truong Chinh 1957, TCVN 1, p. 15.

[61] ND 1957d. It should be pointed out that the plan to complete economic recovery in fiscal 1957 was proposed at the Eleventh Plenum in December, 1956 (HT 1957a, p. 5).

[62] HT 1957c, p. 1. The Twelfth Plenum confirmed the policy of gradual socialization of the North.

[63] HT 1957a, p. 5. These "mistakes" were discussed at the Eleventh Plenum. Deficiencies were pointed out in the following areas: rehabilitation and development of light industries, production of consumer goods, efforts to develop the potential of handicrafts and of family side jobs in rural districts, and utilization of the positive aspects of private-sector commerce and manufacturing.

[64] HT 1957c, p. 5.

in "educating and stimulating the people to engage more actively in production and to struggle to execute all the urgent duties incumbent upon them."[65]

Literature was expected to make its due contribution to these efforts as "popular literature." Specifically, writers were expected to diversify their activities to better meet the needs of villages, companies, and military camps, and to contribute to the creation of cultural life by delivering lectures on such subjects as reading, current topics, and experiences and technologies related to production activities.[66] Also emphasized repeatedly throughout 1957 was the need to intensify political education and discipline both in universities and in lower-level schools.[67] Thus, the literary policy presented at the Congress on Art and Literature was aimed primarily at mobilizing writers to serve as the nucleus of a VWP-led cultural revolution. This was based on the Party's belief in the importance of literature as a means of promoting production activities and state policies.

It should be borne in mind that Truong Chinh did show some respect for the individuality, the style, and the independence of individual writers though with some conditions. One instance is his elaboration of a passage of the VWP letter that emphasized the need to allow "freedom of creative activity" and "sound criticism" for the sake of the development of literature and the arts.[68] Commenting on this passage, Truong Chinh asserted that "writers are free to choose the theme, the form, the subject matter, and the methodology of creative writing in accordance with their own strong points and taste" as long as they followed the guidance of the Party and adopted the above-mentioned "position," which was incumbent upon all writers.[69]

At several other points in his speech, too, Truong Chinh evinced flexible views. Commenting, for instance, on the proper conduct of literary guidance, he stated that guidance should be limited to matters concerning political orientation, policies, programs, and organizational structure; that administrative orders should not be used; and that there should be no interference in professional matters, such as the choice of theme and artistic form. He also declared that writers should study Marxism-Leninism voluntarily and that the Party line should not be forced upon writers who were not party members.[70]

In addition, Truong Chinh pointed out that the slogan "Freedom of creative activity" had been proclaimed in response to the demand for implementation of the "hundred flowers" policy and that there was no basic difference between this policy and that of the VWP. "Just like our policy of ensuring the freedom of creative activity," he declared, "the Chinese policy of 'Let a hundred flowers bloom' in essence is meant to ensure the exercise of freedom of thought, freedom of expression, and freedom of creative activity among the people and to encourage all meaningful pursuits and creative activities in the areas of ideology, scholarship, and the arts."[71]

It is true that the views expressed by Truong Chinh had something in common with those in Lu Dingyi's "hundred flowers" speech. Nonetheless, it would be a

---

[65] ND 1957b.

[66] Ibid.

[67] ND 1957c; Doan Trong Truyen 1957, pp. 43–45.

[68] HT 1957b, p. 10.

[69] Truong Chinh 1957, TCVN 2, p. 14.

[70] Ibid., pp. 4–5.

[71] Ibid., pp. 14–16.

mistake to characterize the VWP's policy of respecting "freedom of creative activity" as a mere imitation of the CCP's "hundred flowers" policy. For one thing, as pointed out above, many of Truong Chinh's contentions were recapitulations of points already made in the autumn of 1956 in response to criticisms raised by literary circles. For another, it was in response to and as a consequence of the debate with the NV and other publications and the Hungarian Revolt that the VWP's literary policy as a whole—including the policy of respecting "freedom of creative activity"—came to uphold the basic principle that the Party should guide literary activities and to propose a cultural revolution. There is no denying, however, that Truong Chinh, by emphasizing the basic similarities between the two policies, was able both to claim that the VWP's policy accommodated the writers' demands and to demonstrate the VWP's respect for the CCP's policy.

The above observations make it clear that the literary policy presented at the Congress on Art and Literature incorporated two different lines of thinking: one oriented toward intensified control over writers, the other oriented toward respecting writers' initiative, albeit conditionally. This was also the case with the policy toward intellectuals that was announced in August 1957. The obligations and behavior stipulated by the latter policy, which intellectuals were expected to follow in transforming themselves, were much the same as those specified for writers. The policy toward intellectuals also emphasized that intellectuals should transform themselves voluntarily, the Party doing no more than assisting their efforts.[72]

It was, however, the more flexible of the two lines of thinking, the one oriented toward respecting the initiative of writers and intellectuals, that was actually implemented throughout 1957; no concrete measures were taken to force writers to engage in political study or take part in production activities. When Truong Chinh referred to the NV for the first time as a Party leader at the Congress on Art and Literature, he condemned the paper severely for "distorting Marxism-Leninism while pretending to uphold it, attacking the Party's supervision while pledging to accept it, and painting the regime completely black while vowing to defend it" and of "taking advantage of and exaggerating the Party's correct view of self-criticism and pandering to the people, gradually expanding its subversive activities from the spheres of ideology and the arts to the sphere of politics."[73] He emphasized the need to continue waging an ideological struggle against the NV. But despite this harsh verbal attack, no steps were taken to condemn personally or punish any of the contributors to the NV or to launch an organized campaign of denunciation.[74]

Another feature of cultural policy in 1957 was the moderate approach taken toward accomplishing policy objectives, an approach that emphasized arriving at a consensus through persuasion and patient discussion. For instance, in dealing with university faculty members whose ideas were deemed problematic, emphasis was placed on giving them a chance to "cure the disease and save themselves" by criticizing them with sincerity and thoughtfulness.[75] In implementing the policy toward intellectuals, those in charge of the policy were warned against acting impatiently.[76]

---

[72] ND 1957c.

[73] Truong Chinh 1957, TCVN 2, pp. 8–9.

[74] At that point, the leaders themselves were not considering the adoption of harsh measures (Truong Chinh 1985, pp. 351–52).

[75] Doan Trong Truyen 1957, p. 50.

[76] ND 1957f.

Moreover, a forum for debate was provided in the pages of a Hanoi newspaper, where teachers, students, and ordinary citizens exchanged views on the purposes of education and the correct relationship between education and labor.[77]

Furthermore, a clear line was drawn between affairs within the Party and those outside it and between party members and nonmembers, so that issues concerning party building were not applied to nonmembers and society at large. At that time collectivism was being emphasized within the Party, and party members were being encouraged to struggle against individualism and bourgeois ideas; but members were strongly warned against directly applying the idea of collectivism to nonmembers.[78] With regard to the relationship between members and nonmembers, too, the VWP, the events of the autumn of 1956 fresh in its memory, was taking a cautious attitude. Upholding the principle of "struggle and unity" through mutual criticism and self-criticism, the VWP emphasized the need to guide nonmembers by means of persuasion and discussion. At the same time, it severely denounced attempts to interfere with or issue coercive orders concerning the affairs of nonmembers.[79]

The moderate cultural and ideological policy pursued in 1957 was in a sense an extension of the "democratization" initiative emphasized by the Ninth and Tenth Plenums. Yet the Party, while endorsing the long-term objectives of promoting socialization in the North and carrying out a cultural revolution, did not dare organize a mass movement toward these ends. This was apparently because the banning of the NV did not necessarily serve to strengthen the Party's hegemony at a time when the Hungarian Revolt and the Suez crisis had made many people, both inside and outside the Party, skeptical of the capabilities of the socialist camp.[80] Moreover, opinions opposing the viewpoint of the Party executive—such as the view that socialization of the North would present a serious obstacle to national unification and the view that favored a neutralist policy as a means of early unification with the South—were very influential.[81] These trends raised fundamental doubts about the legitimacy of VWP rule.

After the denunciation of Stalin it became increasingly difficult to maintain a monolithic, universal view of socialism. To cope with this difficulty, at the Tenth Plenum the VWP adopted a policy of accommodating to the actual situation; but only very limited progress in this direction was made during 1957, and the Party remained unable to present a model that could convincingly explain the fundamental issues of the superiority of socialism over capitalism and the necessity for the DVR to pursue a socialist policy. Moreover, the CCP's "hundred flowers" policy could easily have repercussions in the DRV, and, as the VWP itself admitted, "ideological struggles within fraternal parties" could immediately spread to the DRV.[82] This situation must have made it extremely difficult for the VWP to formulate programs and policy guidelines that could win the support of all party members or to mobilize the masses in a party-led movement.

How did writers respond to the literary policy of the VWP? The Congress on Art and Literature adopted a resolution to support the letter from the Party executive,

---

[77] Thoi Moi 1957.

[78] Dao Duy Tung 1957, p. 31.

[79] Pham Van Dong 1957, pp. 6–10.

[80] HT 1956d, p. 3; Dao Duy Tung 1957, p. 28.

[81] ND 1958b.

[82] HT 1958a, p. 8.

but the resolution did not denounce the NV by name.[83] None of the contributors to the NV and the GP were expelled from literary organizations; on the contrary, some were even elected to the executive committees of the Association of Writers, the Association of Musicians, and the Association for Fine Arts, established as part of the restructuring of organizations after the congress. Moreover, Tran Duc Thao remained chairman of the History Department of Hanoi Teachers College and Truong Tuu retained his post at the same college.

In 1957 the journal of the Association of Writers (Hoi Nha van), the *Van*, became the target of VWP criticism. Upon publication of this journal's tenth issue the Party's theoretical journal, the *Hoc Tap*, began to criticize the *Van*'s editorial policy. The point at issue was the descriptive methodology used by many writers published in the *Van*. Many of the works in the *Van*, contended the *Hoc Tap*, dealt with trivial matters and were excessively inclined toward artifice.[84]

Among the works criticized was an essay on a typical Hanoi dish, *pho*, by Nguyen Tuan, secretary general of the Association of Writers, describing with a light touch many varieties of the dish as well as different methods of cooking it.[85] In denouncing this essay, the *Hoc Tap* maintained that writers should describe present-day people and their way of life. The people worthy of description, according to the *Hoc Tap*, were those who "fight the dark forces that go against the stream of history, intimidating mankind with atomic bombs, violating humanity, and subjecting nations to indignities; defend the people's right to life, justice, and lasting peace; and struggle to achieve national independence and socialism." The way of life worthy of description consisted of "collective life, impartiality, friendship among nations, and the courage to accept sacrifices."[86] The subject matter of works of creative writing considered appropriate by the Party was thus made clear.

There was no further criticism of the *Van*. This does not mean, however, that literary circles began to produce only the kinds of works that the VWP would find satisfactory. Consider, for example, a poem by Phung Quan titled "Mother's Instructions" (Loi me dan), in which he expressed his own position by describing his mother's instructions. Asserting that for him the ideal person was one who "can clearly tell good from evil," he expressed his determination to engage in creative writing with this ideal person in mind.[87] Similarly, Tran Dan, in his poem "March Forward!" (Hay di mai), expressed his will to press forward resolutely, never giving in to obstruction or becoming a passive observer.[88] A short story by Phan Khoi titled "Mr. Nam Chuot" (Ong Nam Chuot) is another case in point. The author drew a sharp contrast between the life of the protagonist, an artisan named Nam Chuot, who was ostracized by his fellow villagers because of his penetrating insight and rich cultural

---

[83] Truong Chinh's speech and the report by the executive committee of the Association of Writers, established after the congress, criticized the NV by name. The resolution, however, did no more than emphasize the need to fight "the mistaken tendency to demand a reappraisal of the basic principles of our literature, denying all its achievements, and the tendency to sever literature from politics and the masses from the leadership of the Party" (ND 1957a).

[84] The Tuan 1957, pp. 64–67.

[85] THDN, pp. 203–10.

[86] The Tuan 1957, pp. 65, 67.

[87] THDN, pp. 120–21.

[88] Ibid., pp. 112–16.

background, and that of public officials and ordinary villagers, who, enmeshed in conventional ideas, were unable to appreciate a man of talent and insight.[89]

Phung Quan, Tran Dan, and Phan Khoi had all contributed to the NV and the GP. Their views were shared by other writers, as well. Nguyen Hong, editor in chief of the *Van*, refused to accept the criticism leveled by the *Hoc Tap* and dared to criticize the *Hoc Tap* openly for its "dogmatic, crude, formalistic," and bureaucratic attitude.[90] Nguyen Tuan took issue with the Party's argument that the lack of lively criticism of literature was due to the prevailing notion that "criticizing writers is a very 'difficult' thing to do"; he asked party officials to be more careful in criticizing literature, since criticizing a work of literature "is often more difficult than creating one."[91] Again writers were resisting the Party's interference and control over them.

IV. THE LITERARY RECTIFICATION CAMPAIGN AND ITS BACKGROUND

The moderate cultural policy pursued after the Second National Congress on Art and Literature changed abruptly in early 1958. Below, I will first summarize the course of events, then examine some of the underlying factors.

On January 6 the Politburo issued the "Politburo Resolution on Literary Affairs," thus signaling its decision to launch a literary rectification campaign. In regard to the situation in literary circles, the resolution maintained that, having assumed an increasingly ambiguous political position, exemplified by the attitude of the *Van*, and having lost their "will for revolutionary struggle," literary circles were serving as a convenient arena of activity for "subversive elements."

The resolution made two specific demands: that "subversive elements" be expelled from literary organizations and that writers study Marxism and transform themselves ideologically, first receiving ideological education and then drawing up plans for participation in production activities and for long-term study of current affairs and policy.[92] Clearly, the "subversive elements" referred to writers who had contributed to the NV and the GP.[93] With this *diktat* the Party effectively repudiated its policy of respecting the initiative of writers and adopted in its stead a policy of imposing mandatory measures.

In late January the Party executive convened an approximately month-long conference attended by a total of one hundred seventy writers who belonged to the Party and cultural cadres, drawn from all over the country, to study the national and international situations, the Politburo resolution, and accomplishments following the Second National Congress on Art and Literature. The purpose was to gain a consensus among the participants on the need to continue to struggle openly against "the antiparty and antisocialist ideological tendencies that still exist among some people."[94]

This conference was followed by a month-long political study meeting that began in early March and was attended by over three hundred people, including writers who did not belong to the Party. At the end of the meeting the participants unani-

---

[89] Ibid., pp. 76–88.

[90] Ibid., p. 211.

[91] Ibid., pp. 210–13.

[92] For the text of the Politburo resolution, see To Huu 1958, pp. 24–26.

[93] Ibid., p. 26.

[94] TCVN 1958a, p. 116.

mously adopted a letter to the Party executive expressing their support of the Party's leadership and pledging to struggle against "the NV and GP group."[95]

A series of developments unfolded in conjunction with these meetings. In January the *Van* was banned. From March through early June a campaign to criticize writers who had contributed to the NV and the GP was carried out in all public organs. Phan Khoi, Truong Tuu, Tran Duc Thao, and Nguyen Huu Dang[96] were condemned especially severely for being antiparty. They were denounced by name on the basis of arbitrary interpretation and criticism of their writings. Tran Duc Thao's emphasis on the importance of safeguarding "individual freedom," for instance, was totally detached from the context of his discourse and scrutinized to determine "whose freedom, and freedom to what end" he was advocating. It was concluded in a slapdash manner that he was advocating "freedom for agents of the United States and Diem and for antirevolutionary elements" and "bourgeois, individualistic freedom."[97] Phan Khoi's "Mr. Nam Chuot" was treated in much the same way. Phan Khoi was accused of having exacerbated the rift between the Party and writers on the basis of one passage: "I don't teach you about literature, so don't try to teach me the business of a goldsmith."[98]

These writers were attacked not simply because of their writings but also because of their backgrounds. Phan Khoi, for instance, had his entire background exposed, including the fact that his father was a civil servant, the "anticommunist" and "obscurantist" nature of his pre–World War II works, his cooperation with the Vietnamese Nationalist Party (Viet Nam Quoc Dan Dang) immediately after the August Revolution of 1945, and his opposition to the Vietnamese-French modus vivendi of 1946.[99] In the case of Truong Tuu, his participation in the Marxist group Han Thuyen, which was active during World War II but pursued a line different from that of the Indochina Communist Party, was cited as evidence of his being a "Trotskyite."[100] Both men were accused of having failed to make use of the precious chance to transform themselves offered by the Party.[101] Given the fact that their backgrounds were typical of those of a majority of the intellectuals who chose to remain in the North after 1954, we can surmise that the literary rectification campaign was not aimed simply at literary circles but was intended to serve as a warning to intellectuals in general, thus inducing them to follow the Party's line and transform themselves ideologically.

The literary rectification campaign more or less ended in June with a report by To Huu to the Union for Literature and the Arts (Hoi Lien hiep van hoc Nghe thuat). One thing that had become clear in the course of the campaign was that nobody would be allowed to criticize or oppose the Party's policies and strategy. Another was that, with the condemnation of the NV's point of view as "bourgeois individual-

---

[95] TCVN 1958b, pp. 87–88.

[96] Nguyen Huu Dang, a VWP member and the former editor in chief of the literary newspaper *Van nghe*, was accused of having played a central role in escalating the political tone of the NV's position (Manh Phu Tu 1958).

[97] Pham Huy Thong 1958.

[98] Nguyen Dinh Thi 1958, p. 28.

[99] Hoang Chau Ky 1958. Although the accuracy of some of the allegations about Phan Khoi's background cannot be verified, they serve to indicate clearly the trend of criticism by the Party.

[100] Hoai Thanh 1958; Bui Huy Phon 1958.

[101] To Huu 1958, p. 26; To Huu 1973, p. 173.

ism," writers were being reminded once again of the types of human beings they should describe[102] and of the need to use socialist realism as their methodology.[103] Writers' freedom to choose subjects and writing methods was now severely curtailed. The flexible attitude manifested in Truong Chinh's speech at the Congress on Art and Literature was nowhere to be found.

At the same time, the VWP, in an effort to reorganize educational circles as well as literary circles, promoted ideological education in Marxism-Leninism, emphasized labor education, and launched a movement to sweep away "hostile ideas."[104] As a result of the argument that "reactionary elements unwilling to transform themselves" should be banished from educational institutions,[105] the principle of giving ideologically misdirected people a chance to "cure the disease and save themselves" set forth in 1957 was in effect repudiated.

In early July steps were taken in line with the Politburo resolution to expel writers who had contributed to the NV and the GP from literary organizations or at least to dismiss them from executive posts in those organizations.[106] Phan Khoi was deprived of his membership in the Association of Writers and was rendered virtually incapable of continuing his writing activities. Truong Tuu was also expelled from the association and was purged, along with his colleague Tran Duc Thao, from Hanoi Teachers College. In July and October writers were mobilized to experience a life of labor in plants, mines, mutual-aid teams, cooperatives, farms, and military camps.[107] In both universities and lower-level schools, teachers and students were mobilized to take part in programs of political study and of firsthand experience of a life of labor during the period from the summer recess through early October.[108]

Thus implementation of the literary rectification campaign marked a radical change in the VWP's cultural policy. Its earlier, moderate policy—which had tried to accomplish a cultural revolution and ideological transformation gradually, by means of persuasion, respecting the initiative of writers and intellectuals and eschewing coercive measures—was replaced by one that pursued these goals by applying pressure from above. In the remainder of this section, I will examine the factors behind this policy reversal, in particular the reasons that literary circles became the target of the rectification campaign.

It should be borne in mind that the literary campaign was in a sense an antirevisionist struggle and that as such it was launched as a campaign to criticize revisionism within literary circles[109] and was carried out in conjunction with activities *both inside and outside the Party* to study the literature on the Moscow Conference of November 1957. The antirevisionist struggle was an offshoot of that conference.

---

[102] To Huu refers to "socialist workers leading an organized and collective life" as "the true persons of today" and "physical laborers, brain workers, worker-peasant soldiers, and socialist intellectuals" as "the true persons under a socialist regime" (To Huu 1973, p. 188).

[103] Quang Dam 1958b.

[104] HT 1958b, p. 6.

[105] Vo Quang 1958, pp. 15–16.

[106] ND 1958d. It should be pointed out that Nguyen Huu Dang was later arrested on the grounds of complicity in espionage and was sentenced in 1960 to fifteen years' imprisonment and five years' suspension of civil rights (ND 1960).

[107] The Tuan 1958, pp. 80–91; Huynh Ly 1962, p. 49.

[108] Ha Huy Giap 1958.

[109] Quang Dam 1958a.

Actually, two major international conferences were held in Moscow in November 1957 in commemoration of the fortieth anniversary of the October Revolution. The one relevant to our discourse is the International Conference of Twelve Communist and Workers' Parties, to which the VWP sent a delegation. Even though the conference failed to gain Yugoslavia's participation, it succeeded in reestablishing a semblance of unity in the socialist camp, which had become increasingly restless and disorganized since the denunciation of Stalin.[110]

The Declaration adopted by the Moscow Conference, affirmed that the international situation was developing to the advantage of the socialist camp and upheld the importance of unified leadership by Marxist-Leninist parties in the process of the socialist revolution and socialist construction. In particular, it emphasized the need to reaffirm the "universal principles of Marxism-Leninism" and to apply them creatively to the actual conditions of individual countries, and the need to wage a struggle against revisionism and dogmatism within party ranks. According to the Declaration, the "universal principles of Marxism-Leninism" included the following features:

1. Guidance of the working masses through the working class, whose core is a Marxist-Leninist party, in carrying out a proletarian revolution in one form or another and establishing a proletarian dictatorship in one form or another
2. Union of the working class, the key part of the peasantry, and other categories of workers
3. Abolition of capitalist ownership and establishment of social ownership of the basic means of production
4. Gradual socialist transformation of agriculture
5. Planned development of the national economy, oriented to the construction of socialism and communism and to the elevation of the standard of living of the working masses
6. Implementation of a socialist revolution in the areas of ideology and culture and building of an intelligentsia serving the working class, working people, and socialist undertakings
7. Abolition of oppression of one nation by another and establishment of equitable, fraternal relationships among nations
8. Defense of socialist achievements from attack by internal and external enemies
9. Solidarity of the working class in one country with the working class in other countries: proletarian internationalism[111]

Revisionism, diametrically opposed to these principles, was perceived to have the following features:

---

[110] François Fejtö aptly assesses the significance of the conference: "Le résultat le plus important de la conférence de Moscou aura été de fournir l'arsenal pour le réarmement idéologique des cadres communistes qui, dans la crise de 1956, avaient un peu perdu la boussole. Elle a servi à ranimer la foi léniniste dans la révolution inéluctable et dans l'efficacité de la dictature du prolétariat" (Fejtö 1969, pp. 152–53). [The most important result of the Moscow Conference was that it offered the arsenal for the ideological rearmament of the communist cadres who had to some extent lost their compass in the crisis of 1956. It (the Conference) served to encourage the leninist faith in the inevitable revolution and in the efficiency of the dictatorship of the proletariat.—My translation.]

[111] *KPSS* 1960, p. 620.

1. Opposition to the need for a proletarian revolution and a proletarian dictatorship during the period of transition from capitalism to socialism
2. Denial of the leading role of a Marxist-Leninist party
3. Denial of the principle of proletarian internationalism
4. Refusal of the Leninist principles of party construction, especially the principle of democratic centralism
5. Demand for transformation of a communist party from a militant revolutionary organization into a kind of debate club[112]

At about the same time as the Moscow Conference, the VWP was being hard pressed to carry out the plan adopted by the Twelfth Plenum to complete economic recovery and proceed to the period of "planned construction," or socialist transformation. Achievement of this target was of crucial importance to the Party, which regarded successful completion of the 1957 economic plan as an especially important prerequisite for promoting socialization.[113] More fundamentally, failure to complete the plan could threaten the prestige and even the very survival of the Party, which had held on to power by proclaiming that its primary task was to lead the nation's "march toward socialism."[114]

While the Party was undergoing this ordeal, questions were being raised both inside and outside the Party about its policies and strategy. Literary circles, in particular, continued to criticize openly the VWP's literary policy even after the Second National Congress on Art and Literature. The Party considered writers and intellectuals important as the driving force of the cultural revolution that was to be carried out parallel to and in conjunction with economic transformation. Such criticism not only threatened to impede the cultural revolution but could even prevent the Party from successfully launching its economic transformation program. In addition, the effectiveness of the VWP's strategy for "socialization of the North" was being questioned by intellectuals outside the Party, as pointed out earlier.

On top of this, apparently no clear-cut consensus had been formed within the Party on basic strategy after the completion of economic recovery. On the one hand, the Thirteenth Plenum, held in December 1957, shortly after the Moscow Conference, reached agreement on fundamental issues, such as the "revolutionary duties facing the entire Party and people";[115] on the other hand, a document used in an intraparty study campaign at about the same time stated that there were some party members who demanded reexamination of the Party's erroneous policies and lines, and who "attack the party and its leadership, echoing vicious elements."[116]

The Declaration of the Moscow Conference was a tremendous encouragement to the embattled VWP leadership. With its emphasis on the "universal principles of Marxism-Leninism" and its definition of the major features of revisionism, the Declaration reaffirmed the legitimacy of building socialism under the unified leadership of a strong Marxist-Leninist party, provided reassurance that the policies the VWP had

---

[112] Ibid., p. 622.

[113] HT 1957c, p. 1.

[114] Vu bien soan Ban tuyen huan Trung uong 1978, p. 269.

[115] Vien Mac–Le-nin 1982, pp. 69–70. Although the full text of the document has not been made public, it can be inferred from other relevant literature that socialization of the North and national unification were the document's major themes (HT 1958a, p. 20).

[116] HT 1958a, p. 13.

been pursuing were correct, and made it clear that the Party's efforts to strengthen its leadership role and to sweep away hostile forces were supported internationally.

The Declaration heartened the Party leadership, which had been holding fast to the belief that the united support of the socialist camp was indispensable to national unification.[117] It was instrumental in reassuring the Party leadership that the international situation was developing to its advantage and in inducing it to reaffirm its decision to proceed toward socialist transformation.[118] Another important feature of the Declaration was its affirmation of the unity and strength of the socialist camp; this must have helped counter the criticisms of the Party's policies and strategy that had been prompted to a large extent by developments within the socialist camp after the denunciation of Stalin, especially the Hungarian Revolt and the CCP's "hundred flowers" policy. The extent of the Declaration's impact on the DRV became clear in a series of developments that began to unfold shortly after the Moscow Conference.

As soon as the conference was over, the VWP identified the Declaration and the Peace Manifesto[119] as the "common programs of the communist parties and workers of all nations" and ordered all party members to study them. The members were instructed to study ways to apply the two documents "creatively to the struggle for gradual construction of socialism in the North and for realization of national unification" and to struggle against "both revisionist and dogmatic ideas opposed to Marxism-Leninism." The purpose of the study campaign was to "enhance awareness of socialism, patriotism, and proletarian internationalism by carrying out education in socialism both within the Party and among the people."[120] In February 1958 the Politburo decided to expand the study campaign outside the Party, identifying this as "the major ideological campaign" of the year.[121]

As for the antirevisionist struggle, the Party's theoretical journal, the *Hoc Tap*, pointed out immediately after the Moscow Conference, echoing the Declaration, that "revisionist tendencies" existed in Vietnam. The typical manifestations of such tendencies in the area of politics and ideology, according to the *Hoc Tap*, were denial or neglect of the proletarian dictatorship, denial or neglect of the role of the working class, denial of the accomplishments of land reform and other undertakings, and compromise with the corrupt ideology of bourgeois democracy. In the area of economics, such tendencies took the form of denial of the accomplishments of economic recovery (1954–1957), opposition to the increased leadership role of the state economic sector, and compromises with capitalist commerce and industry. Revisionist tendencies in the area of literature included disparagement of the Party's leadership role, advocacy of "absolute freedom of creative activity," denial of the Party's literary policy, and approval of the decadent artistic viewpoint of the bourgeoisie.[122]

---

[117] Kho Shi Min [Ho Chi Minh] 1956.

[118] HT 1958a, pp. 6–10. In regard to economic achievements, it was reported at the Fourteenth Plenum, in November 1958, that by the end of 1957 both agricultural and industrial output had more or less returned to their 1939 levels (Dang lao dong Viet-nam 1958, pp. 5–6).

[119] The Peace Manifesto was adopted by the Conference of Sixty-four Communist and Workers' Parties of the World, which followed the International Conference of Twelve Communist and Workers' Parties.

[120] ND 1957g.

[121] ND 1958a.

[122] HT 1957d, p. 10. Some scholars interpret the antirevisionist struggle emphasized in the Declaration as being targeted at Yugoslavia (McCauley 1987, p. 165); but in the light of the subsequent actions of the VWP, this interpretation is not altogether convincing.

It is immediately clear from this list of unacceptable phenomena that the primary purpose of the antirevisionist struggle was to have party members and nonmembers alike endorse the VWP's leadership role and approve the various policies it had undertaken since 1954. The features of literary circles deemed problematic were exactly the same as those for which the NV and the GP had been criticized during the literary rectification campaign—evidence that the Party leadership had begun preparing for the rectification campaign before the Politburo resolution of January 1958.

Some of the reasons that literary circles were singled out as the major target of the antirevisionist campaign have already been referred to briefly. Another factor worth noting is the Politburo's perception of literary circles; in its view, literary circles had become the refuge of antiparty elements and writers were behaving in ways that ran counter to the important duties with which they were entrusted in the implementation of the cultural revolution.

Why were the NV and the GP, banned more than a year earlier, chosen as the targets of the antirevisionist campaign? The explanation seems to lie in the fact that aside from banning the two periodicals, the Party had taken no concrete steps to deal with those who had contributed to them even though these writers had engaged in revisionist activities as defined by the Declaration by openly challenging the Party's leadership role and policies. The situation in early 1958 was very different from that in 1956. Both the Soviet Union, which had inspired the NV and the GP by its denunciation of Stalin, and China, which had done the same by its "hundred flowers" policy, had signed the Declaration, thus expressing their support of the antirevisionist struggle. What is more, the "hundred flowers" policy had turned into an antirightist campaign in China.

These changes in the situation meant that the writers who had contributed to the NV and the GP had been totally deprived of the theoretical justification for their position. Ready proof of this is the fact that in the course of the literary rectification campaign the NV was criticized for its attitude toward the Soviet Union and China. For instance, Nguyen Dinh Thi charged that the NV "distorted the Chinese slogan 'Let a hundred flowers bloom' to make it seem as if the Chinese line on literature and the arts was in conflict with that of the Soviet Union. As soon as it realized that China was opposed to revisionism, it searched for 'national communism' elsewhere."[123] The NV was also accused of having "attacked China and the Soviet Union"[124] and of having called for revising the policy of cooperation between the DRV and socialist countries based on proletarian internationalism, asserting that the DRV should follow a neutral course and receive aid from both the capitalist and the socialist camps.[125] That accusations of this sort were being voiced for the first time since the autumn of 1956 indicates that the VWP had found the job of refuting the contentions of the NV and the GP, which had been based on the policy lines of the CCP and the CPSU, very difficult and sensitive.

The campaign to study the two documents and the campaign of literary rectification (which was an antirevisionist campaign) emphasized the Party's leadership role and the legitimacy of its policies, rendering the blueprint of socialization clearer. On March 13, 1958, Truong Chinh delivered a report at a meeting of the Central Commit-

---

[123] Nguyen Dinh Thi 1958, p. 7.

[124] To Huu 1973, p. 173.

[125] Truong Chinh 1985, p. 249.

tee of the Fatherland Front in which he identified the "overall tasks to be completed in the period of transition to socialism" as planned development of the national economy, gradual socialist industrialization, development of both the state-run economic sector and the cooperative economic sector, promotion of agricultural collectivization, socialist transformation of capitalist commercial and industrial firms, and "the implementation of a cultural revolution, the transformation of the intelligentsia, and the building of a new type of intellectual."[126] He also discussed the need to mobilize the entire nation to accomplish state plans. He emphasized the ideological aspects of such a mobilization effort: the importance of raising the people's awareness of their role as masters of the state; setting a high regard for labor; educating them in collectivism, organizational discipline, patriotism, and proletarian internationalism; and enhancing their caution against class enemies.[127]

The following month, Prime Minister Pham Van Dong presented to the eighth session of the National Assembly the outline of the Three-Year Plan, to run from 1958 through 1960, and at the same time provided a clearer description of the tasks in the spheres of ideology and literature. In line with the Declaration, he added a new task with regard to the cultural revolution: "the transformation of the intelligentsia and the building of a new type of intellectual loyal to socialism." In elaborating on the question of transforming the intelligentsia, he stated that intellectuals would be required to "understand the position and the role of culture and cultural organizers during the period of transition in the North, and do so from the Marxist-Leninist standpoint and by means of a Marxist-Leninist methodology and viewpoint." This, he emphasized, was a "necessary and meaningful struggle and trial" for intellectuals. "This is so fundamental an issue," he declared, "that there is no room for compromise." No trace remained of the moderate policy of a year earlier, which had respected the initiative of writers.

Pham Van Dong also clarified the roles that literature and education were expected to play in the country's transition to socialism. Literature was charged with the task of "serving workers, peasants, and soldiers and of describing socialist construction."[128] He emphasized that writers should assist the socialist transformation of society by propagating its importance among the people, encouraging them, educating them, and mobilizing them to work for it. As for the role of education, emphasis was placed on the linkage between education and daily life, the economy, and production activities, as well as the need to train cadres capable of meeting the requirements of socialist transformation.

It suffices to say that the socialization program announced in March and April emphasized the ideological education and mobilization of the masses and charged writers and intellectuals with a pivotal role in the implementation of ideological education.[129] A program with much the same orientation had been advocated in

---

[126] ND 1958b.

[127] Ibid.

[128] ND 1958c.

[129] In preparation for socialist transformation, the Fourteenth Plenum, in November 1958, adopted a resolution defining the basic tasks of the Three-Year Plan for Economic Development and Transformation and Cultural Development. This resolution pointed out that the task of cultural affairs was to "mobilize and organize all the forces of culture, science, education, and the arts in order to educate the people in socialist thought and encourage them to vie with one another in striving for the construction of socialism in the North and for the struggle for national unification, [and to] raise the cultural and technological standards of the people and

early 1957, as already pointed out, but it had never gathered momentum, having failed to define the nature of socialization in even a vague way. A little over a year later, a blueprint for socialization combining the economic and the cultural spheres was presented for the first time since 1954. At the same time, both the literary rectification campaign and the campaign to study the two documents helped reinforce the Party's leadership role and the imposed transformation of the intelligentsia, and thus helped pave the way for full-fledged mobilization of the masses in the socialization effort.

CONCLUSION

The literary policy of the VWP was first formulated to deal directly with criticisms of the Party voiced by literary circles in 1956 and 1957. Subsequently, the Party shifted toward viewing the literary sphere as the driving force of an ideological campaign to mobilize the masses to carry out socialist construction. It is important to note that the twists and turns in the VWP's literary policy in 1956 and 1957 were closely related to, and significantly affected by, developments unfolding in the socialist camp during that period, including the denunciation of Stalin, the CCP's "hundred flowers" policy, the Hungarian Revolt, and the Moscow Conference.

In concluding this paper, I would like to note some of the historical implications of the shifts in the VWP's literary policy and the questions raised by writers and intellectuals in the 1956–1958 period.

First, the literary rectification campaign of 1958 began what may be called a process of expansion of the intraparty lifestyle to society as a whole. Up till 1957, the lines had been clearly drawn, by the VWP itself, between affairs pertaining to the Party and those not, and between party members and nonmembers. In the course of the literary rectification campaign, however, study of Marxism-Leninism, VWP policy, and the two documents—subjects whose study would previously have been assigned only to party members—was decreed for party members and nonmembers alike.[130] This was also the case with the program for firsthand experience of the life of labor on the part of writers and intellectuals. It was also during the literary rectification campaign that the NV was criticized for having advocated "bourgeois individualism" and that the importance of the concept of collectivism began to be emphasized not only within the Party but in society at large, on the grounds that this concept was crucial in promoting the idea that socialist construction was an undertaking of the entire people.[131] The literary rectification campaign was followed by a series of rectification campaigns in other spheres of social life. For instance, a debate on the "two roads" held in rural areas (1959) spread the intraparty lifestyle to village communities, while an enterprise management improvement movement (1958–1959) expanded it to the shop floor.

One noteworthy concurrent development was that socialist construction was increasingly manifesting a spiritualistic tendency to mobilize mass participation. As

---

foster intellectuals loyal to the Fatherland and to socialism in order to meet the requirements of economic and cultural construction and of state administration" (Dang lao dong Viet-nam 1958, p. 43).

[130] Writers' obligations, subsumed under the term "party orientation," were required not only of writers with party membership but also of those not affiliated with the Party (Truong Chinh 1986, pp. 129–31).

[131] Nguyen Chuong 1958, p. 12.

pointed out already, this tendency was seen in the very terms in which the VWP conceptualized the cultural revolution. The primary purpose of the revolution was defined as reformation of literature and education so that cultural and ideological activities would lead the masses to display as much initiative as possible and would then channel that initiative into production activities. This tendency became even more pronounced during the Le Duan era, which began with the VWP's Third Party Congress, in 1960, at which he was elected first secretary of the Party. Le Duan emphasized the importance of collectivism and human factors through such concepts as the "right of collective mastery" and the "new person"; he also emphasized the spiritual side by placing importance on the ideological and cultural as well as economic factors of the socialist revolution.[132] In the light of these developments, we can say that a series of events in the first half of 1958 foreshadowed the political culture that was to take shape during the Le Duan era.[133]

Second, the demand made by writers and intellectuals in the autumn of 1956 for the return of the right to supervise literary matters and the critical views they expressed at that time about the relationship between "politics and professions" remain relevant today; these issues are still debated in socialist countries whenever conflict erupts between intellectuals and communist parties. In the DRV, after the literary rectification campaign of 1958, writers were frequently mobilized to participate in ideological study programs and production activities, and training courses were inaugurated for young people aspiring to careers in literature. It is also true that the types of articles and works of creative writing once published by the NV and the GP ceased to appear either in literary journals or in book form. But it would be a mistake to conclude from these facts alone that the Party's literary policy was working well or that writers were engaging in creative writing following instructions from others.[134] On the contrary, the questions raised by writers and intellectuals in the autumn of 1956 have remained unanswered.

Third, the transition from the "period of economic recovery" to the "period of socialist transformation" was accompanied by various phenomena similar to those regarded by students of Soviet history as characteristic of the change in Soviet economic policy from the New Economic Policy to the First Five-Year Plan. For instance, Lenin's moderate policy of gradual socialist construction, which was in effect during the NEP period, was replaced by Stalin's "revolution from above," which tried to achieve both industrialization and the collectivization of agriculture rapidly.[135] In the DRV, too, following the adoption by the Fourteenth Plenum, in November 1958, of a

---

[132] Le Duan's emphasis on ideology and culture was later formulated into an ideological and cultural revolution, which constituted one of the "three revolutions," along with the technological revolution and the revolution in production relations. In regard to the relationship between economic development and ideological and cultural standards, Le Duan continued to argue that whereas economic development should take precedence over ideological and cultural affairs, the latter need not be always subordinated to the former. He referred to this current of thought in his political reports to the Third, Fourth, and Fifth Party Congresses, held in 1960, 1976, and 1982, respectively (Le Duan 1976, pp. 16–18; Le Duan 1980, p. 64; Le Duan 1984, p. 82). A similar opinion was expressed as early as January 1958 by Do Duc Duc, then the vice-minister of culture (Do Duc Duc 1958).

[133] Le Duan became politically active in the Party executive at about the same time. He became an assistant to Ho Chi Minh in 1957 and attended the Moscow Conference in November that year as a member of the VWP delegation.

[134] On this point, see Sy Ngoc 1987; Nguyen Duy 1987.

[135] Tucker 1987, pp. 51–71.

policy of rapid socialization, the collectivization of agriculture and the partial buildup of heavy industry were vigorously promoted.[136]

There were similarities in the area of culture, as well. In the 1920s Soviet intellectuals were treated fairly generously, prepublication censorship standards were lenient, and many different schools of literature were allowed to follow their own stylistic preferences.[137] When Lenin spoke of the necessity of launching a cultural revolution to raise the cultural standards of the peasantry as a prerequisite to organizing cooperative farms, he perceived this revolution as a gradual, long-term undertaking to be carried out by means of persuasion and education.[138] In contrast, the cultural revolution implemented in the 1928–1931 period on Stalin's orders, which was a kind of rectification campaign, purged "bourgeois intellectuals" from their posts in higher education, public administration, and management, replacing them with Party cadres of working-class origin.[139] This forceful step was certainly "a means of training a future corp of elite communists and creating a new Soviet intelligentsia,"[140] but it also served as a breeding ground for Stalin's cult of personality.[141] In the DRV, too, after the literary rectification campaign, the children of workers and peasants began to advance in great numbers into institutions of higher learning,[142] significantly altering the composition of the intelligentsia.

As socialization proceeded in the DRV from 1958 onward, many Stalinist features became evident. This suggests that if we wish to understand in its totality the process by which agricultural collectivization, industrialization, and the cultural revolution unfolded in the DRV, we should not be content to analyze it only in relation to the socioeconomic conditions of the DRV and the domestic and international political developments during the period concerned but should analyze it in relation to Stalinism, as well.

This paper was originally published under the title "Betonamu rōdōtō no bungei seisaku tenkan katei (1956 nen–58 nen): Shakaishugika no naka no sakka, chishikijin" [The process of change in the literary policy of the Vietnamese Workers' Party (1956–1958): Writers and intellectuals during socialization], in *Ajia, Afurika gengo bunka kenkyū* [Journal of Asian and African studies] 36 (1988): 1–26.

---

[136] Furuta 1980, pp. 21–23. Furuta also discusses the influence of the CCP's "great leap forward" policy on the VWP.

[137] Fujii 1976, pp. 166–202.

[138] Lenin 1964, pp. 369–77.

[139] Fitzpatrick 1978, pp. 8–12.

[140] Ibid., p. 11.

[141] Zaslavsky 1982, pp. 10–13.

[142] According to government statistics, university students from workers' and peasants' families accounted for 25.4 percent of the total university student body in 1956–1957. The ratio rose to 40.7 percent in 1959–1960 (Murano 1969, p. 104).

ABBREVIATIONS USED IN NOTES AND REFERENCE LIST

GPMT II: *Giai pham mua Thu*, vol. 2
HT: *Hoc Tap*
ND: *Nhan Dan*
TCVN: *Tap chi Van nghe*
THDN: *Tram hoa dua no tren dat bac*

REFERENCE LIST

Bui Huy phon. 1958. "Chan tuong phan cach mang cua Truong Tuu." *ND* 16–4.

Dang lao dong Viet-nam. 1958. *Nghi quyet Hoi nghi Trung uong lan thu 14* (11–1958). Ha Noi, Ban chap hanh Trung uong Dang lao dong Viet-nam.

Dao Anh Kha. 1956. "Gap cac ban tri thuc va vien chuc." *ND* 28-29–10.

Dao Duy Tung. 1957. "Chong tu tuong tu san xam nhap vao trong Dang." *HT* 9, pp. 23–32.

Do Duc Duc. 1958. "Chong nhung te nan xa hoi cu nhu the nao?" *ND* 30–1.

Doan Trong Truyen. 1957. "May y kien ve viec xay dung nen dai hoc." *HT* 5, pp. 41–52.

Elliott, D. 1976. "Revolutionary Re-integration: A Comparison of the Foundation of Post-Liberation Political Systems in North Vietnam and China." Ph. D. dissertation, Cornell University.

Fehér, F. and A. Heller, 1983. *Hungary 1956 Revisited: The Message of a Revolution—A Quarter of a Century Later*. London: Allen & Unwin.

Fejtö, François. 1969. *Histoire des démocraties populaires*. Vol. 2, *Aprè Staline*. Paris: Éditions du Seuil.

Fitzpatrick, S. ed. 1978. *Cultural Revolution in Russia, 1928–1931*. Bloomington: Indiana University Press.

Fujii, Ikkō. 1976. *Shakaishugi to jiyū* [Socialism and freedom]. Tokyo: Aoki Shoten.

Furuta, Motoo. 1980. "Betonamu ni okeru 'jishu' rosen no mosaku" [Vietnam's search for an independent line]. *Rekishigaku kenkyū* [Journal of historical studies], no. 478: 15–26.

Giai pham mua Thu. Tap II. 1956. Ha Noi: Minh Duc.

HT 1956a. "Ra suc hoan thanh nhung nhiem vu cong tac nam nay." 2, pp. 6–11.

HT 1956b. "Mot cuoc Dai hoi co y nghia lich su trong dai." 6, pp. 12–40.

HT 1956c. "Thong cao cua Hoi nghi lan thu 10 (mo rong) cua Ban chap hanh Trung uong Dang Lao dong Viet-nam." 10, pp. 6–12.

HT 1956d. "Tang cuong doan ket, nang cao tinh to chuc va boi duong chi khi chien dau trong Dang." 11, pp. 1–8.

HT 1957a. Thong cao cua Hoi nghi lan thu 11 (mo rong) cua Ban chap hanh Trung uong Dang Lao dong Viet-nam." 1, pp. 4–6.

HT 1957b. "Thu cua Ban chap hanh Trung uong Dang Lao dong Viet-nam gui Dai hoi van nghe toan quoc lan thu hai." 2, pp. 7–11.

HT 1957c. "Boi duong quan diem lao dong moi, day manh thuc hien ke hoach nha nuoc." 4, pp. 1–5.

HT 1957d. "phan dau cho su toan thang cua chu nghia Le-nin o Viet-nam va the gioi." 12, pp. 1–11.

HT 1958a. "Tang cuong doan ket nhat tri trong Dang, ren luyen tinh Dang, nang cao y chi chien dau, lam tron nhiem vu truoc mat." 1, pp. 4–20.

HT 1958b. "Bao dam cho mien Bac vung buoc tien len chu nghia xa hoi." 5, pp. 1–8.

Ha Huy Giap. 1958. "Buoc tien dau tien tren duong xay dung truong dai hoc xa hoi chu nghia." *ND* 28–10.

Hoai Thanh. 1958. "Mot ke nghich ve tu tuong." *ND* 26~27–3.

Hoang Chau Ky. 1958. "Bo mat that cua Phan Khoi." *ND* 17–4.

Hoang Van Chi. 1958. *The New Class in North Vietnam*. Saigon, Cong Dan.

———. 1964. *From Colonialism to Communism*. London, Pall Mall Press.

Honey, P. J. 1957. "The Revolt of the Intellectuals in North Vietnam." *The World Today*, vol. 13, no. 6, pp. 250–60.

———. 1963. *Communism in North Vietnam*. Cambridge, Mass.: The M.I.T. Press.

Hong Chuong. 1956. "Chinh tri va van nghe." *HT* 10, pp. 33–47.

Huynh Ly, Tran Van Hoi. 1962. *Giao trinh lich su van hoc Viet-nam, tap IV*. Ha Noi: NXB Giao duc.

Le Duan. 1976. *Cach mang xa hoi chu nghia o Viet Nam, tap I*. Ha Noi: NXB Su That.
———. 1980. *Cach mang xa hoi chu nghia o Viet Nam, tap III*. Ha Noi: NXB Su That.
——— 1984. *Cach mang xa hoi chu nghia o Viet Nam, tap IV*. Ha Noi: NXB Su That.
Manh Phu Tu. 1958. "Nguyen Huu Dang, moi ten pha hoai dau so." *ND* 15–4.
McCauley, M. (ed.) 1987. *Khrushchev and Khrushchevism*. London: Macmillan.
Murano, Tsutomu. 1976. "Kita Betonamu no tochi kaikaku" [Land reform in northern Viet-
nam]. In *Ajia tochi seisakuron josetsu* [An introduction to land reform policies in Asia], ed.
Hitoshi Saitō. Tokyo: Institute of Developing Economies, pp. 67–114.
———, trans. 1969. *Betonamu Minshu Kyōwakoku: Keizai, bunka kensetsu no go ka nen* [The Demo-
cratic Republic of Vietnam: Five years of economic and cultural construction]. Tokyo:
Institute of Developing Economies.
Nakajima, Mineo. 1971. *Gendai Chūgoku ron* [Modern China]. Rev. ed. Tokyo: Aoki Shoten.
ND 1956a. "Thong cao cua Ban thuong vu Hoi Van nghe Viet-nam." 6–10.
ND 1956b. "Phat cao ngon co yeu nuoc va xa hoi chu nghia, nhan dan Hung-ga-ri da de bep
bon phan cach mang, tay sai cua de quoc." 5–11.
ND 1956c. "Dan chu va chuyen chinh." 9–11.
ND 1956d. "Sac lenh ve che do bao chi." 15–12.
ND 1956e. "Quyet dinh cua Uy ban hanh chinh Ha-noi ve viec dinh ban va cam luu hanh bao
[Nhan van]." 19–12.
ND 1957a. "Nghi quyet cua Dai hoi van nghe toan quoc lan thu hai." 3–3.
ND 1957b. "Day manh cong tac van hoa va kien thuc pho thong cua quan chung." 9–3.
ND 1957c. "Tang cuong ky luat o nha truong." 20–4.
ND 1957d. "Thong coa cua Hoi nghi lan thu 12 (mo rong) cua Ban chap hanh trung uong Dang
lao dong Viet-nam." 23–4.
ND 1957e. "Chinh sach cua Dang lao dong Viet-nam doi voi tri thuc." 29–8.
ND 1957f. "Tham nhuan va thuc hien dung dan chinh sach cua Dang doi voi tri thuc." 29–8.
ND 1957g. "Nghi quyet cua Hoi nhgi Ban chap hanh Trung uong Dang lao dong Viet-nam ve
Ban tuyen bo va ban tuyen ngon hoa binh cua Hoi nghi cac dang cong san va dang cong
nhan." 6–12.
ND 1958a. "Lanh dao va tien hanh tot viec hoc tap hai van kien lich su." 3–2.
ND 1958b. "Tang cuong doan ket de xay dung mot nuoc Viet-nam hoa binh, thong nhat, doc
lap, dan chu va giau manh." 17–3.
ND 1958c. "Bao cao cua Thu thong Pham Van Dong tai khoa hop thu tam cua Quoc hoi."
18~19–4.
ND 1958d. "Cac hoi van hoc, nghe thuat tien hanh viec chan chinh to chuc." 9–7.
ND 1960. "Toa an nhan dan Ha-noi da xu vu gian diep Nguyen Huu Dang van Thuy An." 21–
1.
Nguyen Chuong. 1956a. "May diem sai lam chu yeu trong bao Nhan van va tap Giai pham
mua thu." *ND* 25–9.
———. 1956b. "Co can cu hay khong co can cu?" *ND* 15–10.
———. 1958. "Chu nghia tap the van chu nghia ca nhan." *HT* 9, pp. 6–12.
Nguyen Duy. 1987. "Phong van cu Nguyen Tuan." *Van nghe*, 37.
Nguyen Duy Trinh. 1956. "Phat trien che do can chu nhan dan va bao dam quyen tu do dan
chu cua nhan dan." *HT* 10, pp. 23–32.
Nguyen Dinh Thi. 1958. "Chong chu nghia xet lai trong van nghe." *HT* 3, pp. 5–22.
Nhu Phong. 1962. "Intellectuals, Writers and Artists." *China Quarterly*, 9, pp. 47–69.
Pham Huy Thong. 1958. "Mat that cua Tran Duc Thao." *ND* 4~5–5.
Pham Van Dong. 1957. "Cai tien va that chat quan he giua Dang." *HT* 3, pp. 5–11.
Quang Dam. 1956. "Giu vung nhung nguyen tac dan chu cha chung ta." *ND* 11–12.
———. 1958a. "Kien quyet dau tranh chong chu nghia xet lai." *ND* 3~8–3.
———. 1958b . "Dap cho nat chu nghia xet lai trong van nghe." *ND* 21–3.
Sy Ngoc. 1987. "Nho nha van Nguyen Tuan." *Van nghe*, 33.
So phan tri thuc mien Bac. 1959. Sai Gon: NXB Van Huu A chau.
TCVN 1958a. "Hoi nghi van nghe Dang." 10, p. 116.
TCVN 1958b. "Thu cua 304 van nghe si va can bo van hoa o lop hoc van nghe lan thu hai gui
Ban chap hanh Trung uong Dang lao dong Viet-nam." 12, pp. 87–88.
Tai lieu hoc tap ve khoi phuc kinh te. 1955. Ha Noi, Uy ban hoc tap Trung uong.
Tap san Dai hoc su pham. 1956. "Thu tuong Pham Van Dong noi chuyen voi sinh vien cac truong
dai hoc o Thu do." 1, pp. 4–10.

The Tuan. 1957. "Tuan bao [Van] va con nguoi thoi dai." *HT* 7, pp. 63–68.

———. 1958. "Can bo van hoa va van nghe si di vao thuc te." *HT* 12, pp. 80–81.

Thoi Moi. 1957. "Nen giao duc cua ta ren luyen hop nguoi moi yeu lao dong." 25–5~14–6.

To Hoai. 1957. "Vao thuc te xay dung sang tac." *TCVN*, 1, pp. 71–77.

To Huu. 1973. *Xay dung mot nen van nghe lon xung dang voi nhan dan ta, thoi dai ta.* Ha Noi, NXB Van hoc.

———. 1958. "Y nghia mot cuoc dau tranh trong van nghe." *HT* 4, pp. 22–28.

Tram hoa dua no tren dat bac. 1959. Sai Gon, Mat tran Bao ve Tu do Van hoa.

Tran Cong Tuong and Huu Trong. 1956. "Ra suc gin giu va phat trien nen dna chu nhan dan cua ta." *HT* 11, pp. 24–37.

Truong-Chinh. 1956. "Sua sai van tien len" *HT* 11, pp. 9-23.

———. 1957. "Phan dau cho mot nen van nghe dan toc phong phu, duoi ngon co cua chu nghia yeu nuoc va chu nghia xa hoi." *TCVN* 1, pp. 3–21; *TCVN* 2, pp. 1–24.

———. 1975. Cach mang dan toc dan chu nhan dan Viet-nam, tap II. Ha Noi, NXB Su that.

———. 1985. *Ve van hoa va nghe thua, tap I.* Ha Noi, NXB Van hoc.

———. 1986. *Ve van hoa va nghe thua, tap II.* Ha Noi, NXB Van hoc.

Tucker, R. C. 1987. *Political Culture and Leadership in Soviet Russia.* Brighton: Wheatsheaf.

Vali, F. A. 1961. *Rift and Revolt in Hungary.* Cambridge, Mass.: Harvard University Press.

Vien Mac—Le-nin. 1982. *Nung su kien lich su Dang, tap IV.* Ha Noi, NXB Thong tin ly luan.

Vo Quang. 1958. "Nha truong cua ta phai tro thanh cong cu sac ben cua chuyen chinh dan chu nhan dan." *HT* 5, pp. 9–17.

Vu bien soan Ban tuyen huan Trung uong. 1978. *Lich su Dang Cong san Viet-nam, tap II.* Ha Noi, NXB Sach giao khoa Mac-Le-nin.

Xuan Truong. 1956a. "Mot thai do phe binh khong dung, mot quan niem sai lam ve nghe thuat." *ND* 9–27.

———. 1956b. "Chong vu khong va xuyen tax." *ND* 10–12.

Zaslavsky, V. 1982. *The Neo-Stalinist State.* Armonk, NY: M. E. Sharpe, Inc.